Waiting for Buddy Guy

MUSIC IN AMERICAN LIFE

A list of books in the series appears at the end of this book.

Waiting for Buddy Guy

Chicago Blues at the Crossroads

ALAN HARPER

UNIVERSITY OF ILLINOIS PRESS

Urbana, Chicago, and Springfield

∞ This book is printed on acid-free paper.

ISBN 978-0-252-04008-5 (cloth)
ISBN 978-0-252-08157-6 (paper)
ISBN 978-0-252-09828-4 (e-book)

The Cataloging-in-Publication Data is available
on the Library of Congress Web site.

For Gill

Contents

Author's Note

The events described in this book took place a long time ago and, I'm tempted to add, in a galaxy far away. It was another world. The Chicago blues I knew and the Chicago blues you might encounter if you visited the city today, more than thirty years later, would be almost unrecognizable to each other. I was fortunate to be there at a time of transition, when elderly musicians born in the early years of the twentieth century were still active, alongside—often literally, on the bandstand—young men and women not much older than I was.

It was understood then, and had been for years, that the Chicago blues was only able to survive as a viable art form thanks to the economic support of white audiences and record buyers. But there was never any question as to whose music it was. It was a black music, and one of America's greatest gifts to the world.

White people have played and sung the blues for years and, for almost as long, their critics have stood up and said that not only can they not play, but they've got no right to. Their supporters counter that it's the music that matters: if it sounds good, what's the problem? Well-worn even thirty years ago, these arguments often gave me pause for thought, but at a time when it was easier to go out and find a black blues musician to listen to than a white one, there didn't seem to be much point in dwelling on it.

Today, though, you can go to a blues festival and see no black faces at all, either in the audience or on the stage. A tectonic shift has taken place, and the debate is more heated than ever. Words like "hegemony" are employed, and "imperialism." People do dwell on it. Books get written on the subject.

This isn't one of them. This is the story of a young, white, British fan's adventures in the noisy, friendly, creative, chaotic, nurturing and overwhelmingly black world of the Chicago blues, a long time ago. As Johnny Dollar used to holler at the end of the night: "I had a ball, y'all!" I hope you do too.

Acknowledgments

My thanks are due to the musicians, club owners, label bosses, DJs, and fellow blues aficionados who gave so generously of their time, hospitality, and wisdom during my visits to Chicago.

I owe a great debt to Laurie Matheson and her publishing team at the University of Illinois Press, and to Alan G. Thomas for putting us together. Brendan Bernhard studied several drafts of the text, and his advice and encouragement were invaluable. David Whiteis and Steve Cushing were patient, painstaking, and insightful readers.

None of this would have been possible without the generosity of my Chicago friends Ann, Steve, and Tony, who without question or complaint simply accepted the fact that I lived on their sofa.

Waiting for Buddy Guy

Blues Fell This Morning

On the first of July 1979, armed with a J-1 temporary U.S. work visa, I boarded an elderly World Airways DC-8 and flew from London to Newark, New Jersey. After a night in Manhattan, I made my way to the Holland Tunnel at the start of Interstate 78 and stuck out my thumb. It was a beautiful morning. I was twenty years old.

English accents were still a novelty for many Americans in 1979. A wealthy young man in a BMW, heir to the family construction firm in New Jersey, invited me home, suggested we try a singles bar to see what effect the accent had on the young ladies—a singularly unsuccessful expedition—and took me to see the newly released *Alien*. He got me three days' work on a building site, lugging heavy sheets of plasterboard. One of my fellow laborers was a huge man from Trinidad, the other a rangy, wizened longhair who wore Levi's and a cowboy hat and took heroin. When I asked him why, he looked at me as if I was faintly deranged: "Because it's so *goood*, man." He made the word last for several seconds, and it seemed to come from somewhere deeper than his larynx.

An elderly couple carried me in their station wagon across New Jersey and into Pennsylvania at a steady 55 mph,[1] and when, after some hours, I unfolded my map, I realized for the first time how big the country was. We had gone about half an inch. I got a ride on the back of a Kawasaki Z900 ridden by a boy who insisted on praying for me when he dropped me off, holding my shoulder and bowing his head at a busy intersection. An absurdly cheerful young man called Coco drove me six hundred miles through the grim industrial landscapes of Ohio and Indiana in his Honda Civic, set me down outside the wooden house he shared with his girlfriend, Beth, in Normal, Illinois, and invited me to stay for a while.

I arrived in Chicago in the early evening of the ninth of July, watching awe-struck from ten miles out as the city's unmistakable skyline loomed ever larger: the black glass ziggurat of the Sears Tower, the white marble obelisk of the Standard Oil Building, and the tapered gunmetal zigzag of the John Hancock Center, which still puts me in mind of an aircraft carrier standing on end. I asked a ragged figure outside a boarded-up storefront for directions, and he looked me up and down contemptuously: "I don't want to talk to you, man." After a nervous encounter in the gloom of an underpass with two men whom I took to be muggers—but who informed me, indignantly, that they were just asking for change—I checked in for the night at the YMCA on South Wabash Avenue, a teeming hostel between Eighth and Ninth Streets with a reputed two thousand rooms.

By mid-morning next day, somewhat to my surprise, a realtor had agreed to rent me a shabby but affordable one-room apartment in a down-at-heel red-brick building at 1807 North Lincoln Park West. I had no money for a deposit and no references, but I did have an English accent. One morning I found an elegant yellow mushroom growing out of the wall.

That lunchtime on the corner of Clark Street and Lincoln Avenue, across from the park, I discovered a sandwich restaurant called Hemingway's Move-able Feast, owned by Michael, an Englishman, and Diane, his American wife. Incredibly, they took me on as a busboy, four shifts a week, for three dollars an hour and 10 percent of the tips. Like all restaurant work, it was sweaty, tough, and relentless. Michael seemed to like having a fellow countryman to talk to, and in the evenings after work we would sit in the office drinking his draught beer and smoking his cannabis, something with which I was not very familiar. On one occasion I found myself looking across at him carefully. "There's a fizz-ing sensation along the top of my skull," I explained. "And this floor is domed. Really, really, domed." He looked at me quizzically. "Alan, you are *fantastically* stoned," he marveled. "I'm going to get you a glass of water. Have a walk around."

The same day I got the restaurant job, I saw an ad for part-time telesales work up in the northern suburbs, phoned the Pioneer Press, and was immediately invited for an interview. I was signed on for four evenings a week, from six until nine. I was a dismal salesman. Even with a script, I found it almost impossible to close a deal, although I had many long conversations with pleasant ladies from Deerfield and Lake Forest who didn't want a newspaper subscription but were happy to chat to a young man from England. I was slightly disturbed to find that it was easier to sell into the poorer areas, where people who manifestly had no need for a paper stuffed with property ads and lightweight local news were often more polite, more prepared to listen to my pitch and, apparently, more gullible than their affluent counterparts in leafier neighborhoods. I earned the sales-related bonus only rarely, but the basic two dollars and ninety cents an hour was worth turning up for.

Within forty-eight hours of arriving in Chicago, I had two jobs and a room. I was euphoric. All that remained was to carefully doctor the date of birth on my British student identity card, because you had to be twenty-one to get into a bar. I needed to be able to get into bars. They were the only places I would find what I came for: the Chicago blues.

. . .

I had probably spent longer in the library than most first-year students at my English university, not out of a fascination for the eighteenth-century novel or the poetry of George Crabbe but because it had the best audio blues archive in the country.

Concealed within an annex called the Roborough Room, huge reels of tape assembled from rare 78s had been carefully cataloged by the librarians. The tapes were recorded and sent in from Canada on a regular basis, I was told, by a mysterious American draft-dodging record collector. They contained hundreds of hours of prewar blues and thousands of songs, not just old classics by legendary figures like Leadbelly and Blind Lemon Jefferson, but obscure, scratchy tracks from musicians with names like Tommy Johnson, Cripple Clarence Lofton, and Tommy McClennan.

Sitting with headphones on at a Formica-topped table, gazing out through leaded windows at the green Devon countryside, you could listen to the Blind Willie McTell version of the Allman Brothers' "Statesboro Blues," the 1930 recordings of 1960s festival favorite Son House, Charley Patton's fabled "High Water Everywhere," and countless others.

It was a priceless education in what B. B. King called "the real old blues,"[2] and for me it continued a process that had started at school, when I discovered that the Rolling Stones' "Love In Vain" was actually a pretty faithful homage to a Robert Johnson song. So were the thrillingly rude lyrics of Led Zeppelin's "Lemon Song"—even though the credits would have had you believe otherwise[3]—while a bit more digging unearthed artists with improbable, otherwordly names like Robert Nighthawk and Clarence Gatemouth Brown. Eric Clapton's more eclectic canon led to the discovery of Skip James and wonderful guitar players like Freddie King.

I didn't automatically like the original songs better than the white bands' cover versions. It was certainly true that a lot of so-called British blues was laughable, but some of it really wasn't bad. Clapton's rendition of "Hideaway" was, I felt, incapable of improvement. If, on a first listen, the sheer primal force of Howlin' Wolf seemed to stray beyond the realms of music and into anthropology, the

Stones' covers were much easier on the ear, and musically, Led Zep were simply phenomenal. But the old songs got their hooks into me, and finding out about this largely forgotten and increasingly obscure music satisfied some urge I had to get to the root of things.

The blues, I quickly understood, underpinned everything—jazz, soul, or rock. Punk? Mere reheated rock 'n' roll. If you were looking for unsuitable role models with which to alarm your parents, virtually any blues singer would fit the bill. When Willie Mabon sang "I'm getting sick and tired of the way you do/Cool kind papa going to poison you," he sounded like he meant it. Little Walter's murderous "Boom Boom, Out Go the Lights" was emphatically not the cheery rock 'n' roll it pretended to be. And how could the Sex Pistols, bravely swearing on British television, possibly measure up to the magnificent, towering malevolence of a bluesman like Sonny Boy Williamson?

I heard the blues everywhere and in everything. I did have friends, but they avoided talking to me about music.

Blues records were hard to find, which was why the university library's collection was so valuable. I spent long afternoons in there, listening to ancient recordings from the 1920s and 1930s that might have come from an earlier civilization. Only gradually did I admit to myself that it could sometimes seem more of a duty than a pleasure. A 78 lasts for about three minutes, and after scouring the ring-bound lists of songs and lodging your requests at the desk, it could feel like a poor return on investment to discover that one Martha Copeland song sounded very much like another. [4]

More satisfactory was the library's collection of vinyl. There was a Paul Oliver compilation, for a start: *The Story of the Blues*,[5] a four-side crash course in thirty-two songs, with copious liner notes. On another album I discovered the hypnotic, retro-Delta sound of R. L. Burnside's 1967 recordings: "Long Haired Doney," "Poor Black Mattie" and his Muddy Waters homage "I Be's Troubled."[6] They also had Mance Lipscomb,[7] several Lightning Hopkins LPs, and some extraordinary music by the Como Drum Band, which sounded African but was recorded in Mississippi. Best of all, there was a three-disc set recorded by Samuel Charters for Vanguard in 1965—*Chicago/The Blues/Today!*[8] This was pure gold.

Charters was a blues historian and writer in the tradition of Alan Lomax, who before the war had made a vital collection of field recordings for the Archive of American Folk Song at the Library of Congress. Charters traveled through the South in the 1950s on the trail of "lost" blues musicians, tracking down Sleepy John Estes and Lightning Hopkins. In the early 1960s, when traditional country blues was being embraced by white folkies—an audience that prompted many a suave city bluesman to put down his tuxedo and Telecaster and dress up in sharecropper's overalls—Charters was among those who realized there was a market for modern electric blues among young white rock 'n' roll fans. In the echoing RCA studios on the Chicago lakefront he assembled the pick of the crop, kicking off with the tight and soulful Junior Wells band, featuring Buddy Guy on guitar. Harmonica master James Cotton was backed by the great pianist Otis Spann, both of them sidemen in Muddy Waters's band. The fat tone of Cotton's harp, his propulsive one-note solos and gruff vocal delivery provided a stark contrast to Wells's contorted delicacy.

Slide guitarist J. B. Hutto sang in a barely intelligible holler and punched his songs across with unstoppable energy, like Elmore James on Benzedrine, his band making far more noise than seemed physically possible for a classic three-piece of guitar, bass, and drums. On disc 2, fellow bottleneck guitarist Homesick James claimed to be the cousin of the late, great Elmore but sounded more like his twin, while Mississippi bluesman Johnny Shines gave the best indication yet of what Robert Johnson might have sounded like if he had lived to play with a postwar Chicago rhythm section. Gleaming amid all this gritty urban blues was the polished lyricism of Otis Rush's lead guitar. The two instrumentals in his session sounded to me like the sort of thing the anemic English band The Shadows[9] had always striven for but never came close to achieving. On disc 3 there was the hard-driving, South Side sound of the laconic guitarist Johnny Young, who also, surprisingly, played a mandolin.

There was something else distinctive about disc 3, but it took me a while to realize what it was. Young's harmonica player seemed to possess unusual subtlety for a sideman, and an extraordinary versatility, coaxing sounds from his instrument I had not heard before. His name was Walter Horton, nicknamed Big Walter to differentiate himself from the younger but more famous Little Walter Jacobs. There he was again in Johnny Shines's band, playing behind the anachronistic Delta vocals, respectful but never overshadowed, taking the lead when invited. He was given a single track under his own name, a playful instrumental called "Rockin' My Boogie," which borrowed its central theme from George Gershwin. On this he was accompanied by Shines, Floyd Jones on bass, and Frank Kirkland on the drums, along with a clearly overawed "Memphis" Charlie Musselwhite on second harp.

With Horton playing on nine out of its thirteen tracks, disc 3 virtually belonged to him. No one on the entire three-record set featured more. His playing was masterful but never brash or intrusive. Above all it was intriguing, full of surprising textures and complexity, and unfailingly melodic. Big Walter Horton was a revelation.

I listened to *Chicago/The Blues/Today!* time and again, musing glumly on being about fifteen years too late to experience this phenomenal music for myself. Then one day a new album set appeared in the library collection, from an unfamiliar label: Alligator Records. Inspired by the Charters sessions of the previous decade, *Living Chicago Blues*[10] retained the same format of three discs with several bands on each, but these were—with a couple of exceptions—younger bands comprising as-yet "undiscovered" musicians. I certainly hadn't heard of any of them.

There was no Junior Wells or Buddy Guy, but Lonnie Brooks was given space to display a powerful and individual guitar style. Big Walter didn't feature, but Carey Bell knew what he was doing on the harmonica. Another harp player, Billy Branch, played alongside Bell's son Lurrie in a rather earnest band called the Sons of Blues. One of their songs was about the Berlin Wall. The young Bell's guitar had a late-night feel, murmuring in your ear. Then there was Eddie Shaw's foghorn saxophone and rambunctious party music, with someone on guitar who was evidently an original: Hubert Sumlin, who along with Shaw used to play in Howlin' Wolf's band. Also standing apart from the legion of B. B. King copyists were guitarists Jimmy Johnson and Left-Hand Frank. Magic Slim's playing, too, had a powerful, room-filling personality. And there were piano players: muscular barrelhouse from Johnny "Big Moose" Walker, fragile, sensitive blues from the elderly Lovie Lee, and harmonic ruminations from the sophisticated Pinetop Perkins.

"The blues men and women of Chicago are singing, shouting, crying, laughing, celebrating," the liner notes declared, breathlessly. "Songs of hard times, heartbreak, loneliness; songs to drive the blue feelings away, to rock the night and let the good times roll." This seemed a little over the top, but Alligator Records' *Living Chicago Blues* series nevertheless made a promise: that these bands were all living and working in Chicago, right now.

Maybe I wasn't too late.

· · ·

What remained of Chicago's famous 1950s and 1960s blues scene was to be found deep in the city's South Side: notably at Theresa's, and also at the more recent Checkerboard Lounge. But the South Side had a fearsome reputation. In the coming months I would take a deep breath and venture down there on the L—Chicago's clattering, antiquated rail system—but on the first night in my grubby little Lincoln Park room I elected to walk a few blocks north, to where I had been told there were some good blues bars in a safe neighborhood.

A neat card in the window of the Wise Fools Pub, at 2270 North Lincoln Avenue, announced forthcoming appearances by Son Seals and Magic Slim. John Lee Hooker had played on Sunday; next weekend it was J. B. Hutto. A block farther on at number 2354, the Kingston Mines had Lefty Dizz and Carey

Bell booked, and Junior Wells had just played the previous weekend. But I kept walking. At 2519 North Halsted Street, where an amateurish-looking hanging sign advertised B.L.U.E.S,[11] a scrawled notice said: "Floyd Jones and Playboy Venson. No cover charge."

I pulled open the heavy wooden door and entered a dark room. There was a small bandstand at the far end and a few tables. A bar ran down the right-hand side, with booths down the left. Sitting in one of these on a high stool with a glass of whiskey was an old, thin black man wearing a short-sleeved white shirt. I saw he had a slight squint, grey hair, pale, deep-set eyes, and a shy suggestion of a smile. As I walked past he caught my nervous glance and put a hand on my arm. "Howdy, blue," he said.

It was Big Walter Horton.

Sunnyland Slim's Birthday Party

I can play 'em, but I don't. The reason I don't get down into the blues like it is, because when you really get out in the blues like it is, partner, you will cry behind 'em.

—Jimmy Walker

I spent two months in Chicago in 1979 and heard a lot of music, sometimes visiting two or three different clubs a night. Income from my two part-time jobs kept pace with outgoings, and I even managed to save enough to buy a cherry-red Gibson SG from its elderly owner on the West Side. He gave me a paper bag to put my camera in, lest it attract unwelcome attention on the bus.[1]

I came back to Chicago for a longer stay in 1982. There was no J-1 visa in my passport this time because I was no longer a student, so there was no possibility of getting a job to subsidize my blues habit. I had worked, saved, and instructed my bank to open an account for me at its Chicago branch, which had seventeen hundred and seven dollars in it. On the plus side, I no longer had to pretend to be twenty-one years old. On the first of June 1982, I landed at Chicago O'Hare, where a large, black and slightly world-weary customs officer directed me to open my luggage. As I fumbled with the locks he asked me what I was doing in Chicago.

"I've come here to listen to the blues," I said, glancing up to see what sort of a reaction that got. He might be a fan. As I lifted the lid of my grandfather's old suitcase I remembered that I had laid all my music cassettes over the top of everything to stop them bashing against each other. There they all were, dozens of them, a plastic mosaic of brittle cases, still chilled from the flight, their labels covered in tiny writing. If you looked hard, you could read the names on them, and the song titles and dates: Jimmy Rogers, Elmore James, Muddy Waters, Little Walter. For a few seconds the customs officer surveyed this musical carapace, which completely concealed the contents of the case, and then he lowered the lid and gazed down at me. "I believe you. You have come to Chicago to listen to the blues," he sighed, and waved me through.

B.L.U.E.S was again the first club I sought out. I remembered it as the perfect blues club: small, dark and smoky, with friendly bartenders and a crowd that was a mix of black, white, old and young, and often seemed to consist more of musicians than fans. There was no cover charge except on Fridays and Saturdays, but music every night, on a schedule that changed every month. And such music: nowhere but B.L.U.E.S could you hope to see an old country bluesman like Yank Rachell, or the harmonica player Snooky Pryor, who was said to have invented the amplified urban style, cupping the instrument to the microphone. Mama Yancey, at age eighty-three, was a direct link to the classic blues years of the 1920s. On my first-ever visit, three years before, I was startled to encounter Big Walter Horton, and he wasn't even playing that night; he was only there to talk, have a drink, and listen to his old friend Floyd Jones. Jones had recorded some of the first-ever Chicago blues back in 1947, and on the nights that followed I would also see Homesick James, Eddie Taylor, Lee Jackson and the piano players Jimmy Walker and Erwin Helfer play at the club. Most of these people didn't play anywhere else in the city. B.L.U.E.S gave them a home, and I had felt pretty comfortable there myself.

North Halsted Avenue was much as I remembered, although the Kingston Mines had moved. From two blocks away on North Lincoln, just up from the Wise Fools Pub, it had relocated to 2548 North Halsted, almost across the street from B.L.U.E.S. I could see it had a board outside advertising Jimmy Johnson. Resolving to check that out later, I pulled open the heavy wooden door of B.L.U.E.S once again and stepped inside, noting the familiar faces of the club's owners, Rob Hecko and Bill Gilmore, and recognizing the singer Big Time Sarah behind the bar. There was a good crowd. Eddie Shaw was on the bandstand down at the end, telling the audience about his recent trip to Paris. He no longer seemed to have Hubert Sumlin with him, and when he introduced the new guitarist, it turned out be his son. On bass, I recognized the unfailingly cheerful Shorty Gilbert, while the most recent addition to his gang was evidently their tall young drummer, "who's been with me thirty long days." Shaw launched the band into "Movin' and Groovin' Man," blowing a harmonica instead of his saxophone, as I settled down at the bar and asked Sarah for my first Old Style in nearly three years. It still didn't taste of anything. Young Eddie Junior could certainly play that guitar.

I stayed for the rest of the set, decided against another beer, and began to think about going across the street to the Kingston Mines to see how Jimmy Johnson was doing. The atmosphere in B.L.U.E.S felt just the same—an easy mix of respect, good humor and alcohol—although the crowd seemed, on average, maybe slightly younger and slightly whiter than I remembered. I couldn't see many of the old musicians who had always been such a fixture of the place, but maybe they would come out at the weekend. Things really didn't seem to have changed much.

But before I left the club on that first night back, I saw that someone had scratched on the toilet wall: "Big Walter Lives." Which, of course, didn't mean that at all.

• • •

The close proximity of B.L.U.E.S, the Kingston Mines and the Wise Fools Pub made these few blocks of the North Side the principal focus for the blues in Chicago. But it was nothing like the old days. There was a map in the back of Mike Rowe's useful and scholarly book, *Chicago Blues*,[2] showing the city's 1950s blues clubs: fifty-three of them, dotted all over the black neighborhoods in the South and West Sides, with clusters marking real hotspots like Forty-Third Street, South Indiana Avenue and Roosevelt Road.

A similar map of Chicago blues joints in the early 1980s would have been pretty easy to draw, thanks to *The Reader*,[3] the free weekly listings newspaper which came out every Friday. Its music section was divided into rock, folk, country, blues, jazz and classical, and stretched to twenty pages. The small ads were free, so you could be pretty sure that every little corner bar with aspirations to be a venue had got itself in there, giving the impression of a city that was bursting with music. Under "Blues" there might be fifty or more places listed. But close scrutiny revealed that some of them only put on music one or two nights a week, while others could be remarkably vague about who was actually playing. If it just said "blues jam" you could be pretty sure you weren't missing much. If a "blues club" was a place that booked blues at least three nights a week, then a 1982 blues map of Chicago would have had just nine marked on it.[4]

And they were spread all over. Chicago was huge. Apart from the architectural drama of its central business district, its vast urban sprawl had transformed a flat, featureless prairie into a flat, featureless city, which even from the top of the Sears Tower, the tallest building in the world, disappeared into the haze as far as the eye could see. Biddy Mulligan's, a lively bar that booked some of the biggest blues acts, was at 7644 North Sheridan Road—seventy-six blocks north of Chicago's "base line" of Madison Street, at eight blocks to the mile—while Theresa's Tavern, the sole survivor from Mike Rowe's map, was at 4801 South Indiana Avenue, forty-eight blocks south. If two out of nine clubs could be separated by more than fifteen miles, to have three within a five-minute walk of each other was extraordinary, especially as they were three clubs that took the music seriously, and two of them, B.L.U.E.S and the Mines, had blues seven nights a week.

No club took the music more seriously than B.L.U.E.S. Bill Gilmore was the partner in charge of booking the bands, a tall, slim, clean-shaven man of thirty-six years, with thick glasses and a bookish air that concealed a dry sense of humor. He had listened to a lot of blues in the 1960s, he explained to me in the club one evening, not just in South Side places such as Pepper's Lounge and Theresa's, but in some of the first white-owned, North Side blues bars like Big John's on Wells Street, and another called Mother Blues.[5]

It was early evening as we talked, and singer and guitarist Buster Benton and his band were setting up at the far end of the room. Gilmore's first club, Elsewhere, opened in 1975 on North Lincoln Avenue, and when that didn't work out—landlord problems—he opened another one on North Clark Street in 1977. Music one night a week soon developed into music every night, and folk music was dropped in favor of blues. By the time the second club fell through—too big, wrong shape, unpleasant neighborhood—he knew what he wanted to do. Rob Hecko had the right place, Gilmore brought the idea, and B.L.U.E.S opened in April 1979.

"Since I don't try to book the best-known blues people, I thought I'd better get a small place," he said. "When we opened, Rob and I, most nights he was working the bar and I was working the door. That was the whole staff, we had no waitress, so we never lost money. I don't think we've had a really bad month." From what I remembered back in 1979, apart from the "B.L.U.E.S Festival" month of August, when every night was different, Gilmore tended to block-book bands: you could see Big Walter Horton every Sunday in July, say, and Eddie Taylor every Thursday. But in 1982, every month seemed to be a festival month. Apart from weekends, when the bigger acts played both nights, and Sundays, when Sunnyland Slim had the stage, there was a different band every night.

"I book an average of twenty-five bands a month," said Gilmore. "I've booked more blues in the last five years than anyone else in the world. I don't even think there's a close second." Finding musicians to book was seldom a problem, but he would still have liked to get out more to look for them: "I can't say I really go to Sixty-Seventh and State and try and find so-and-so who hasn't played in twelve years: I'm just too busy, unfortunately," he admitted. "I tend to talk to people. Otis 'Big Smokey' Smothers brought his brother Abe 'Little Smokey' Smothers in, who hadn't played in some years: things like that I follow up on. I try to read *The Reader* each week, and talk to Jim and Amy of *Living Blues*. I do get leads on people." He had recently started to book Magic Slim after hearing several people recommend him, and he also tried to make sure Hubert Sumlin played at B.L.U.E.S whenever the guitarist was in town. Acts he didn't know had to audition: "I try to hear people in person: either hear him sit in with the band I have playing, or sometimes we'll bring whole bands in to sit in."

There was certainly no more eclectic blues club in Chicago. "I do feel an obligation to bring up people who would not otherwise play on the North Side, like

Smokey Smothers, Homesick James, or Eddie Taylor: some of the older guys who are not currently as well known perhaps as some of the people I also book, like Jimmy Johnson, Johnny Dollar, Phil Guy, Magic Slim," said Gilmore. "I try to keep it varied: I book Little Brother Montgomery, John Davis, mostly people I like personally." He acknowledged a certain obligation to his business partner to book acts that brought people through the door to buy beer. "I also listen to what the employees say, I listen to my partner, I listen to the customers." Like most clubs, the music at B.L.U.E.S started sometime after nine-thirty and went on until two in the morning on weeknights, and until four at weekends.

I remembered Smokey Smothers from 1979. Back then I saw him play only a couple of times, once accompanying the singer Jeanne Carroll and on another occasion sitting in for a loosely assembled set with J. B. Hutto's band, the New Hawks. He was often in the club, and usually drunk. People told me who he was: a popular singer who recorded numerous sides for Federal in the early 1960s and had a few local hits. He had a following and knew what it was like to hear his own records on the jukebox. He played rhythm guitar on some of Freddie King's singles, and Freddie King returned the compliment by playing lead on some of Smokey's. But those days seemed to be over. He wasn't old, particularly—according to my weighty and compendious copy of *Blues Who's Who*,[6] he was born in Mississippi in 1929—but sitting in B.L.U.E.S, oblivious, he looked like a relic, lost to music and himself.

Something had happened in the meantime. In 1982 Smothers was still a regular at the club, and with his perpetually sleepy expression and gentle smile he might still have been taken, at first glance, for someone who was present in body only. But he was sober, and he was back on the bandstand: B.L.U.E.S booked him regularly, and his quirky songs and rooted, Mississippi guitar playing provided a textural contrast to the flashier styles of many of the younger musicians. No other North Side club would have booked him—he just wasn't noisy enough— and I doubted there were many places elsewhere in the city where his old blues would find favor. It seemed obvious to me that he had made his way back from the brink thanks to the possibilities offered by B.L.U.E.S.

"Seem like to me the people, the style of music, the blues, it's like they coming back to 'em," Smothers agreed. "I started back playing my style where I left off: the blues. It's different now. It seem like it catch on a little bit, and my style of blues more so now." We were sitting in his girlfriend's car outside the club. It was a Sunday, around midnight. After his success as a recording artist—and he was sufficiently bankable for the King label to release a compilation album of his 45s in 1962[7]—Smothers made a couple of sides for the obscure Gamma Records, but then the work dried up. "Jobs was kind of bad," he remembered. "During the sixties they had rock 'n' roll. The big blues artists, they only could survive. I was trying to play, but I wasn't doing nothing. I could have changed my style and kept on playing, maybe. Instead, I just quit."

Smothers left music and took up a variety of different jobs, including, according to local legend, selling ice cream: now his part-time band called themselves The Ice Cream Men. But with his musical career apparently over, his life also lost its focus. "I was drinking for a spell, pretty heavy," he admitted. "Most blues musicians drinks, and in other fields they get high off other things. I started drinking heavy. I didn't think I was drinking that much really, but I started thinking about my career, my kids, family. No doctor, nothing told me to stop drinking. I stopped myself. People give me credit for that willpower."

It was clear that Smothers didn't feel especially comfortable answering such personal questions. I wasn't sure I had any right to be asking them of a man the same age as my father, but he tolerated my clumsy inquisition and answered with shy good manners, anxious to explain himself. Whatever damage his drinking might have inflicted on his personal life, it was music that made him realize how far he had sunk. "I get up there and play, drunk, I think I'm playing good. And then I taped myself, and heard it the next day when I was sober. I say, 'Gee, that sound terrible.' And now I play, and I come down and folks say, 'You sound good.' I'm not at my best, but the audience like it."

We listened to a demo tape he had made in the hope of exciting the interest of a record company. He had recently put out a single with Rooster Records,[8] but what he really wanted was another album release. He was practicing, and writing songs: "Now, I have a idea, I write it down, fix the guitar up, get me a sound, and keep that," he said. "It's better to be sober. Drink too much, you can't think. You can't perform your job."

Most blues clubs in Chicago attracted mixed crowds of black and white fans, and I always felt that the crowd at B.L.U.E.S was more mixed than most. It was also the North Side club least likely to book a white headline act.[9] Bill Gilmore was very clear about it: "Most white guys cannot sing the blues," he said. "They mean well, and they try, and there are a few exceptions, but there's a real voice that you have to have. If I tried to do it, or if you tried to do it, it would sound vaguely ludicrous: as opposed to blues guitar, where a lot of the young guys can obviously do the chords and the changes and play guitar very well." I tended to agree. In fact, I was pretty sure rock music had been invented by white blues bands to shift attention onto the instruments and away from dodgy vocals in faux-Mississippi accents. But the reasons behind this aspect of the B.L.U.E.S booking policy were not just artistic but altruistic, according to Gilmore. "I tend to feature black artists because I feel that by and large most of them have not worked that much, they're overlooked," he said. "They have not received the recognition due. Mainly, they're older, and they're more interesting." He stopped to think about that. "Possibly if there were whites in their fifties and sixties I'd book them. Charlie Musselwhite comes to mind as someone who's in his forties—he's sort of the senior citizen among the white Chicago blues guys. I think a good deal of it is just plain age, you know."

· · ·

Sunnyland Slim was one of the elder statesmen of the blues, with a performing and recording career that went back to Chicago in the 1940s and beyond that to Memphis and the turpentine camps and barrelhouse bars of the rural South. Sunnyland sang in a style that belonged to the pre-amplification era, sometimes described by music scholars as "declamatory," but it was really just a kind of tuneful shouting. A car accident had limited the mobility of his right hand, so his playing style wasn't as accomplished as it had been, but that made little difference to the effect of a Sunnyland Slim performance. He was an entertainer, and he knew how to get an audience's attention, whether through his music or with Woody Woodpecker impressions between numbers. He wrote good songs. One was "Be Careful How You Vote":

> Please be careful how you vote on every election day
> Be careful how you vote on every election day
> Cos the one you vote for won't do a damn thing he say

I talked to him sitting in his Oldsmobile during an open-air gig at the Delta Fish Market on the West Side, while the Chicago singer Little Wolf—one of several performers who used the name—was up on stage. Seagram's Crown Royal was Sunnyland Slim's tipple of choice, and he passed the bottle across. "Little Wolf's singing pretty good," remarked Sunnyland. The old piano player had lost patience with the record business and set up his own label, Airway. He had recorded with numerous companies over the years, starting with JOB, best known for the Eddie Boyd hit "Five Long Years" in 1952. "I never made no money with none of them," he said dismissively. "I made a little bit with Prestige, Hy-Tone. Hy-Tone made my big record, 'Brownskin Woman,' 'The Devil is a Busy Man': the radio take that over. I didn't make shit with Chess, just session money. And Jewel, I got ripped off with Jewel."[10]

I had a copy of Airway's latest, a Sunnyland album called *Just You and Me* on the front and *Tired But I Can't Get Started* on the back, which had Hubert Sumlin playing on six of its ten tracks plus a number of other notable musicians, including Muddy Waters's guitarist Bob Margolin. It was a remarkably good record for such an obviously low-budget effort, but Sunnyland played the label down: "I ain't trying to make no big job, man," he said. "I got three albums out on it, and a couple of 45s."

The whiskey was medicinal. Sunnyland was feeling his age. "This is just one of my bad days," he sighed. "The doctor say I got a touch of pneumonia. I got to try to get me feeling a little better." The man was like a walking encyclopedia of black popular music. He'd played in movie theaters during the silent-picture era and at the Hole in the Wall in Memphis. I even read somewhere that he did tent shows with Ma Rainey, one of the greatest of the classic blues divas, back in 1931. "Oh, I was just a week with her," he said. "I put her down at Little Rock. I was making a dollar a night. Shit, I was making two dollars mostly at that time when I play a joint by myself, but I just wanted the experience. I liked doing the shows, but I didn't have a chance to make no other tip money or nothing. The side men wasn't making it, she was making all the money that came in the tents, you know. She was making it from the white folks they had out there; she had a name, see. I left at Little Rock and come on home. I was playing in places like Portersville, Missouri, and Memphis and all up and down Highway 61." He also worked with John Lee "Sonny Boy" Williamson. "Yeah, we played some joints, but we played parties mostly. We made good money, back in the early forties before I started getting a band together. We was playing here in Chicago. We played on the West Side. House parties, that's where the money was. We'd get twenty-five dollars apiece in some places. That was a hell of a lot of money."

Since the 1950s, though, Slim had found himself playing increasingly for white audiences. "Me and Big Bill [Broonzy] had been playing up there, and Big Crawford, for the white folks. It was paying more money," he remembered. "We had to play boogies, and some few sweet songs, and blues, they like that." He had left his black audience behind with few regrets, and when I suggested that black people just didn't listen to his kind of music much anymore, he disagreed: "They listen to the blues, man. I could be playing at these joints and that," he said, gesturing vaguely at the surrounding West Side, "but it just don't work up to nothing. They don't have no PA system, they don't have this, they don't have that. You get so much stole. I just quit playing for them mostly. You get more money with the white peoples: it's just a very earthly thing, you got to live."

Sunnyland Slim celebrated his seventy-fifth birthday party in B.L.U.E.S one Sunday night, starting early, because there were a lot of musicians in the house. He opened with a typically lively, strident set of barrelhouse and jump blues before stepping aside for fellow piano veteran Jimmy Walker, whose boogie-woogie was backed by the jazz drumming of Fred Below, in his customary beret, along with Sunnyland's regular band. The jazz singer Bonnie Lee took the microphone for a few numbers, then S. P. Leary took over the drums as the sixty-eight-year-old John Davis sat down at the piano. Davis looked frail and elderly, but there was no better piano player in Chicago: he spent years as the session pianist for legendary blues producer Lester Melrose, made records with Lonnie Johnson, and in the early 1950s was reputedly the first blues pianist to tour Europe, in company with Big Bill Broonzy. Few musicians could match his experience or his repertoire. At B.L.U.E.S he began with some ragtime, until someone shouted out a request for "Saint James Infirmary." He obliged. Then someone else—presumably joking—shouted out "Caldonia!" The blind, grey-haired musician paused, and a hush fell. On the drums, S. P. watched and waited, and then Davis began boldly playing some chords in an unfamiliar rhythm, which didn't make much sense at first. The audience stayed quiet. S. P. listened, caught the mood, and as he joined in on the snare suddenly there it was, Louis Jordan's big-band rabble-rouser, recreated out of thin air for piano and percussion. The applause at the end was intense.

You could wait a long time before you saw anything like that in any other club in Chicago. B.L.U.E.S had its off-nights, of course, but not very often. The atmosphere in the club was unique. "On the average, say, Tuesday night, I usually have twenty-five to thirty musicians in the place during the course of the evening, and that keeps the level of the music up," Bill Gilmore contended. "They know the people out there know the difference, and they're not just going to go up and play crap and assume no one's going to know. Certainly on the North Side I think we get more blues musicians than any other club. It's a nice feeling, because obviously they have a good time: a lot of people have said, 'This is my home base when I'm in Chicago.'"

I had heard musicians talk respectfully of the "tight sets" required by Gilmore. Rarely would a singer allow himself to ramble on for too long between numbers, and sets started and finished more or less on schedule. The one exception was Sunday afternoons, when the music started at five thirty, and for a few hours before the main act the stage was open to all comers, within reason. These sessions were reminiscent of the old Blue Monday parties of the black working-class neighborhoods, which would often start even earlier, before noon, in order to catch night shift workers on their way home from the steel mills and the stockyards.

"The problem with blues jams on the North Side is you get a lot of young white kids who think they can play, but quite frankly they can't play that well," admitted Gilmore. "They're not Johnny Dollar or Phil Guy or Magic Slim or Jimmy Johnson or Eddie Taylor, and they should know they're not. The other problem is you've got four or five different guys up there. They really don't know a whole lot of things they can play together unless they just do the standard changes. And there's not really a community feeling the way there used to be, as I understand it, on the South Side and the West Side," he concluded. "Yeah, Sunday varies—it can be fascinating or it can be dreadful." At B.L.U.E.S, the

Sunday afternoon sessions were often hosted by the genial drummer Kansas City Red or by the gentle and mild-mannered Smokey Smothers. "Smokey'll let virtually anyone up there," Gilmore sighed. "He's just not going to say no."

Buster Benton's band were all set up. It was nine thirty, and right on cue, the music started. As Gilmore and I moved out into the street to finish our talk, a young white man swerved toward us out of the darkness, catastrophically drunk yet at the same time quiet and courteous. As we watched, he began a methodical reconnaissance of the front of the building. "Is this the door?" he wondered. "Yes," said Gilmore, deadpan. "The handle is right here . . ."

• • •

The Kingston Mines differed from its near-neighbor B.L.U.E.S in several ways. It was bigger and had two rooms, each with its own bandstand. It had a counter where you could order sandwiches, and it had a slight air of anarchy, as if no one knew who was in charge.

The idea of the second stage was that a second band or soloist could keep the crowd entertained while the main act took a set break. Sometimes this worked. Sometimes the soloist was piano player Detroit Junior, a great musician and a fun performer who served in Howlin' Wolf's band and wrote "Call My Job," which was a hit for Albert King. But while he could be brilliantly entertaining, he was sometimes too drunk to know that the music with which he was filling the room was neither as brilliant nor as entertaining as the music he heard in his head.

The other drawback of the second stage was that it could encourage the main acts to extend their breaks and occasionally go AWOL. I met plenty of musicians sitting comfortably drinking in B.L.U.E.S, or even up on stage, playing, whom I planned to catch later at the Mines. They were on their set breaks. A waitress would have to dash across the street to drag them back to work.

I liked the Mines and spent a lot of time there. Because of its size it was a comfortable place just to hang out, and you could bump into plenty of musicians doing the same thing. It was owned by Doc Pellegrino—an actual, practicing medical doctor—who was stocky and wide, with the rolling gait of a sailor on leave and a big-featured, pockmarked face surmounted by a helmet of long, dark hair. He was fifty-seven. As we sat down together in his back office very late one night, he looked, and sounded, completely exhausted, as you might expect of someone with a full-on day job. "I guess it's the Italian in me that wants to have a party seven nights a week," he joked, slumping down deep in his chair.

The Mines, Doc explained, had its origins in a not-for-profit theater and coffeehouse that opened in 1970 down on North Lincoln. "We went from a coffeehouse restaurant to a folk music and poetry kind of a center, and then we went into bluegrass and finally into blues itself," he recounted. "We were there for eleven years and eleven months and eleven days—and it was November eleven when the roof fell in." With the building unusable he moved the club to a more upmarket site down near the Loop,[11] but high overheads and a terrible winter put paid to that, and after six months he moved the Mines again, to its new home across the street from B.L.U.E.S, in early 1982.

There were blues clubs in Chicago's white neighborhoods in the 1960s and early 1970s, but not many, and Doc believed that the Kingston Mines had been a pioneer in bringing black blues bands into the North Side. He even felt that the club had influenced the music: "Many of them had never worked in front of a North Side audience, or an audience that was mostly white, and it was a matter of learning a whole new technique and a whole new type of music. So many of them went from being rhythm-and-blues bands to blues bands, and the conversion was done at our club."

That seemed unlikely to me. Although the Mines had opened in 1970, it didn't start booking blues acts regularly until 1975—at least not according to the 775-page *Blues Who's Who*, which at six pounds two ounces seemed pretty authoritative. Big John's and Mother Blues, on the other hand, were booking major blues acts, including Muddy Waters, Howlin' Wolf, Magic Sam and Otis Rush back in the early- to mid-1960s. By 1975 there was nothing new about black blues musicians playing for white audiences, in Chicago or anywhere else.

Either Doc was indulging in a little mythmaking, or he was confused. There certainly had been instances of bluesmen changing their playing styles to suit white audiences. During the folk-blues boom of the early 1960s, plenty of musicians who for years had worn suits on stage and played Telecasters suddenly found they were expected to don overalls and use acoustic guitars.[12] But as Doc went on I began to realize that maybe the music itself wasn't his strongest suit: "We concentrate mainly on up-beat, Chicago-type, or urban, blues," he continued, asserting that "club-like blues for a long time was centered in the more rural type of Delta blues, which is a softer and slower type of music. There has been a move in the last several years to fuse the two: the rural Delta blues has become a more forceful, upbeat music, and the avant-garde type of blues has picked up kind of a softer tone, and they have sort of gone a distance to acquire a Delta sound, and the Delta people have gone a distance to acquiring a Chicago sound." There were probably strands in this confused tangle that could be woven into a theory of sorts, but I let it go. He was very tired.

What interested Doc most was creating a friendly, comfortable atmosphere, and in this he had been entirely successful. "It's a kind of place where people walk in and say, 'Hey, this is really nice.' And they enjoy themselves," he said. He was right about that. Whether by design or as a direct result of a management style that would give laissez-faire a bad name, the Kingston Mines had far more in common with a place like the Checkerboard Lounge, down on the South Side, than with B.L.U.E.S, just across the road. It had the authentic feel of an edgy blues club, without any of the actual edge. It was a winning formula.

Like many traditional blues clubs, the Mines had a house band, an accomplished outfit called the All Stars. At weekends, big names brought their own musicians, but during the week the All Stars usually backed up the featured artist, whether or not that artist had his own band. That didn't sound to me like the most effective way of getting the best performances out of these artists, but Doc was unmoved. It was Kingston Mines policy. "The reason is, the All Stars have been chosen for their ability," he explained. "Bob Levis, the lead guitar, is considered one of the best guitarists in the business. Bobby Anderson, formerly with Koko Taylor, has played with many of the top names in blues. Robert Covington, the drummer and vocalist, has been in the business about fifteen years. And then we fill in: for instance, Ken Sajdak is the piano player with Lonnie Brooks. So we have a band that is essentially tight, it works together, it rehearses together, they're able to back up anybody. And if we have problems with the guest star, they can fill in the gap."

On stage as well as off, Doc ran a relaxed regime. In most clubs, bands were happy to let other musicians sit in occasionally, whether to let a friend gain some exposure or just to give the guitarist a break to chat up a girl at the bar. At the Mines, sitting-in seemed to be ingrained in the culture. I asked Doc what his policy was. "In general I let the bandleader decide," he said. "When the bandleader doesn't care particularly, we try to hold sitting-in to the last one or two sets."

I suppressed the thought that only the Kingston Mines would employ a bandleader who didn't care particularly, but I had seen how this easygoing approach could have corrosive consequences. It was a source of pride to Doc Pellegrino that musicians enjoyed coming to his club, and one of its most eminent regulars was the harmonica player James Cotton, who was always ready to take a turn on stage if invited, and sometimes even if he wasn't. This, obviously, was good news for the crowd, because Cotton, by Chicago blues standards, was a huge star. One night with Jimmy Johnson on stage, supported by the house band, the All Stars, Cotton strode up in his pale safari suit, fresh from an early-evening festival gig and clearly still in the mood to play. Johnson moved aside with good grace, and Cotton launched into a concentrated blast of the best blues harp playing I had ever witnessed, directing the musicians as he went. A James Cotton solo could last for twenty-four bars and still only consist of one note, beaten percussively out of the harp: it was all about rhythm and the building of tension, and there was nowhere for the band to hide. But Jimmy Johnson was a superb musician, as comfortable playing soul or jazz as blues, and the All Stars were quick on the uptake. It sounded as if they had been rehearsing with the harp man for weeks.

When after three numbers Cotton finally got off the stage, to enthusiastic hollers and whoops from the crowd, Johnson stepped back to the microphone. He had been completely upstaged, and he knew it, and in an effort to win back our allegiance he wound the band up into a blitzkrieg performance of "Caldonia" at about two hundred miles per hour. It worked, but he was not pleased. When I talked to him later, he didn't mince his words: "That wasn't right. I really didn't like that," he said angrily. "He wouldn't like it if I did it to him. He's supposed to be a big deal, but to me he's no big deal, not like that. This is my gig, man! He was very high, too. You can't do that, man, that's not pro."

Doc was beginning to fade, and appeared, if possible, to have sunk down even deeper into his chair. As I gathered up my things he started telling me about the Mines' latest discovery. "We have a young blues musician called Sugar Blue who is a fantastic harmonica—or as it's called in the business, 'harp'—player," he explained, pleased to display this nugget of blues expertise. "He does stuff with the harp that I've never heard before. He's a new experience; he's taken blues, and he has added a dash of jazz, and a dash of pop, and a lot of high energy, and he has come up with something new. I think the man is fabulous, absolutely fabulous."

There was a long pause, and I looked up from my notebook. Doc Pellegrino was asleep.

• • •

I was intrigued by Jimmy Walker. He wasn't as big a name as Sunnyland Slim, but he was even older, and his distinctive boogie-woogie style was firmly rooted in the 1920s. "I'm seventy-eight," he told me.[13] "I've been seventy-eight since March." He invited me down to his apartment, at 750 East Forty-Sixth Street. He lived alone, but there was a fire station across the road, and the firemen had adopted him: "They watch me a like a hawk watching a chicken," he chuckled. "If something happen to me, if I get sick or something like that, they grab me up and run to the hospital with me. I'm not used to that. Some of them cats, they think I should do nothing but eat, but I don't want to eat. Man, we have a time. I just left from over there." He was talkative, with an impish air, and wore denim overalls and a baseball cap.

Walker played at rent parties in Chicago during Prohibition and had a four-piece band—harmonica, drums, and Homesick James on guitar—in the 1930s. He learned piano in his teens: "Back around 1917, 1918, guy used to come from New York, a female impersonator, he was a black guy," he remembered. "Called himself Gloria Swanson. This guy that played with him, his name was Willie something, he always played down there at Eighteenth and State Street, used to show me. I'd catch him where he was rooming. And I run into another guy, Lorenzo Murphy, he had been playing a little bit, so he tried to show me a little."

He might not have been a major artist, but Jimmy Walker was a living link to the Chicago of King Oliver[14] and Al Capone. He had lived in the city since 1907, arriving from Tennessee with his family at age two, several years before the first of the "great migrations" that swelled the black population of the city. Chicago in those days was racially segregated, not just economically but by decree: "No colored on the east side of State Street," as he explained it. He was fourteen at the time of the 1919 race riots[15] on the South Side but insisted that in his experience, Chicago seemed less divided along race lines back then than it was in 1982: "Way I was raised, I don't know nothing about no color. I look at you as a man, and I try to treat you that way. It's just that easy." He elaborated: "I remember when my mother was living down at Twenty-Seventh and Dearborn, whites was living next door, understand? And blacks was living on the other side of them. Blacks was living across the street, and whites was living next door, and all that. And nobody had nothing to say about it."

Walker's father died when he was six. "My mother had it pretty hard—maybe she would make at times about two and a half a day, sometimes a dollar and a half a day." When Walker was seven years old, she sent him to live with a Jewish family on Fifty-Third Street, where he would go to school in the mornings and work afternoons and all day Saturday on a horse-drawn wagon, delivering milk and cream around the South Side. On Sundays, he was taken home to see his mother. "I had a good time," he said. "I had everything a poor boy wanted. I always wanted to work, see, I never been in jail." He stayed with the Jewish dairyman for about ten years, until he found he could make money playing piano at rent parties. "Times was hard. You got fifty cents a night. Sometimes, if they sold enough moonshine, you got maybe a dollar. That was good money: you could take a dollar then and go to the store and you couldn't hardly get back home with the food."

Jimmy Walker never got a serious record deal, but he kept busy, making money sub-letting rooms, selling his own moonshine whiskey, and working in a steel mill. He played alongside Lonnie Johnson and Big Bill Broonzy, and developed his piano style. "There's a few guys that try to play like me, but you got a job on your hands trying to copy, see, because I don't play nothing twice the same way," he said. Walker admitted to fourteen daughters and thirty-six grandchildren, and had a fifty-two acre farm in Michigan, which since his divorce had been rented out. In 1964 he recorded an album on Testament, accompanied by Erwin Helfer.

When he was starting out as a musician, blues was less in demand than boogie-woogie, jazz, and jump. The success of a performance was measured by how many people danced and how much illicit whiskey they drank. "I don't play blues like it's supposed to be played, see, because I've got an up-tempo. That's not proper blues," Walker explained. "Because the blues is something that you live, see. You take the people over there in those countries that's starving: now those people are having the blues, you understand? Now you wouldn't consider me having the blues, you wouldn't consider yourself having the blues, you wouldn't consider somebody else having the blues where they've got money, and they're capable of getting just almost anything they want. See? It would be hard for them to have the blues." Over the years his style hadn't really changed. He still played mainly good-time music. For him the blues was something different, something powerful: "I can play 'em, but I don't play them, because everybody's playing this up-tempo. The reason I don't get down into the blues like it is, because when you really get out in the blues like it is, partner, you will cry behind 'em."

Walker was demonstrating techniques on his piano when the door burst open and a wave of huge white firemen surged in, wearing enormous boots and jackets. They seemed to fill the small apartment, wall-to-wall and floor-to-ceiling. The old musician looked up from the keyboard, smiling: we were cordially invited across to the station. Time to eat again.

• • •

Doc Pellegrino's favorite harmonica player was a new face on the North Side. With his earring, jewelry, floppy denim cap, and background in New York, Paris and the South of France, the thirty-two-year-old Sugar Blue brought an air of international glamor to the Kingston Mines. And of course there was also the Rolling Stones connection, the one thing everyone seemed to know about him: he had done session work on a couple of their recent albums and had played the riff that kicked off "Miss You."

His real name was James Whiting, and he was an extraordinary musician. His technical ability and his musical ideas seemed far too big not only for the harmonica but for the blues itself, and he seemed intent on seeing how far he could push them both. Two things struck me when I first heard him play: that he was not playing blues but jazz, and that the instrument cupped in his hands sounded less like a harp than some kind of miniature synthesizer.

"Well, I'm so much of a jazz baby," he explained. "But as a harmonica player I owe very much to cats like Big Walter and Little Walter. When they first started playing, it was very evident their jazz influences, like the big bands. If you sit down and listen to Little Walter, you can hear saxophone parts from big bands, and guitars are doing the horn lines." Sugar Blue's mother worked as a singer and dancer at the Apollo Theater in Harlem, and his father was a serious jazz fan. As a child he tried the saxophone, the violin and the drums before discovering an affinity with the humble harp. He spoke quickly and with quiet intensity as ideas tumbled over each other on their way out. He had suggested meeting at a favorite cafe, the aptly named Franco-American at 2845 North Clark Street, and we sat in the window one Friday afternoon taking nothing stronger than coffee to lubricate the conversation.

Three unhappy years in the U.S. Army had radicalized the young musician— he avoided Vietnam because he was AWOL when his company shipped out— and he spent much of the 1970s in Paris. Busking in the streets led to session work, and eventually he recorded two albums on Disques Blue Silver. It was while in France that Sugar came to the notice of the Rolling Stones. It didn't end well. Bluesmen down the ages have complained about being ripped off, and Sugar was no exception: "When I first met them it was a great big kick because it was the Rolling Stones, the world's biggest rock group, blah blah blah. But after I got to know them . . . it was a little thing so minor as a few hundred dollars which marred the situation," he said. "Simply for a few lousy dollars, man, it's insane, because finally the money's not important, it's the music."

A lot of older Chicago blues musicians might have put it differently, I thought. Sugar was philosophical: "Actually I think it was good for me, because if I'd got too sucked up into that thing it might have weirded me out. I've seen some of their sidemen that are constantly in their world, and as a result they've lost their musical identities," he said. "Maybe they did me a favor."

He certainly seemed to be focused on carving out a career in the Chicago blues. Since moving to the city earlier in the year, he had begun working regularly in Willie Dixon's band, and sitting-in at the Kingston Mines had also got him noticed, not least by Doc Pellegrino. *The Reader* granted him the rare honor, for a blues musician, of a respectful three-page profile,[16] which drew attention to the harmonica player's "ethereal-sounding bitonality . . . the perfectly defined swirls and contours of his melody" and his "floating, modal harmonies and slightly off-blue soloing." The young musician had just come back from the 1982 Montreux Jazz Festival, where he performed on the main stage, supported by Koko Taylor's band, before going on to jam with B. B. King. While there he also played with up-and-coming jazz giants Wynton and Bradford Marsalis.

Sugar Blue's instrumental technique was out there, and his soloing was fearless and full of ideas. He seemed hungry for change. "There are very few young people in the blues," he insisted. "At thirty-two I'm one of the babies of the music, and that's ridiculous. If there was more input from the younger generation, then it would change, because then you've got young ideas and a different approach to the music. Cats like Lurrie Bell: he's one of about three or four young blues guitar players, and the rest of them are thirty-eight, thirty-nine, forty, fifty. The music is becoming a little geriatric."

That was true. No doubt change would be necessary to keep the music vibrant, but I wondered how much change a typical North Side audience might actually be prepared to put up with. A lot of people liked the blues because it was old. Just as certain songs were standard fare, so were certain phrases and certain sounds, while the primal feel and emotional connection that so engaged its devotees had to be regarded, surely, as non-negotiable.

Sugar Blue seemed to understand that. Whenever I saw him perform, however wild and intricate and challenging his solos might have been, he always remembered to cover Chicago harp classics like "Help Me" or "Don't Start Me To Talking." If he was going to succeed in changing this music without alienating its fans, he would have to tread carefully. One step at a time.

2

Can Blue Men Sing the Whites?

Hoodoo Man Blues was premature. For some reason it took the whiteys a little bit longer to get into black Chicago blues than white.

—Bob Koester

After a long night on the South Side, I found myself in the basement apartment of a bearded, balding academic at the University of Chicago. It amazed me how this leafy, stone-built campus could exist in its protective bubble of academia and old money, an oasis surrounded on all sides by parched ghetto. The windows of the lecturer's living room looked out at ground level across a perfect, lantern-lit lawn. A skyline of Gothic towers and buttresses was just establishing itself against the first glow of day. We were twelve blocks from Theresa's.

Responses to Britishness usually went one of two ways: aggressively uninterested, as in "England, eh? Is that Prince Charles as dumb as he looks?" (Treasonably, on that occasion I could only respond, in surprise, "Oh, more so, I imagine.") Or simply interested, often guilelessly, like a huge man named Grizzly I met in a truck stop in Barstow while hitchhiking in 1979, and with whom I spent the best part of the night talking, fuelled by endlessly refilled cups of watery coffee. When we couldn't take any more of it, he let me sleep across the front seats of his car while he reclined in the back, two enormous feet protruding from the open door. "England, eh?" he said. "What language do they speak over there?"

An evident Anglophile, my Chicago faculty friend clearly regarded me as a rare prize: someone with whom to try out funny voices and talk about places neither of us had been. It was the accent. Even though, after several weeks in the city, mine was starting to swerve and wobble like a bus on a skidpan, it still seemed intact enough for him.

We had become acquainted as the only two white faces in the Checkerboard Lounge that night. Typically, there were only about a dozen other people there, and although billed, Buddy Guy was nowhere to be seen. My academic had a car, which promised a safe passage out of Forty-Third Street, and he didn't seem to be gay, which would have been awkward. There were beers in his fridge. We went through Monty Python for a while, although my knowledge of the classic sketches was far from complete. Had he wanted to move on to The Goons,[1] I would have been skating on thinner ice, although if required I could have obliged with Derek and Clive, being word-perfect in their entire oeuvre. Fortunately, he hadn't heard of Peter Cook and Dudley Moore's foul-mouthed alter egos.[2]

After a couple more beers, he suddenly remembered something and crouched down over his record collection. What would it be: a rare fifties bootleg of Buddy Guy playing at Silvio's? An original Robert Johnson 78? With the exaggerated care of a connoisseur bringing to light something unspeakably precious, he produced his collection of Bonzo Dog Doo-Dah Band albums.[3] My heart sank.

I knew about the Bonzos, and they worried me. I did agree that as an album title, *The Doughnut in Granny's Greenhouse* was unlikely to be bettered, but there was that picture of Roger Ruskin Spear on stage, doing a sax solo while holding a cardboard thought-bubble above his head: "Wow! I'm *really* expressing myself!" These English satirists could seemingly play in any style that suited them, and they pillaged anything—even the blues—not for inspiration but for comic effect. They selected some worthy targets, admittedly—pink-cheeked English boys singing about ridin' de blinds—but to this earnest fan they seemed dangerously close to taking the mickey out of the music itself. After one of his tours to Europe in the early 1960s, Sonny Boy Williamson remarked, "Those English boys want to play the blues so bad. And they do." The Bonzos would have liked that. I often wondered what they talked about with Eric Clapton when they found themselves supporting Cream in London in 1967.[4]

"These guys were just so talented they couldn't take anything seriously," my academic friend enthused. "Listen to this." And as the stylus popped in the groove, his basement room filled with a searing bottleneck scream: part homage to Elmore James, part merciless piss-take. It was "Can Blue Men Sing the Whites?" and I had forgotten how good it was:

> Oh I'm lyin' in my bed, pull the silken sheets up tight
> I gotta keep my strength, I got a show tonight
> I have a sip of coffee while I'm taking in the news
> Don't need to have a shave because I got to sing the blues

It put me in mind of The Bob Levis Question. A few nights earlier I had been sitting in the bar section of the Kingston Mines, scribbling notes during one of their interminable set breaks, when I got talking to a white man and his girlfriend. She was pretty and interested—I was pretty interested myself—while he wore a goatee and a black beret. He didn't seem quite the right age to have hung out with Kerouac or Ginsberg, but the anachronistic beat poet look was clearly intended to mark him out as a North Side liberal intellectual. We talked about the book I was supposedly writing. I said that I thought the portly, magnificently accomplished and manifestly white Bob Levis, who always played sitting down, was one of the best guitar players in Chicago: indeed, one of the best I had ever heard.

"And you'd *say* that?" the beatnik asked, surprised. Well, yes, I would. Of course. Why not?

I couldn't pretend I didn't know what he was talking about. The blues was a black musical form, or used to be. For a white observer to single out a white practitioner—even one who was usually the best guitarist in the room—felt like expropriation, and there had been quite enough of that down the years, as all fans knew. Many books about the blues, including my own university dissertation, began with an anguished recounting of the music's origins in slavery and oppression. Nonetheless, Mr. Beatnik's well-intentioned desire to differentiate black blues from white was basically just, well, you know. . . . Actually, wasn't he being racist?

It was easy to get muddled. Eric Clapton, for example, was one of my favorite musicians, and I loved to hear him play the blues. But to me there did seem to be an important difference between some young suburbanite who learned about the blues from records and, say, Floyd Jones, who learned his trade as a street musician in the Mississippi Delta. With a background like that, anyone listening out for it couldn't help but imagine—or was it real?—that in the music of Jones and his contemporaries they could hear a crucial extra depth of emotional content and feeling. Here was the "authenticity" that blues fans craved.

The implications were at once racial, cultural, historical, geographical, and, for all I knew, culinary, but more important, this was a view that seemed to encourage a distinction between the musician's credentials and the music itself. Which mattered more? What were you actually paying for when you handed over your two dollars at the door?

The quality of the argument could be depressingly low. I owned a disreputable-looking LP called *An Offer You Can't Refuse*,[5] which featured Big Walter Horton on one side and Paul Butterfield on the other: two harp players, one black and one white. The sleeve notes began:

"Seems an odd coupling? We think not, the root plus it's [*sic*] source derivation. Purists should not attempt to be subjective on non-black blues outfits because:

(a) Its [*sic*] racism.
(b) We are immersed in the digression of blues now, thus we cannot view it retrospectively, but as it becomes history, the vast change this musical hybrid has initiated will be obvious to all."

To any young and passionately anti-racist blues fan looking for a steer on the whole troubling "authenticity" business, impenetrable tosh like this was no help at all. Even proper writers, who had mastered the mysteries of the apostrophe and had their work published between hard covers, could be dogmatic on the subject. In the "Whites Versus Blacks" chapter of his 1976 book *Blues and the Poetic Spirit*,[6] the entertaining Paul Garon simply dismissed the idea that anyone white could perform the blues, practically exploding with blimpish rage: "The most baffling aspect of the entire phenomenon of 'white blues' is the legitimacy and relevance with which its perpetuators would like to see it endowed. This single fact is evidence of the cretinously low level of mental activity which is forced upon us under the guise of the creative process in so-called youth culture today. . . . The question, then, is not 'Can whites play (or sing) the blues?' but simply, 'Why do they bother, and who cares?'"

Again, not much help.

In the abstract, respect for the black American experience ran deep in most white blues fans, as did respect for the art form that seemed most poignantly to address it. It was a small step from there to regarding "authenticity" as more important than musical accomplishment. Meanwhile, the real question— whether this notion was anything other than sentimental claptrap—was the elephant in the room.

There was a passage in Charles Keil's *Urban Blues*[7] in which he sought to skewer this position by poking fun at the European "folk blues" tours of the early 1960s. He attended a London concert organized by a goateed German promoter—presumably Horst Lippman or Fritz Rau[8]—whose lineup, it seemed to Keil, "might best be described as a third-rate minstrel show. The same show presented to a Negro audience in Chicago . . . would be received with hoots of derision, catcalls, and laughter." And yet, he noticed, "the packed audience was appreciative to the point of reverence, listening to each song in awed silence; the more ludicrous the performance, the more thunderous the applause at its conclusion."

It was a point well made, but as a graduate student at the University of Chicago, Keil could hardly have imagined how British blues fans, forced to make do with home-grown talent, would have felt just to be in the same room as any singer who didn't have to fake the American accent, let alone in the same room as Sonny Boy Williamson or Howlin' Wolf, who were headliners on this "minstrel show." To react in awed silence, it seemed to me, showed commendable restraint.

More pertinently, when he wrote that passage in the early 1960s, Keil could not be expected to know how important such shows had been for fellow audience members like Keith Richards, Eric Clapton, and Jimmy Page, or the impact their responses were to have on popular music. Keil watched that London show and quite understandably thought he was witnessing the blues of the past, which he contrasted with the smooth, modern sounds of artists like Junior Parker and Bobby Bland. "A minority group," he conceded, "still like the dirtier down-and-out styles of Muddy Waters and Howlin' Wolf." In fact, in ways that would not become clear for some years, he was actually glimpsing the future of the blues. It was thanks largely to English R&B bands that British blues fans in particular, and white blues fans in general, would come to focus on Mississippi and Chicago, with Chess Records stars like Waters and Wolf at the top of the pyramid, and Robert Johnson lurking in the background like a specter at a dark, country crossroads.

This blinkered view would have far-reaching consequences, one of which was the rise of the "blues purist," the sort of fanatical fan who came to regard any blues that didn't fit the template as somehow inferior, watered down, or shamelessly commercial. As this specious distinction gained currency among white record buyers, it became self-fulfilling, imposing a kind of tyranny of white taste. This discouraged both artists and labels from taking creative risks and would ultimately stunt the growth of the blues as an art form. It became surprisingly pervasive: in his otherwise unimprovable *The Arrival of B. B. King*[9] even the erudite Charles Sawyer felt able to describe one particular album as "the purist's B. B. King"—meaning that on this occasion, uncharacteristically, the great man was accompanied by just piano, bass, and drums, as if this somehow made the music more "authentic."

As I sat in the bar section pondering the "authenticity" question for the hundredth time, the Kingston Mines All Stars finally got the next set underway. Bob Levis's flawless blues guitar came through clear and soulful, backed by the steady stride of Aron Burton on the bass. Then Lavelle White took to the microphone. Mr. Beatnik and his pretty girlfriend had gone. A pity: I would like to have asked him what he thought about Bob's playing.

Then again, maybe he was just winding me up.

• • •

The British had always been mad for American music and had discovered the Chicago blues long before their white counterparts in the United States. Their enthusiasm for blues grew out of imported rock 'n' roll, a brief craze for skiffle, the liberal idealism of the folk revival, and a kind of genetic predisposition for jazz that pre-dated Louis Armstrong.[10] Among the first bluesmen to make an impression was Lonnie Johnson, who played the Royal Festival Hall, while the singers Josh White and Big Bill Broonzy also spent time in England in the early 1950s. White was given his own BBC radio show. Thanks to small but adventurous jazz record labels like Vogue, it was possible to buy 78s by John Lee Hooker and Muddy Waters in the United Kingdom as early as 1952.

It wasn't easy for promoters to bring American musicians to U.K. venues because of Musicians' Union rules designed to protect its membership from foreign competition. However, these were gradually relaxed, and later in the decade Chris Barber's jazz band backed several tours of American acts, including the gospel singer Sister Rosetta Tharpe, country bluesmen Sonny Terry and Brownie McGhee, and, most famously, in October 1958, Muddy Waters[11] and his pianist Otis Spann. These performances were recorded and later broadcast nationally on BBC radio. This was two years before Waters's earthshaking show at the Newport Jazz Festival, which is generally credited with first drawing the attention of white America to the existence of Chicago blues, a process not completed until the "British invasion" of the mid-1960s.

British blues bands sprouted, modeling themselves on the classic Chicago combination of guitars, harmonica, bass and drums. The extravagantly side-burned guitarist Alexis Korner and balding harmonica player Cyril Davis, both veterans of the Chris Barber band, formed Blues Incorporated and played gigs in support of trad jazz acts. They recorded an album in 1962, *R&B from the Marquee*,[12] which included four Muddy Waters songs among its twelve tracks. Their band served as an academy for fledgling English blues musicians, including future Rolling Stones Brian Jones and Charlie Watts, and was followed in 1963 by John Mayall's Bluesbreakers. This was the ivory tower to which the twenty-year-old, blues-obsessed Eric Clapton would flee after his traumatic brush with grubby pop success in The Yardbirds. These bands were serious about their blues, sometimes painfully so. But in Clapton, Mayall secured one of the best young guitarists in London, and their sole album together was to prove one of the three defining blues albums of the period.

The *Beano* album, or as it was more properly known, *Blues Breakers* by John Mayall with Eric Clapton,[13] on which the guitarist was shown reading a comic while his bandmates concentrated on looking soulful, embodied the English blues sensibility. It was well read, moderately adventurous, and illuminated by flashes of brilliance. There was a studious performance of Robert Johnson's "Ramblin' on My Mind," a Mersey-beat version of Mose Allison's "Parchman Farm," and an enjoyably noisy attempt at Little Walter's "It Ain't Right." The vocals were of variable quality and rendered in not very convincing American accents. The songwriters were credited, so you knew whose records to look for at Dobell's on Saturday.[14] A pedestrian drum solo on "What'd I Say" was allowed in, presumably, because everyone else in the studio was too polite to object.

There was more to this album than careful carbon copies of Chess Records 45s. Like the Rolling Stones before them, the Bluesbreakers played with a certain attitude, and that attitude was expressed not in the leering pimpsqueak of Mick Jagger's vocal delivery but in lead guitar of improbable quality. Given equal billing with his bandleader, Clapton was granted plenty of space to perform on almost every song. Several showed what he could do as a sideman, but for me the best tracks, by a long way, were those included solely to showcase the young man's talents as a soloist: the Otis Rush cover "All Your Love" and, especially, the instrumental gems "Steppin' Out," which even I could figure out on my Epiphone acoustic, and "Hideaway," which I couldn't.

Clapton's take on the Rush guitar classic was a straightforward homage to one of his heroes, with few departures from the script. His arrangement of "Steppin' Out" showed real verve, as he took the piano, saxophone and guitar parts of the original Memphis Slim tune and made it sound like it was written for solo guitar. On "Hideaway" he started with a virtuoso vignette by Freddie King and built upward, adding twenty-four bars, a raft of new ideas, and somehow contriving—in a solo instrumental—to take three guitar solos.

If he could do that in the studio, it was easy to imagine how seeing the diffident young Surrey bluesman play live at the Marquee in Oxford Street[15] could be a life-changing experience. For me, age six, that was not an option, but a decade or so later I bunked off school with a friend and hitch-hiked up the M1 to the De Montfort Hall in Leicester. It was a markedly less atmospheric venue than the Marquee, but after seeing the guitarist play it didn't surprise me at all that fans in the 1960s had daubed "Clapton is God" all over London's Blitz-ravaged brickwork. Those of a train-spotterish bent enthused about the tone he achieved on the *Beano* album with his appropriately Anglo-American combination of Gibson Les Paul guitar and Marshall amplifier. A picture on the back cover showed Clapton, all Mod hairdo and manly sideburns, tuning the Les Paul as a cigarette smoldered in its machine heads, which explained the burn marks that seemed to scar most of the second-hand guitars I saw for sale in Denmark Street.[16]

· · ·

The second of the three defining mid-1960s blues albums I encountered was *The Paul Butterfield Blues Band*,[17] whose cover typeface made the Ts look like Gs, raising the odd snigger at school. This one seemed to offer a more realistic Chicago blues experience than the Bluesbreakers' effort, with a black rhythm section comprising Sam Lay and Jerome Arnold from Howlin' Wolf's band. It too featured a white virtuoso on guitar in the shape of twenty-two-year-old Mike Bloomfield, and rhythm guitarist Elvin Bishop didn't sound too bad either. Butterfield's harp was raucous and confident, and his vocals were occasionally reminiscent of Junior Wells. Respectful standards from Elmore James, Little Walter, Willie Dixon and Muddy Waters competed for groovespace with a smattering of lively originals. It thumbed its nose at the "British invasion" with a swaggering opening track called "Born in Chicago." There were no slow blues. Two tracks, "Waiting for Mr. Poobah" and "Screamin,'" were improvised instrumentals showcasing the guitars and harmonica, which hinted at what the band might be like to see in a live setting.

Bloomfield's guitar playing seemed more solidly grounded in the Chicago blues than Clapton's. It was easy to imagine him lurking in South Side clubs, absorbing lessons from great sidemen like Louis Myers and Jimmy Rogers, rather than sitting at home playing along to Freddie King 45s. But it wasn't a guitar album in the way that the Bluesbreakers' was. It couldn't be: the bandleader was a harmonica player.

According to the notes on the record sleeve, Paul Butterfield played in Chicago's blues clubs regularly, "in the company of some of the city's better young Negro bluesmen." Perhaps inevitably, the liner notes went on to tie themselves in knots on the issue of "authenticity," arguing that by concentrating on modern Chicago blues and ignoring the older, "country" styles, Butterfield had "neatly bystepped the problems that have prevented other young blues interpreters from attaining a comparable degree of fluency, ease, conviction and utter authority." Not only could the privately educated Butterfield, the son of a Hyde Park[18] lawyer, apparently claim "a long intimacy with the culture that produced the music," but also the music itself "was much less bound up in a maze of sociocultural factors than is the country blues of another time and place." But this didn't mean that Chicago blues was simply easier to play than country blues, being "devoid of significance or emotional content." Certainly not, as the notes explained: "The modern style is more readily assimilable simply because these factors are not operative in the contemporary blues to the same degree, or in the same way, as in the older blues. They are the music of here and now."

Well. After wading through that lot, it was relief to get the record onto the turntable. The music, at least, knew what it was trying to say. Butterfield was a good singer and a terrific harp player, and Bloomfield was fantastic on guitar. An arch little note advised playing the record at the highest possible volume, some years before such exhortations could be found on the back of virtually every rock album.

The Butterfield Blues Band were different from the Bluesbreakers in lots of ways, the main one being that the Americans learned their trade in Chicago's clubs, while the Englishmen—apart from occasional gigs in support of touring American blues acts—had learned by listening to records in their bedrooms. It showed in the overall quality of the two albums. There were noticeable areas of weakness in the English effort, and a couple of duff songs, but no such shortcomings with the Butterfield album. It was solid. They were good.

I still liked the *Beano* album more. Notwithstanding the two instrumentals, Butterfield and his band seemed just a little too respectful. Their album was an excellent, faithful, and notably lively reproduction of an urban blues style that had reached its apotheosis ten years before the record came out. It had little to offer that you couldn't get from a compilation LP of Muddy Waters's or Little Walter's singles. The only thing new about the band was that its front men were white: whereas in Eric Clapton, John Mayall appeared to have found a musician capable of something genuinely special, whose instrumental virtuosity looked to the future, even if the album's repertoire did not.

The same week that the *Beano* album came out, Clapton left the Bluesbreakers, and the blues, to form Cream with Jack Bruce and Ginger Baker. Not long afterward the second Butterfield album was released. *East West*[19] was very different from their first, with long, exploratory instrumentals inspired by John Coltrane and Indian music, short liner notes, and covers of songs by Nat Adderley and Allen Toussaint. As if acknowledging that they had arrived at a dead end with the first album, Butterfield's band was leaving Chicago and the blues behind and, like Clapton and Cream,[20] like Jimi Hendrix and countless other blues, pop, and folk bands on both sides of the Atlantic, moving on to bigger things.

The Bluesbreakers, meanwhile, without their star soloist, kept the faith. Their follow-up to the *Beano* album featured a new guitarist, as Mayall explained apologetically in his liner notes: "The personnel of the Bluesbreakers having changed since our last LP . . ." he began. That glorious subjunctive, like some clunking schoolboy translation of Tacitus, laid bare the essential English propriety that the Bonzos lampooned so gleefully. But Mayall didn't need to apologize. Clapton's successor was Peter Green.

· · ·

In the Checkerboard Lounge one evening I settled down to listen to the dreadlocked support band, fronted by the brilliant guitar player Buddy Scott, with the promise of soul singer Syl Johnson as the main attraction. I knew little about Johnson except that he was Jimmy Johnson's younger brother, and according to the colorful cardboard poster nailed to the wall outside the club, he'd had some chart success with versions of "Take Me to the River" and "Fine Brown Frame." I had an ulterior motive for being there. With an eminent headliner booked, I was hoping that Buddy Guy might also show his face. He was billed as an "extra attraction." As I was beginning to learn, a Buddy Guy billing didn't necessarily mean anything at the Checkerboard, but the five-dollar cover charge, and the sight on the stage of an amplifier I knew to be his, seemed to be grounds for optimism.

Another hopeful sign was that the beer was also more expensive than usual. I was resigning myself to making a warm can of Old Style last all evening when

Bob Koester marched through the door and bought me another one. The forty-nine-year-old owner of the Jazz Record Mart and founder of Delmark Records was in an enthusiastic mood, clearly ahead of me in beers, and chaperoning two young Italian blues aficionados around the South Side. He sat down and asked me who the band were. I filled him in as best I could, but he was probably just being polite, since he surely knew who Scotty was.

Rotund, bearded and avuncular, Koester was also restless. One drink and he suggested moving on somewhere. The young Italians were enthralled by their surroundings but equally happy to tag along behind a man who probably knew the Chicago blues scene better than anyone. He assured them that we could come back to the Checkerboard, because they, too, were hoping for a sight of the elusive Mr. Guy. Then we piled into Koester's car and headed off in the direction of 5944 South Halsted Street, the New Excuse Lounge, formerly Porter's, taking a detour via Theresa's Tavern for no reason that I could discern until Koester confessed he had done so unintentionally and purely out of habit, as though the car were on autopilot. At the small and pleasantly shabby-genteel New Excuse we found a good soul-blues band featuring Pete Allen, an excellent guitarist who was more often to be seen playing in the considerable shadow of Magic Slim. Our host and driver bought more beers, and after fending off a tipsy young woman who had taken a shine to the Italians, we were back in the Checkerboard in time for Syl Johnson's last set. Buddy Guy didn't appear.

As we left the Checkerboard the second time I grabbed the Syl Johnson poster off the wall as a souvenir and we climbed back into the car. Koester dropped the Italians off at their hotel in the Loop, and we continued north, calling in at the Jazz Record Mart so he could pick up some records, and again at a White Castle restaurant so he could satisfy a sudden craving for their weird miniature hamburgers, which were sold by the bagful. They were nicknamed "sliders," I was told, because they slid right in and then they slid right out again. Actually, they were pretty tasty. Steve Cushing's late-night blues show was murmuring on the radio.

"You should have been out with me last night," said Koester, driving with one hand and feeding himself sliders with the other. "Willie Johnson was playing on the West Side."

I knew that name. Would that be the Willie Johnson who played guitar on Howlin' Wolf's Memphis recordings, long before Hubert Sumlin joined the band? Sumlin was something, but Willie Johnson was something else. His amplifier on "How Many More Years" sounded like someone had reversed a truck over it. He used distortion, played power chords: invented rock guitar, as far as I could tell, in 1951. That Willie Johnson?

"That's the guy."

"He's still alive?"

"Certainly was last night. Great show."

Damn.

The car pulled up outside the friends' Wicker Park apartment where I had installed myself on the sofa for the summer. At the end of the street the sky was beginning to brighten over the L tracks, and with a cheery farewell Koester drove off: "You're all right, Harper!"

· · ·

Bob Koester might well have been in the habit of buying beers for total strangers, but in fact he and I did know each other a little. I had bought records at the Jazz Record Mart, and a couple of weeks earlier I'd interviewed him there. A woman standing in line as I took a photograph of him at the cash register asked, "Are you famous again, Bob?"

It was some time after hearing the *Beano* and the first Butterfield record that I discovered the third in my defining, mid-1960s set of blues albums. And it was Koester who recorded it, on the Delmark label: *Hoodoo Man Blues*,[21] by Junior Wells's Chicago Blues Band. "I thought, 'Here's a beautiful sound, and it's getting wasted,'" Koester told me. At the time, he explained, Wells was in dispute with his label, USA: "So I happened to come along at exactly the right time, and he did this relatively quiet record. Pete Welding in *Down Beat* gave it two stars, said it was a terrible record: it wasn't noisy enough, in effect, it should have had another guitar. Well, that wasn't what was going on at the club. The Buddy Guy trio plus Junior is what it really was: Buddy had the trio at Theresa's, and Junior was the separately hired feature artist, which is how Theresa's always works."

Koester had an enduring passion for old jazz and blues, a compendious memory, and, apparently, plenty of time. "I should be sitting in there knocking out royalties statements right now," he said, pointing to a corner office. "I'd rather talk." We were perched on stools in the Jazz Record Mart at 4243 North Lincoln Avenue,[22] hemmed in by rack upon rack of records, where customers roamed like grazing buffalo. The Delmark offices were upstairs.

Released in 1965, *Hoodoo Man Blues* wasn't the first Chicago blues album, but it was in the first half-dozen, Koester explained. In 1960 Chess released *Muddy Waters Sings Big Bill*,[23] which he reckoned was probably the first time that anything that could be described as Chicago blues was recorded for LP release. It bombed, he said, but in the same year, the same band played the Newport Jazz Festival, where instead of excerpts from the Broonzy songbook they did a knockout South Side set of straight-ahead Chicago blues. *Muddy Waters at Newport 1960*[24] was critically acclaimed and hugely influential.

Then, said Koester, there was *Folk Festival of the Blues* in 1963. This was a hard-to-find live album recorded by Chess in a West Side club with a couple of studio tracks dubbed in. In 1964 Prestige came out with albums by Otis Spann, Homesick James, and Billy Boy Arnold,[25] and Pete Welding's Testament label also released its *Modern Chicago Blues* compilation: twenty-one songs by eight different Chicago artists, including Johnny Young and Big Walter Horton.[26]

Although *Hoodoo Man Blues* put Delmark on the map, it was the twelfth album Koester had made. The label dated back to the early 1950s, when as a student at Saint Louis University he recorded his favorite band, a Dixieland outfit called the Windy City Six. At the same time, he found himself dealing in records in order to finance his own collecting. "It's like a drug addiction," he explained. "You become a dealer out of need." He started tracking down and recording old country blues singers like Speckled Red, J. D. Short and Big Joe Williams, and he released their material, initially, on ten-inch LPs. "There were no blues LPs in the early fifties: blues as blues, and not as folk music. And even the folk music audience was tiny then," Koester recalled. "My approach was that I'd record blues, and they wouldn't sell very well, but I'd have no competition."

He moved to Chicago in 1958 and bought a record store, Seymour's Jazz Mart, which provided some financial stability for the record label. After several changes of address and a new name, the Jazz Record Mart was still the bedrock of the business: "I've not missed any meals, basically, since buying Seymour's," confirmed Koester. "The struggle was always to get enough money to record something and then get enough money to release something. Delmark, with very few exceptions, has never really had a year in which it's showed a profit." For every successful record, he estimated, there might be one that broke even and then maybe two or three loss-makers. Looking only slightly pained, he remembered one by the avant-garde jazz saxophonist Anthony Braxton: "It sold, I think, two hundred copies."

Blues in the 1950s, as far as the album-buying public was concerned, was performed by singers like Big Bill Broonzy, Josh White, and the duo of Sonny Terry and Brownie McGee. In the early 1960s "rediscovered" bluesmen like Skip James, Mississippi John Hurt and Son House joined the circuit. With his own clutch of singers on the Delmark roster, Koester immersed himself in this strange, hybrid, folk-blues world. He had fond memories of the 1964 Newport Folk Festival, when he shared a house with the blues musicians: "It didn't have any furniture in it, and they brought in army cots. It was a hell of a place, man. Imagine—I slept in a room with Sleepy John Estes, Yank Rachell, and Hammie Nixon, and in the next room Lightning Hopkins shared with—I forget, he might have had his own room—and upstairs was Skip James. In the back, Jesse Fuller slept in a car with a shotgun by him—he had all the shit in the car and didn't want to unload it—and who the hell else was there? Son House, Fred McDowell and Annie McDowell, just a lot of real good people. At night every room was a different blues group playing, and I think they decided, 'Fuck it, let's get a dollar from everybody who comes in.' The guys asked me to collect the money. I remember an extremely famous white blues singer refused to pay. Turn your tape recorder off and I'll tell you who." I did as I was told. "Maybe he thought I was going to keep it!" Koester's laugh echoed across the store.

The happy times didn't last long. "The white blues singers were coming in. The John Hammond Juniors and Dave Van Ronks were dominating the concert scene[27] and getting gigs, and the Big Joe Williamses and the Sleepy John Estes were doing about three jobs a year. Or they were offered coffeehouse gigs for ten dollars a night. That sort of shit. It just pissed me off," Koester spat. Always simmering on the subject of racism, he came quickly to the boil: "I don't argue with a [white] guy's ability or desire or right to do it, but it was the perfect willingness of supposed liberals and old-left people to just cater to this fucking dominant racism that even today is still there in what's left of the folk music world," he fumed. He remembered a prominent folk music school in Chicago's Old Town asking for his help to find a blues guitar teacher. He suggested Big Joe Williams. "And they said 'No, no, we need somebody white—he won't be able to teach.'"

Koester glared down at the memory as if a dog had done something on the carpet. "Fuck it!" he exclaimed, as nearby customers glanced up nervously. "Joe's taught more goddam white blues guitar kids than he should have. He's generated his own fucking competition, and he's done it, just like Junior Wells has, very unselfishly." The teaching job went to Mike Bloomfield, who, according to Koester, quit after two days: "He said, 'They want me to teach them how to play like Broonzy.'"

The folk-blues phenomenon was short-lived. "Black country blues singers were doing business for a very few years in the early sixties," said Koester. "Sixty-four was about the high-water mark." But times were changing.

• • •

Koester was hands-off as a producer: he preferred to leave the music to the musicians. Of Junior Wells's *Hoodoo Man Blues* he said: "I thought it was a very unique sound. I do not bring any musical concepts to the studio, other than the idea of recording a band that I heard somewhere and liked. If the musician doesn't have his shit together, I sure as hell can't—I'm no bandleader, I'm not an arranger, I'm no musician. I'm just a fan with a checkbook."

Amos Wells Blakemore Jr. arrived in Chicago as a boy and made his first records in his own name in 1953, aged just eighteen. Elmore James and Muddy Waters served as session men. He learned to play harp at the feet of Sonny Boy Williamson, and he fronted The Aces—Louis and Dave Myers, and Fred

Below—one of the finest of all Chicago blues bands. By the mid-1960s Junior
Wells was at the forefront of the city's blues scene, a veteran of the Muddy
Waters band and the resident headliner at Theresa's Tavern. When I saw him
at the Hammersmith Odeon[28] in London, the next day's review in *The Guard-
ian* began: "Junior Wells has achieved the trick of making the very idea of his
existence seem impossibly exotic." This was true. He was a genuine star, born
to perform: a brooding and almost sinister presence during a slow blues, an
eccentrically electrifying dancer, and a mesmerizing singer who would punctu-
ate an impassioned tenor wail with weird, guttural clicks and growls. He sang
and played as if totally possessed. When Junior Wells was up on stage, nothing
else in the room could hold your attention.

When it came to musicianship, the band on *Hoodoo Man Blues* made the
Bluesbreakers sound like gifted amateurs and even put Butterfield's people in
the shade. If there were any question of "authenticity," this lot had it by the
bucketful. Next to these white bands, I felt, this one had to be the real deal, a
true representation of the Chicago blues. Trouble was, it didn't sound much like
the Chicago blues I thought I knew.

The opening track, "Snatch It Back and Hold It," reminded me of "Brand New
Bag"—even before Wells's sardonic reference in the lyrics to James Brown's huge
summer hit of 1965. The album's sound engineering had a spacious, architectural quality, giving parts of the session the feel of modern jazz. The music had
a precision that was new to me in a blues record. Silences between phrases were
like white space. It was spare, and it was funky. And the next song, "Ships on the
Ocean," a beautiful, slow, twelve-bar blues—lyrically opaque, to be sure, but full
of feeling—dispelled any doubts about what sort of album it was. Throughout
the album, Jack Myers's bass was jazzy and melodic. On the drums, a flamboyant Billy Warren seemed to have been plucked from some razor-sharp 1940s
dance orchestra, but he was just as adept at shepherding a song along with no
more than a delicate tap on the ride cymbal. As for the guitarist: how could
anyone that good be content to play with such discipline, as a sideman? It was,
of course, Buddy Guy.[29]

The album had clearly been influential. Junior's version of "You Don't Love
Me" had inspired the Allman Brothers to cover the song on their live *At Fill-
more East* album.[30] What I had previously assumed to be a quirky Californian
rendition by the Grateful Dead of "Good Morning Schoolgirl"[31] turned out to
be a note-for-note lift from *Hoodoo Man Blues*. Other standards like "Yonder
Wall" and "Hey Lawdy Mama" were delivered with an equally powerful twist of
individuality. Wells's grunts, moans and sighs were potent with sexual suggestion. Every track on the album was about Wells, his harmonica, and his unique
and soulful vocals.

Hoodoo Man Blues came out in November 1965, a few weeks after the first Butterfield album. The Bluesbreakers' *Beano* LP followed in mid-1966. Here were three contemporary albums of Chicago blues that not only made radically different demands on their listeners but also revealed crucial differences in their artists' approach to the music. The *Beano* album was polished and reverential, and it came to be regarded as a pinnacle of quality for British blues. *The Paul Butterfield Blues Band* was something of a pinnacle for the Paul Butterfield Blues Band, at least as a blues act, because almost as soon as it came out they, like Eric Clapton, moved on. They had studied the blues, graduated with honors, and their album had the dutiful feel of a final exam. The Junior Wells album was the most grown-up and least self-conscious of the three. It was created by musicians who were steeped in the traditions of their music, who were also prepared to play around with it, willing to look forward as well as back. They weren't trying to sound like anybody else. They were concerned mainly with creating something new and interesting.

Paul Butterfield sang, with a certain braggadocio, about being "Born in Chicago," as if it were a badge of honor. Sung by a rich white boy, the lyrics sounded idiotic,[32] but it was hardly surprising if he wanted to buff up his streetwise credentials, if only to trump the claims of the irritating British invaders who were making such a noise about their "discovery" of the Chicago blues. But of course his "credentials" also trumped those of Wells, Guy, and the other musicians on *Hoodoo Man Blues*, because they weren't from Chicago either. They'd moved up from the South—from Louisiana, from Arkansas, from Mississippi—like the blues itself. They were the music.

And that, to me, trumped everything. If it was a question of "authenticity," then *Hoodoo Man Blues* had it. This was the real Chicago blues. And yet it sounded so modern. How strange it was that the real thing had overtaken its imitators.

• • •

Delmark's first foray into modern, electric, Chicago blues was not an immediate success, but *Hoodoo Man Blues* was certainly noticed. "It started a thing," said Koester. "Sam Charters came to town shortly after the record was out and recorded those three Vanguard things. That led to the whole Vanguard involvement." The huge New York label was known for its jazz, folk and country blues, but Charters's massively influential three-album set, *Chicago/The Blues/Today*, recorded in Chicago in the winter of 1965, spurred it on to release solo albums by Wells and Guy, along with James Cotton and Charlie Musselwhite.

"*Hoodoo Man Blues* was premature. For some reason it took the whiteys a little bit longer to get into black Chicago blues than white," said Koester acerbically. "I have to say that the interest in Chicago electric blues was profoundly increased upon the appearance of the Paul Butterfield band at Newport, behind Bob Dylan, when Dylan got into an electric band thing."[33] The album's sales figures backed up this view: *Hoodoo Man Blues* sold only about fifteen hundred copies in its first year of release, but a lot happened during the next twelve months, not least the *Beano* album and Bob Dylan's blues-rock *Highway 61 Revisited*, with Mike Bloomfield on lead guitar. *Hoodoo Man Blues* then sold twenty-five hundred in its second year. After that, sales settled at around twelve hundred a year.

Never one to be discouraged by modest sales, Koester looked around for more Chicago blues to record, and in the years following Wells's first album he recorded Magic Sam, Luther Allison, J. B. Hutto, Jimmy Dawkins and Carey Bell, not forgetting the older blues styles represented by Roosevelt Sykes, Sleepy John Estes and, of course, Big Joe Williams. There were also three more Junior Wells albums. As the label's reputation grew, and with it the market for Chicago blues albums, according to Koester sales improved to the point where a new Delmark release could be expected to sell as many as five thousand copies in its first year.

The business of recording also became more sophisticated. As I spoke to Koester, the most recent sessions had been for Jimmy Johnson's second Delmark album, *North//South*, which was due out later in 1982.[34] "There were three or four sessions, and mixdowns. Even on a blues album, recording now can sometimes involve an hour of mix time to an hour in the studio, or even sometimes two hours. I think anything over an hour of mixing versus an hour of recording is obscene, really," said Koester. "Jimmy's new album is a much more polished kind of thing than I personally could do. Steve Tomashefsky produced it."

Delmark had produced some notable blues records. In 1981 it brought out a beautiful-looking double album of live Magic Sam performances from the 1960s,[35] which contained some real gems, in particular a timeless, rocking boogie from the Ann Arbor Blues Festival called "I Feel So Good." Another Delmark album, with terrible cover art, came close to musical perfection: Otis Rush's *So Many Roads*,[36] recorded live in Japan in 1975. For musical quality and emotional punch, I rated it second only to B. B. King's untouchable *Live at the Regal*.[37]

But it was the Jazz Record Mart, not Delmark Records, which remained the foundation of Koester's business. "If Delmark's twenty-eight years old, I doubt if there's been more than six or seven [years] in which we showed a profit," he said. As we sat on our stools among the ruminating customers, Koester explained that he had just put the label to one side, temporarily, while he concentrated his energies and money on an expansion of the main West Grand branch of the record store. Incredibly, *Hoodoo Man Blues* and several other important Delmark albums had been deleted: you couldn't buy a copy, even in the Jazz Record Mart.

"I regretted doing that, but when we re-issue *Hoodoo Man*, we'll probably have a five- or ten-thousand piece year on that, and that will more than make up for the sales we missed in the interim. In fact, it can be damn good business to do that once in a while."

Blues albums, it seemed, really weren't a good way of making money. "Musicians can't really believe a blues record can sell as poorly as two thousand, or one thousand," said Koester. "They find five thousand unbelievable. I'm sure most of the artists that we record do not believe the numbers. It's another good reason not to do royalty deals. The artist we have never had an exclusive contract with is the best-known artist on the label: Junior Wells. Some of the best records on the label. Never a bad one."

At the Court of King Luther

I spearheaded black musicians mixed with white musicians.
Promoters always kicked against it: "Bring black musicians."
The hell with you: play your own fucking concert.

—Jimmy Dawkins

The "West Side" style of guitar playing, which had so influenced rock music, was much discussed by blues fans, although much of the discussion centered on whether it actually existed. There was a long quote by Jimmy Dawkins in Mike Rowe's book *Chicago Blues* in which the guitarist explained that because there was less money on the West Side than the South Side in the 1950s, the bands there were smaller, so the guitarist had not only to play both lead and rhythm but also to supply fills and choruses from imaginary horns and keyboards. This made for a wonderfully exciting and noisy style, characterized by Robert Palmer as "gospel-tinged blues sung in minor keys . . . bursts of high-note guitar paced by bass-string riffs that still retained a little of the Muddy Waters feel."[1] But I suspected that its origins had more to do with generation than geography.

The musicians' generation, primarily: the classic proponents of the style, Otis Rush and Magic Sam, might have first found fame on the West Side and first recorded for Cobra at 2854 West Roosevelt Road, but they played in clubs all over the city, as did Buddy Guy, who was to become the most exciting "West Side" guitarist of them all. While in their teens, they were exposed to the urban buzz of Gatemouth Brown, Guitar Slim and B. B. King, not just the old rural blues of Charley Patton or Robert Johnson. Although they lived in the same Mississippi-steeped city as Muddy Waters, the electric blues that blared at them out of jukeboxes and the radio hailed from Houston, Los Angeles, Memphis and Detroit, not just Chicago. It was hardly surprising that these young players sounded different.

The blues writers who first latched on to the idea of giving this style of blues guitar a geographical name were also from a new generation. Early researchers had classified the old country blues according to its place of origin—the Piedmont, Texas, the Mississippi Delta—and so later writers like Mike Rowe perhaps felt it natural to do the same thing for this new kind of guitar playing they had identified in Chicago. It was a legitimate distinction, but a misleading label.

Right Hand Frank Bandy introduced me to Jimmy Dawkins as we stood at the bar in B.L.U.E.S. "This guy's from England," explained the genial bass player. "He's writing a book about the blues." I knew Dawkins by reputation, owned some of his records, and had seen him play in the club a couple of times. I never once saw him smile. The guitarist looked across at me like a bird of prey: "Everybody's writing a damn book."

But he agreed to talk. Dawkins, age forty-five, recorded his first album for Delmark Records in 1968[2] after making a name for himself in Chicago's West Side clubs alongside contemporaries like Sam and Rush. One thing he and I were agreed upon was that the "West Side" style was exciting for a reason: to play it well was phenomenally demanding. "You had a lot of three-piece bands around. We had to play hard, and we had to play the rhythm, and we only knew two or three chords," he told me. He had seen his fellow West Sider Luther Allison recently having to revert to the three-piece sound because his keyboard player didn't show up: "He had to play harder because he had to concentrate, and he had to play the keyboard changes and the sounds, you see: the pressure. He sounded good."

What I really wanted to talk about was blues and race. We were sitting in Dawkins's burgundy Cadillac outside B.L.U.E.S, where there were always black musicians on the bandstand and always black people in the audience. Yet the club was in a comfortably prosperous area of the mostly white North Side and was owned by two white men. "The whole thing just flipped like a coin," conceded the guitar player. "The black musicians are playing in the white clubs, owned by whites. The bands have bought into the white audiences' territory." There had to be a reason: perhaps the Chicago blues no longer spoke to the black community in the way it used to, I suggested. Maybe it was simply seen as old hat, superseded by newer and more exciting sounds. "I don't think that the black peoples turned their back on the blues," countered Dawkins. "I know what you're maybe driving at is this thing about blues music oppressed the black people." Indeed I was: the fairly commonplace idea that a music rooted in Southern slavery, with its passive acceptance of misery and misfortune, was hardly relevant to the prickly and assertive racial politics of the modern era. "I think it was a thing of pride," he said. "At one time blacks was thinking that blues music didn't take much education in music: anybody could just sit on the back porch and pick a guitar, blow a harmonica, and moan the blues. So they wanted to move up into a caliber that they figured was a rich man's music more, I guess. But I don't think it was anything down against the blues."

For Dawkins there were more concrete causes for the blues' migration from one side of town to the other. "It's dangerous times. People now, black and white, are going to the liquor store and the grocery store, and going back home. You know: knocks on the head, and you break a ten-dollar bill at the bar now and you can't walk out the door unless you pay for protection. The clubs have changed, the clientele have changed," he explained. "Now what you got? Educated college white kids, being newly exposed to the blues, their friends bringing them out to hear it because we're playing in a white club. Might have wanted to hear it before, but it was in a black neighborhood, and they was told don't go down there because the blacks all carry knives and will cut your throat."

It was true that many white people viewed Chicago's black ghettos with an almost mythic dread. If the South and West Sides had ever enjoyed a golden age of peace and prosperity, it was long forgotten. The city's transition from industrial leviathan to rust-belt relic had been remarkably rapid, with catastrophic consequences for the traditional laboring jobs that had brought most of the city's black population, and their music, up from the South. Steel jobs peaked at two hundred thousand in 1970. The vast Union Stock Yards, a pungent square mile of pork and beef production that employed fifty thousand people in its heyday, closed down in 1971. The Yards were still marked on my dog-eared street map of Chicago, between Halsted Street and Ashland Avenue, bounded to the north and south by Thirty-Ninth and Forty-Seventh Streets, a few blocks from where some of the South Side's most famous blues clubs had been.

Summer race riots were pretty much an annual occurrence in America's cities during the 1960s, and in April 1968, after Martin Luther King Jr.'s assassination, the chaos in Chicago lasted more than forty-eight hours. Eleven people died, and Mayor Richard J. Daley authorized the police to shoot to kill. By the end some twenty blocks of Madison Avenue and Roosevelt Road on the West Side lay in ruins—two of the main commercial strips of black Chicago. The South Side also suffered. Some of the inner-city's black neighborhoods in 1982 still sported a freshly-blitzed look, and the impoverished cores of the South and West Sides had a reputation for crime and violence. The blues scene in black Chicago had not recovered: "Years ago all the bands up and down Roosevelt Road," said Jimmy Dawkins. "Now, we got Theresa's, the Checkerboard, a few others, but you don't have the avenues that you used to have." He wasn't looking at me as we spoke. He was looking into the past straight out of the car windscreen, southward down the endless length of Halsted Street.[3]

There was a surprising element of Jim Crow[4] to the white-owned venues that started to book black blues bands in the early days, Dawkins remembered. "They used to tell us, 'If you all going to play here, just the band come,'" he said. "They thought I should not bring a woman with me, especially if she was white. And most times the band was always black, and you'd get shelved off into some sad boot, in some room built onto the bandstand, then they'd send this guy in to take orders of what you want. That was right here in Chicago on Broadway and North Clark Street in the sixties and fifties. Luther Allison, myself, Freddie King—we played them sometimes."

As more white fans discovered the music, alerted by the likes of Butterfield and the Bluesbreakers, the Chicago blues began to spread beyond this esoteric handful of white clubs, and into festivals and concert venues. Dawkins remembered the 1969 Ann Arbor Blues Festival as a tipping point. "Sixty-nine was a big year for the black blues musicians to get going some recognition," he said. "Luther Allison got his pick-up there; even my recognition come up better. Freddie King, certainly." The festival line-up included Muddy Waters, B. B. King, Big Mama Thornton, T-Bone Walker and Son House, as well as Dawkins, Luther Allison and Magic Sam. Howlin' Wolf came on stage riding a moped. The guitarist also acknowledged the importance of musicians like Paul Butterfield and Eric Clapton. "That mainly was a big help for the blacks. It got us recognition,[5] them saying, you know, 'I like Howlin' Wolf.' I think both can help each other."

One audience arrived as the other drifted away, but for Dawkins and his contemporaries there was more to this cultural shift than simply playing to white faces instead of black faces. The Jim Crow attitudes might have gone, but complex racial undercurrents still lurked beneath the surface of the Chicago blues. "I'm always kicked around for having a mixed band," Dawkins explained. "But I hire whites and I hire blacks. I don't have time to look for colors, I look for good musicians." Many successful bluesmen in Chicago did the same, but not everyone could see it in such straightforward terms: "You get blacks who say, 'Why don't you give some of these poor blacks a job, they need it bad.' And then you get the whites that come up and say something to some of my fellers, 'Why you playing with these niggers, you're too good, you should have your own band.' You get it on each end."

He got it from European promoters, too, only theirs was a reverse racism. It might have been a well-meaning attempt to secure a payday for some black musicians, but I suspected the real reason was a monochromatic view of "authenticity" that I recognized: audiences in Frankfurt or Lille or Nottingham who were paying to see a real blues band flown in from the blues capital of the world would simply expect it to be black. They had plenty of white bluesmen of their own who were regarded, literally, as pale imitations. Whatever the reason, Jimmy Dawkins wasn't interested: "I spearheaded one of the biggest things, taking black musicians mixed with white musicians into Europe, because the promoters always kicked against it: 'Bring black musicians.' I took who was in the band: ever who was in the band, that's who go. Other than that, the hell with you: play your own fucking concert."

• • •

I walked into the Kingston Mines at about eight fifteen to find the club cool and dark and busy with quiet activity as it was readied for another long night. I had an appointment with Luther Allison. "Sure, I do interviews," he said. "Come early tomorrow and we'll have a nice talk, man."

There was no sign of him. An air conditioner was being put in, and rubble from the wall was spread across the floor. Behind the bar Sharon was pulling out hundreds of bottles of Old Style and loading them into the iceboxes, while in the music room Diane was laying out candles and ashtrays and straightening chairs. The equipment on stage was still in position, and Luther Allison's collection of spare plectrums was still stuck in place on the microphone stand, somewhat depleted after the rigors of the previous night. It had been a good gig. His band was tight and professional. Allison was a stupendous musician who played blues, rock, and reggae, and had three pastel-colored Fender Stratocasters and a roadie to look after them.

I sat down and asked Sharon for a coffee. Steve Ditzell, Junior Wells's guitarist, was sitting at the bar with his guitar case, also waiting. People wandered in and ordered beers and food, and slowly the club began to fill up. I looked at my watch. Michel, the band's piano player, arrived and ate a sandwich. Hannibal, Allison's roadie, tuned his boss's guitars, arranged them in a neat row on their stands, and settled down to a game on the Pac-Man machine. Junior Wells strode in, brisk and businesslike beneath a huge hat, signaled to Steve, and walked out with him. The noise level in the club rose in competition with the jukebox, and Bill MacFarland, the horn arranger with the All Stars, was soon fully occupied taking money at the door.

With about ten minutes to go before the gig was due to start, Luther Allison came in through the back door in jeans and a white tee shirt, looking slim and fit, younger than forty-two, and confidently cosmopolitan with his purse and sandals: he had lately been living in France. He glanced at me, remembered, and put an apologetic finger to his temple. We agreed to talk during his set breaks.

He liked talking. He spoke of himself in the third person: "A lot of people don't understand Luther Allison." He had a lot of opinions, and one led inexorably to another as his train of thought continually derailed itself. He had his son Bernard with him, age sixteen, who was beginning to play guitar and would sometimes join his father on stage. When I asked what future he saw for his son as a blues musician, his answer went on for several minutes and took in white blues clubs, audience reactions, the burden or otherwise of being the son of a famous father, the bass player Aron Burton (Bernard was wearing an Aron Burton tee shirt), and the importance of Jimi Hendrix and the Rolling Stones. By the end of it I was no longer sure where we were and neither, apparently, was Luther Allison: "So you're still fighting the same battle," he concluded, irrelevantly. "But it's all the same music."

We were talking in the club's cluttered and windowless back office, Allison sitting regally on Doc's antique office chair. As if suddenly remembering what we were talking about, he added: "If he gets his high school diploma, he can always pick up a couple of years in college if necessary, later. But right now I want him to concentrate on music." Young Bernard looked up from his newspaper and smiled. He was already a good guitar player. I had seen him on stage.[6] When he took a solo and played the guitar with his tongue, his dad covered his face in mock embarrassment, and then did the same. The crowd loved it.

Luther Allison went into the studio to cut his first album in 1969, just a few weeks before playing a blistering set in front of several thousand people at the Ann Arbor Blues Festival. But since this promising start, his career had struggled to gather momentum. He was renowned for a while in the 1970s as the only blues artist signed to Motown Records, releasing three albums on Motown's Gordy label that were well-produced and mixed high-energy, guitar-led Chicago blues with a bit—sometimes a lot—of soul and funk. They were very good in places, capturing his committed and soulful singing style and the kind of powerful guitar playing that made him so watchable on stage. But they didn't make him into a star. Since moving to France he had built a strong reputation in Europe, helped by a series of live albums, but he wanted more. "It's been a real tough uphill battle for Luther Allison," he complained. "All I need in the States is a record label. I'm free right now. We're trying to negotiate with Rounder Records. Rounder and Alligator are the only two that's doing something, and I will not go with Alligator. I can't discuss it, but I just don't see nothing he could do for me." Alligator Records was home to the guitarists Son Seals, Albert Collins and Lonnie Brooks: Luther Allison could have been a good fit, a fourth musketeer. But he wouldn't elaborate.

Like Jimmy Dawkins, Allison had been playing for both black and white audiences for much of his career, but he didn't agree that black demand for the Chicago blues had entirely disappeared. "You still got some black clubs," he said. "Certain bars I play now, like Biddy Mulligan's, I get quite a few blacks coming in. Up here on Lincoln Avenue, far as blacks are concerned in the Kingston Mines, it's a little different. You're getting more blacks across the street at B.L.U.E.S: that's just like being in the West Side or the South Side, in a typical black bar." Along with his older West Side colleague he also employed mixed bands, although he hadn't always been too impressed by some of his white sidemen. "They're spoilt," he said. "We used to do a Sunday morning until four o'clock, go home, take a bath, and get ready for the blue Monday party, which starts right around seven in the morning. That's what it takes: we all used to do these things. And you get these guys from Wisconsin, Minnesota, from these little places that have to close up at one o'clock, they can't do it. They be bitchin' and bitchin' and bitchin'. But when the paycheck come, no problem."

According to Allison some of these young white musicians also found Chicago's black blues scene rather overwhelming. There was one in particular: "I took him down to the Checkerboard," he said. "He was from Minneapolis, a wonderful guitar player. He got scared: 'Luther, I want you to know, man, I'm just a suburban white boy.'" The club was rowdy, Allison recalled: "People were drunk, acting the fool and having a good time. If they had their three-piece suits on and tie, they had their three pieces on. If they was ragged and dirty, they was that too. Nobody was introducing nobody on stage: people was up and doing their thing. He couldn't understand that." Allison attempted to explain to his nervous young protégé that this was part of the reality of working in black clubs: "This is what we have to deal with. Ain't nobody bothering you. You wants to pay your dues." But apparently he didn't, and his boss was contemptuous: "I say, 'From now on you shouldn't tell people you play the blues: because you're not understanding it or feeling it at all. That's why you won't be *nothing*, see?'"

It wasn't just the young musician's timidity that seemed to so infuriate Allison but his reluctance to engage with an experience the older man clearly regarded as a rite of passage. It was as if immersion in this rowdy, low-rent Bacchanalia was some sort of cultural baptism, an essential requirement for admission to the dark underworld of the blues.

In the sunny uplands of the Kingston Mines back office, meanwhile, the presence of Luther Allison had not gone unnoticed. A succession of old colleagues and acquaintances peered round the door to say hello, and he greeted them all from his chair like an emperor receiving tribute from the provinces. When the time came for the final set, there was a crowd of musicians in the house ready to help out. Guitarist Eddie Clearwater took to the stage for a couple of numbers, with Bernard accompanying on rhythm. The young singer Valerie Wellington, a vivacious new arrival on the North Side and a great favorite in the Mines, got up to do "Wang Dang Doodle," her party piece, and a couple of other numbers from the Koko Taylor songbook. Finally, as Doc Pellegrino stood at the microphone and said that he would let the music go on for a few more minutes if we hurried up and finished our drinks, an old friend of Luther's whose name I didn't catch sat himself in the spotlight and made some extraordinary sounds with an eight-string lap steel guitar, which sounded alternately like an organ, a synthesizer, and a slide guitar. It shouldn't have worked, but it did. With a pipe clenched between his teeth, he sang "The Thrill is Gone."

• • •

Dynamic, ballsy blues guitar was once the soundtrack of Chicago's West Side, and as I walked along Wilcox Street one steamy afternoon, two blocks south of Madison Street, I fancied I could hear its echo. I was looking for Hip Linkchain's house, and when I got closer, I realized it wasn't my imagination: I really could hear a Gibson 355 at full throttle, working through the chord changes and loosing off staccato bursts of notes like gunfire. His wife opened the door with a smile. He was practicing in the kitchen, sitting on a steel chair in his dressing gown, slippered feet up on the amplifier.

Hip Linkchain was a cheerful, tubby man of middle height, with a boxer's arms, a bone-crushing handshake, and a ready smile that revealed a rabble of undisciplined teeth. "There'd be a band on every corner: every corner, middle of the block, nothing but blues," Linkchain remembered, when I asked him about the neighborhood. "This was back in fifty-six to sixty-one. Then all of a sudden, boom: everybody went to DJ.[7] Dancing stuff, stuff they hear on the air, you know, folks would go crazy about that. They could get a disc jockey much cheaper than they could get a live band."

But he didn't miss the old clubs one bit. "There was always a fight, somebody shooting, you got to put your guitar down and fall on the floor, and you get sick of that. You get scared. Every night. Terrible place. They throw chairs at each other. It just got that I didn't want to play for black people."

Linkchain came to Chicago from Jackson, Mississippi, in 1954. His fellow West Side guitarists Otis Rush, Freddie King and Magic Sam were already there, and Jimmy Dawkins and Buddy Guy followed close behind. "We were all about eighteen at the same time," he said. He didn't mind disagreeing with his friend Dawkins on the subject of West Side style. "There ain't no difference," he said. "We're all playing the same thing: them guys in the South pull a string, over here we pull a string. It don't make you play no different because you've moved from one side of town to the other. Only thing I know is that two guitar players never sound the same way: you play the blues, I'll play the blues, it's all different, like the fingerprints on your hands." His own guitar playing was quite distinctive: less fluid than Rush's, more intense than Dawkins's, more conservative than Guy's.

His real name was Willie Richard, and he had a new record out: *Change My Blues* on Teardrop Records.[8] It was his first studio album, a pleasingly solid effort—although like most blues albums, it didn't even come close to the spark of a live performance—recorded with his regular band of Rich Kirch on guitar, drummer Fred Grady, guest appearances on piano by Pinetop Perkins, and produced by bassist Frank Bandy. He had cut a few singles on a label called Lola in the 1960s, without much success, and during that lean decade for the blues, when many players left the business altogether, Linkchain quit too, before trying his luck with other music: "Mostly R&B, and soul stuff," he said. "It just wouldn't work. It gets too boring, because they ain't saying nothing. I wound up coming right back to the blues. It's just in you, there ain't no way to get around it." Because down in Mississippi, he explained, he was brought up listening to his father's records: Robert Johnson, Blind Lemon Jefferson, Peetie Wheatstraw, Sleepy John Estes. "I started playing when I was eight years old," he said. "I was in the cotton fields then. I used to listen to people way back, like Fats Domino and then, later years, Little Richard and Muddy Waters, Jimmy Rogers, Little Walter. In 1952 B. B. King came out, and I used to listen to Bobby Blue Bland. Everything that came out good, I would listen to it."

Linkchain didn't give up factory work until the mid-1970s, when he began getting gigs on the North Side. Now he played gigs all over the United States and had just come back from nine weeks in Europe. At B.LU.E.S he and his band earned $250 a night, and I wondered how much he could expect if he got a booking in a black club: "Nothing," he snorted. "Twenty-five dollars for a sideman, and somebody big like Junior Wells, they're paying him forty dollars to stop by and do a show. Junior Wells can go up to Biddy Mulligan's on the North Side and make seven hundred dollars a night. That's why when you go to Theresa's he won't go up and play: he ain't making no money."

Linkchain was happy to be a regular at B.L.U.E.S. "He's mostly keeping the blues alive up there," the bluesman remarked approvingly of the dark little club. "People treat you nice there, all your whiskey, free, place is crowded all the time. You can have fun, and people be happy. If they was to have more places like this in every town, the blues would be real, real big."

• • •

I lugged my copy of the *Blues Who's Who* over to Johnny Littlejohn's because I wanted him to sign it for me. It was a bright morning and already hot by ten o'clock, when I arrived at the front steps of his house on North St. Louis Avenue. He was impressed with the book: "Man, this got everybody in it," he remarked, flicking through. "I ain't seen but one white man. Everything the black man created, the white man taken and put money behind it and made money out of it, which is what they're trying to do with the blues. If they could sing, we'd be out of the blues." He turned a page. "Here's another honky," he laughed. I lent him my pen and he signed beneath his photograph in an unsteady script: John W. Funchess.

Littlejohn was a jovial personality on stage, but in conversation his sense of humor was easily overwhelmed by his sense of persecution. Almost as soon as we sat down in the front room of his well-kept bungalow, with its television set under the window, plastic covers on the furniture, and his wife clinking crockery in the kitchen, the telephone rang in another room. It was a short conversation: an offer of a gig in Canada, somewhere near Toronto, he explained as he came back: "Eight hundred dollars: what the hell am I going to pay the band?"

he complained. He said he had turned it down. "Take a whole band for eight hundred dollars? That man is sick."

Despite this invincible sense of self-worth, Johnny Littlejohn was not a big star. The only major label to have shown an interest in him was Chess Records, but the four sides he cut there in 1969 were never released. As well as a few singles for minor labels in the 1960s, he recorded an outstandingly good album for Arhoolie in 1968,[9] another on the ABC subsidiary Bluesway in 1973, and a couple of others for French labels. No bluesman ever got rich that way, but Littlejohn was not one to be philosophical about the economics of the record business. Although he had signed contracts with all these labels, he was not a literate man, and he was convinced he had been cheated. "You can't trust nobody. You can't take nothing for granted. They don't need you: sell all your shit and make money off it, all these big shots getting rich off the poor people. Motherfuckers eating high off the hog, you know, and you got to eat his foots or his damn chitlins or his guts or something," he lamented bitterly.

Although not a big recording artist, Johnny Littlejohn was well known and respected in Chicago and worked regularly on the North Side, especially in B.L.U.E.S, as a front man, sideman, and singer. On Thursdays, when the club booked two bands who played alternate sets, Littlejohn was often paired with Jimmy Dawkins, and the generational contrast in their singing and playing styles was instructive. Dawkins played dirty, distorted chords with incisive arpeggio breaks and sang his low, plangent vocals close to the microphone, which brought out the timbre of his voice. But when Johnny Littlejohn took to the stage, he played a clear and expressive style of lead guitar inspired by B. B. King, but also stupendous slide with the pure, raw Delta sound of Elmore James. In his slow blues you could hear, in both his voice and his instrument, powerful echoes of the Mississippi plantations. The more I saw of Littlejohn, the more I came to think of him as the consummate Chicago bluesman. He was born in 1931 and grew up in Jackson, Mississippi, leaving the South at age eighteen. He was only a few years older than the high-energy West Side guitarists, but artistically he belonged to Muddy Waters's generation. His music had deep roots, as he was well aware.

"We got lots of bands here now that's listed as blues players, but they don't play no blues," he asserted. "Lonnie Brooks is one: he's a rock 'n' roll man. Mighty Joe Young, he's a rock 'n' roll man. Buddy Guy is listed as a blues player, but he went to James Brown and all that kind of shit. Magic Slim, he's a blues player. Eddie Taylor, he's a blues player, Sunnyland Slim, he's a blues player. Muddy Waters, Little Walter before he died, Jimmy Rogers is a blues man. These guys helped to make the blues, and they never tried to go nowhere else. Blues is played one way, and that's blues."

Littlejohn made a name for himself in Gary, Indiana, in the early 1950s and was soon working Chicago clubs too, mainly on the West Side. By the 1970s he was getting regular bookings at the Wise Fools Pub, Biddy Mulligan's and the Kingston Mines, and he became a fixture at B.L.U.E.S once Gilmore and Hecko opened their club in 1979. "B.L.U.E.S is taking care of business," he said. "They have hired more musicians in Chicago than anybody in history. They give everybody a chance: every night it's a different band, there's something going on. B.L.U.E.S is something like home, you know, where white and black go together. You don't have no fights."

A musician who could afford to turn down eight hundred dollars for a night's work was obviously doing OK. I knew he couldn't be earning anything like that at B.L.U.E.S, and I seldom saw him listed playing anywhere else, but Littlejohn's bullish self-confidence had been boosted by a recent trip to Japan with Carey Bell, where they were fêted by blues-mad crowds and apparently paid serious money: "I went to Tokyo on the sixteenth and was back on the twentieth. I was over there five days and I made eight thousand dollars: they took care of the hotel, plus food." By contrast, on a six-week tour of Europe he had earned less than half that.

It was some years since Littlejohn had been inside a recording studio. He claimed he wasn't interested. "I don't know no company now I would cut with, unless he got two or three hundred thousand dollars, flat money," he pronounced. I looked at him, slightly incredulous. This was such a fantastical amount that I couldn't quite believe he was serious. I began to suspect he simply couldn't resist kidding a young blues fan who had brought along a book for him to sign.

I asked him about his musical influences. He learned about slide guitar, he explained, by listening to country music on the radio. Then he said: "I was playing slide before Elmore." I looked at him again. One glance at the *Blues Who's Who* on his coffee table could have given the lie to that, as he must have known, even if he couldn't read it. Elmore James was born in 1918: the great slide guitarist was playing with Robert Johnson and Sonny Boy Williamson when Littlejohn was still a child. But he went on: "I was playing around Club Woodrow in Jackson, and somehow or other he come in and heard me." Somehow or other? Johnny Littlejohn met my gaze with a round-eyed, innocent expression.

As I walked back to Chicago Avenue to catch the bus, I thought back over the interview and came to the reluctant conclusion that even though Johnny Littlejohn was among the finest bluesmen in Chicago, it would be unwise to trust a single thing he'd said.

A couple of weeks later I heard he was out of town, doing a gig in Canada, somewhere near Toronto. Good money, apparently.

4

Peeling Potatoes at Carey Bell's

I'm just beginning to play more for black audiences,
and it's like it brings you back home – makes you feel
like you're getting back with your groove again.

—Lurrie Bell

One Thursday evening I went up to B.L.U.E.S on North Halsted Street to catch the first set by Brewer Phillips and Ted Harvey, Hound Dog Taylor's old band. The dark little club was packed: three deep at the bar, hot and smoky. The veteran Houserockers[1] didn't play the North Side very often and were accompanied by a bass player. In Hound Dog's day they never worried about such niceties. They had also given themselves a name, the Atomic Souls. The rangy guitarist tortured his Telecaster with a stiff-fingered, no-nonsense boogie that was pure Chicago, interspersed with surprisingly fluent lead breaks. Phillips's playing hinted at the intensity of the so-called West Side style but never delivered on the promise. Just as a solo seemed about to escape, he would slam the door. Floor-filling, roughneck urban blues was their stock in trade, not emotional self-expression. These men weren't out to impress anyone, just rock the house.

Carey Bell was headlining up the street at the Kingston Mines, so I was surprised to walk in there and find Sugar Blue sitting in at the start of the set, blowing, as ever, as if his life depended on it. The intense young performer could often be found in the Halsted Street club, but it seemed out of character—provocative, even—for him to take the stage on a night that belonged to another harmonica man.

I sat down a few tables back from the stage to await developments. Carey Bell was nowhere to be seen, but when I next looked round he was sitting next to me, leaning forward in his chair, waiting to go up. I made some inconsequential remark and received no more than a polite acknowledgement. Bell didn't take his eyes off the stage, as though steeling himself for the night's work ahead. Here was a young upstart who needed to be put in his place. At the end of the song, the two of them traded the seat: the older man got going with his big chromatic harmonica and Sugar Blue settled himself to listen. Such rivalry as existed between them was tempered by good-natured banter, for the house was far from full this early in the evening. But Bell opened with a heavy instrumental piece, walking up the aisle to where we were and standing there, shoulders hunched, hands clasped around his harp, looking down at Sugar Blue and blowing up a hurricane of sound. All eyes were on the pair of them, because the show had just become a contest.

I had recently bought Carey Bell's album *Last Night*, released by Bluesway in 1973, with a back-up band comprising Eddie Taylor, Willie Smith, Dave Myers and Pinetop Perkins.[2] As well as the musicianship of these consummate bluesmen, it was an album notable for Bell's inventive, exploratory soloing. It opened with the full-toned Little Walter title track but also contained many a nod toward the lyrical precision of Big Walter Horton. There was a cheeky, Cotton-esque vignette on the instrumental "Freda" and on at least a couple of songs—"Leaving in the Morning" and "Mean Mistreater"—Bell seemed to be trying his hardest to sing like Junior Wells. But the album also showcased his individualism, and one song in particular made my ears prick up, "Love Pretty Women," where the harp made exuberant leaps from one octave to another and picked out phrases in an unusually frenetic arpeggio. It was a harp style I had come to think of as distinctively Sugar Blue's, but on an album recorded years before anyone had heard of the young New Yorker.

Bell could be a surprising musician. I was reminded of the fact again one night when I called in at B.L.U.E.S for a set by Jimmy Rogers, only to find Bell on the bandstand too. It was a rare chance to see Rogers, who had worked alongside the greatest artists in Chicago, had played on some of the most famous blues records ever made—Muddy Waters's "I'm Ready" was one, Sonny Boy's "Don't Start Me to Talking" another—and recorded throughout the 1950s under his own name for Chess. His reputation was cemented by a long association with Muddy Waters, and he was held in high esteem not just as an instrumentalist, sideman and singer, but also as a writer of truly original blues songs. "Walking By Myself," an irresistibly catchy, classic pop tune, was a hit. "That's All Right" also made it into the charts. Both had become standards, and you could bank on hearing one or the other somewhere in Chicago pretty much every night. Fifty-eight years old, Rogers had a beguiling tenor voice, impeccable diction, and a fluid, finger-picking guitar technique straight out of prewar Mississippi.

I was watching Rogers, naturally, and only gradually did it dawn that something unusual was happening at the other microphone. Carey Bell held one note on his harp for what at first seemed slightly too long—maybe four bars—and then for what became an improbably long time—another four—gazing out over the top of his instrument with an amused expression. Finally, I shifted my attention away from the guitarist and looked over at Bell as the long, drawn-out, single-note solo steered the song back into the turnaround. He didn't even seem out of breath. I realized I had witnessed an example of circular breathing, something I had only seen demonstrated before on children's television, with a didgeridoo.

A disciple of Walter Horton's—virtually an adopted son—Carey Bell was the obvious choice as second harp back in 1972 on the album that bore his mentor's name.[3] It was Alligator Records' second-ever foray into the studio, with Eddie Taylor on guitar. Horton's singing was full-voiced and confident, with an occasional hoarseness that underlined his efforts with a weary gravitas, and his playing was never less than sublime. But on the instrumental duets, with Bell on the right-hand channel and Horton on the left, according to Bruce Iglauer's[4] helpful liner notes, it was the student's big chromatic sound that more often took center stage, while his teacher was apparently content to provide elegant fills and harmonious instrumental commentary. It was an album that burnished the reputations of both men.

Back at the Kingston Mines, the applause at the end of Bell's opening solo was intense, with Sugar Blue applauding as long and as loud as anyone. The older man had made his point. Not that he had much to prove.

• • •

"I used to live with Big Walter, years ago. He was a heck of a harp player," said Carey Bell. We were sitting in the front room of the Bell family's brick-built bungalow on South Elizabeth Street, a long bus ride south on Halsted, followed by a short walk. So, was Bruce Iglauer right when he wrote in the liner notes about Horton being more comfortable as a sideman than as a leader? "Well, that's his version. I don't know whether he feel that or not. To me, he was OK. Walter's nervous anyway. He need some pills. His nerve was gone."

Summer sunshine streamed through the windows, and the affable bluesman was slouched comfortably in an armchair, addressing my questions thoughtfully and with an air of amused detachment. I mentioned how much I liked the Alligator record. "Yeah, me and him did a lot of rehearsing on some of that stuff. Some of the stuff we did off the top of our heads. The part that we rehearsed I was playing bass: I'm playing bass on some of that album." Bell was due to go to Europe later in the year, as part of the American Folk Blues Festival, for $250 a week. I had heard musicians complaining about the money on these tours, but Bell was dismissive: "They can't make that much money in the United States. They just talk a lot of stuff. You can't make two-fifty a week here in the States unless you got a big hit record out. I don't have a big hit record out, but I do have a couple of records out. They're not hits. The money's all right, you know."

The harp man's attitude to the economics of blues life seemed commendably pragmatic, but he was not without his principles. He would always insist on a royalty agreement with a record company, he told me, rather than the one-time session payment that so many of the older musicians lived to regret. "I never did that yet, and I don't think I never will. If I can't get no royalties, I don't want to record. You could, a lot of guys did that, I know that. If there's enough money up front, you could do it. But if I do my own material they have to give me royalties, or I won't do the record."

Bell had recently been in the studio again, recording a new album with his twenty-three-year-old son Lurrie for Rooster Records,[5] a label co-owned by *Living Blues* magazine's Jim and Amy O'Neal. Of its twelve tracks, three were instrumentals and no fewer than eleven were credited as originals, including a new arrangement of "If the Ocean Was Whiskey." Of the new songs, one at least was performed with all the swagger of a future standard: Lurrie's "I'll Be Your .44." The soon-to-be-released *Son of a Gun* was recorded over four days in May and June at the Odyssey Sound Studio in Chicago.

"They're going to push it because it's a small company," Bell explained. "Musicians, got to pay them, studio, got to pay that, and you got to go back in the studio for the mixdown, and all that stuff, then they got to have the record pressed, they got to get the jackets—so that's a lot of money. So they got to push the record, all in order to get their money back. They gotta hustle to sell the record. They've got to stick the record in every little place they can get it in. Where it's good on my part, I can get gigs because I got a new record out."

Bell was particular when it came to gigs. He said he could personally make twenty-five dollars for a night's work in, say, the Checkerboard Lounge, but fifty at the Kingston Mines. "That's why I try to stay up that way," he explained. "The black clubs ain't gonna pay you nothing. First thing they tell you, 'Well, we didn't do so good in here tonight, but I bet you next week it'll be loaded.' You can tell when you ain't going to make no money," he added, leaning back in his armchair in resignation. "First goddam thing he do is bring you half a pint, and two cherries sticking up in it, and four or five glasses for the band: 'Be better next week.' I used to play in clubs that had no white faces, period. Black got to use their head. Ain't no way in the world you can do anything without the white faces. Black don't own shit. When he go to work, he go to work for the white man, only way you can make a living."

The rise of the North Side blues clubs mirrored the fall of the working-class neighborhoods in the south and west of Chicago, but a handful of bars on North Halsted Street and Lincoln Avenue could never replace the buzz of the Chicago blues in its heyday, and as far as Carey Bell was concerned, business now was bad all over the city:[6] "People ain't working—ain't no jobs. They ain't got no money to go out with, so that cuts down on the club business, cuts down on the musicians, and everything else. I'm not kicking on fifty dollars: fifty dollars is all right with me. At one time I wasn't making but fifty cents a night, and half a pint of whiskey. Sometimes I wouldn't get that, and play all night long. Oh yeah."

The Bell family house was a busy one. There was clattering in the kitchen where Dorothy, Carey's wife, was preparing lunch. Children dashed in and out, and on the front steps Lurrie was talking to a friend, the rhythm guitarist Eli Murray. From somewhere within came the sound of a baby. Carey Bell surveyed the scene with equanimity. He was born in Macon, Mississippi, in 1936, taught himself harmonica as a child, ran away from home, and started playing in clubs around Meridian in a band led by his stepfather, the pianist Lovie Lee. "I started off playing western and country, doing the train,"[7] he explained. "On my first harmonica. That's what I started off on. Then I left the train and I started to learn something else, you know, listen at the radio and records. I was listening at Hank Williams, all them guys. I was playing gospel, too. I play a little jazz, too." He remembered first playing blues in 1953 and arrived in Chicago three years later. He took factory jobs and played on the street, gradually building enough of a reputation to get work alongside some of the biggest names in the business— on bass and occasionally drums, as well as harmonica—including Eddie Taylor and John Lee Hooker, and the guitar virtuoso Earl Hooker. From the end of the 1960s he was in demand as a sideman, both in the studio and on the road, and he found regular work in Chicago, at festivals, and on overseas tours.

"I was working with the big guys, Muddy Waters, Willie Dixon, Howlin' Wolf," he recalled. "They always had work, so I was steady making money." More recently it hadn't been so easy. "I just had a band two and a half years. This is the worstest year I had, since I had the band."

Carey Bell's preference for playing in the white-owned clubs wasn't just about the money. "They appreciate the music more better," he contended. "More than the black peoples do. You play all night long, you never see a black person do one of these here," he said, clapping his hands. "They don't show you nothing." Applause was a stimulant that fuelled a performance: "It make you play much harder, and more better, and stay on the set more long! Up on the North Side, they know about the blues. And so much is happening in the last couple or three years, like ChicagoFest and all this stuff. Were you here for ChicagoFest?[8] Right, they got a blues stage, they got all kinds of acts down there," he said. "They pay like six or seven hundred for two sets, and you pay the band off it. Any time you work for something like that, or a college, it pay way more money than a club do."

North Side clubs, college dates, festivals: Carey Bell knew where to find his audience, and it wasn't in the traditional heartlands of Chicago's black neighborhoods. The young men on the street outside might be walking around with suitcase-sized radios on their shoulders, but they weren't listening to the blues. "They're not really listening at their mom and dad, either," the musician observed wryly.

• • •

Lurrie had a gig that night with the Sons of Blues,[9] way down at East Eighty-Third and South Cottage Grove in a place called the New Living Room. He invited me to come along with him and Eli Murray, and we would meet bandleader Billy Branch and the rest of the band at the venue. This gave me an excuse to hang around for the afternoon and watch the comings and goings of the Bells' chaotic household. There was a daughter in her twenties, with a very young baby who was sick on Carey's shoulder as he picked her up. Two teenage girls were polite and not at all surprised to find a British visitor in the kitchen. A boisterous set of young boys careered about: musicians, I was told, with their own band, The Ding-Dongs. One of them was dismayed to be left holding the youngest member of the family, and stood at the bottom of the stairs shouting up at his sister, "Come and get your baby!" Two little girls, ages about five and two, seemed to find the general mayhem most satisfactory, looking around with wide eyes but breaking off occasionally to have territorial disputes with their brother. There was an old man sleeping on the couch in the living room and another sitting on the stairs by the kitchen door, to be part of the conversation. Two sharp-looking girls, friends of the older sister, were laughing and passing round a joint as Lurrie and Eli, like young princes, kidded with them and teased the little ones. At the center of it all was Dorothy, stoking the washing machine and stirring the stew, feeding the family in stages and cheerfully juggling the duties of cook, mother and sounding board. Eli and I were handed a large saucepan of potatoes and told to get on with it.

When it was the grown-ups' turn to eat, we sat down at the table and Dorothy dished out the stew, potatoes and greens. She looked quizzically down at her British visitor, with his two-handed knife-and-fork technique. He was, in turn, looking quizzically at his plate. "Do you even know what you eatin'?" she laughed. "Them's neckbones."

After lunch Lurrie took his seat by the window and I put a new cassette in my tape recorder. I was familiar with his 1978 recordings for Alligator's *Living Chicago Blues* series, when he played not only as a member of the Carey Bell band and the Sons of Blues but also accompanied Lovie Lee alongside Eli and his father. Then, just nineteen years old, he played with a confidence and maturity that seemed to mark him out as one to watch. Now, four years later, it was clear from seeing him perform that he was not content to be just another blues guitarist.

"I guess I've been moving pretty fast," he said earnestly. "I've advanced. I've had the chance to go overseas about four times. I've worked with Little Milton.

It makes me feel good, it makes me feel like, 'Well if you want to do what you're setting out to do, Lurrie, you can do it—look how fast you're moving.'"

It was hard, he agreed, to create a distinctive and personal style on the guitar. "I play a lot of B. B. King licks. Me and Eli was talking about that. That's a challenge. If you can get a sound of your own, the same groove that B. B. King put, and get away from that B. B. King sound, and make people know that it's your sound, that's what I want to learn. I'm not trying to sound like nobody else. I learned a lot from B. B. King, and Albert King and Muddy Waters, they really inspired me, but when I play the blues I put my own feel into it." It was difficult to have a conversation with a blues guitarist without the name of B. B. King cropping up. "They say he work like three hundred and some days out of a year," said Lurrie admiringly.

Playing with Little Milton had given the young bluesman a taste for the more formal, big-band style still favored by the stars of the black blues circuit, many of whom had yet to make an impression on the white market. "Most black peoples like B. B. King, Little Milton, Bobby Blue Bland, Tyrone Davis," Lurrie explained. "I got plans of like, recording with horns, and keyboards, that feel of playing behind a big orchestra: really blues, but everybody getting off, you know what I mean? I want to know that feel, that feel of the big sound. I'm standing up there, and I'm the magic of it all, creating it, trying to put the fire to it."

He might have grown up playing alongside Carey Bell, but Lurrie was clearly his own man when it came to musical tastes and attitudes. His love of the modern city blues exemplified by these smooth, tuxedo-wearing crooners could perhaps be explained by the fact that he was a guitar player. You'd be more likely to meet Junior Wells playing on a street corner than see a harp player in an orchestra like Bobby Bland's, which owed far more to the sophisticated groove of the great dance bands than to the down home country sounds that gave birth to the Chicago blues. More important, and although it might have puzzled his father, Lurrie had an ideological attachment to the idea of being black, which was typical of his generation. As a twenty-three-year-old Chicagoan he had grown up against a backdrop of social unrest, simmering civil disobedience, and the fiery rhetoric of black politicians fighting to create a more equal society. Meanwhile, his father was dealing with the realities of putting food on the table in an unequal one.

If Carey preferred white clubs because they paid better, Lurrie liked to play black clubs because to him it felt right. But his own rich blues heritage, steeped as it was in his father's music, was practically unique for someone of his age; the new black attitudes engendered in the 1960s and 1970s were expressed in new music. There were hardly any black clubs left in Chicago that were prepared to book a blues band: not if they could offer soul, funk, or disco instead. This put Lurrie and his fellow Sons of Blues in the interesting position of being musical missionaries, spreading the gospel of the blues in its own heartland.

"I figure that if I'm playing for black people, and I love what I'm doing, hope-fully somebody gonna like it," he said. "And lately that's what we've been doing, me and Billy. We've been playing for these black clubs four nights a week, sometimes more, and the crowd, every night, seem to be getting off into it real tough." One of these clubs was the New Living Room, where we were headed that night. Another regular haunt of the SoBs was the House of J Lounge, at 2518 East Seventh-Ninth Street, and for several months they had played the Blue Monday slot at the Taste Entertainment Center on South Lowe.

"I love playing for anybody, period," Lurrie continued. "But I've been playing for white audiences, professionally, since I've been out here. I'm just beginning to play more for black audiences, and it's like it brings you almost back home, you know, makes you feel like, hey, you're getting back with your groove again, and the young people are relating to what you're doing. Finally."

But just as the clubs had grown out of the blues habit, so had their clientele. "When you look at them you figure they're on the disco level," Lurrie mused, smiling. "I'm looking at it like I might have to change the one-two-three blues, the one-two-three pattern. I don't know what I would call it, rock or whatever. It would be blues to me. It would have to be in order for me to play it. The feel of it, you know what I'm saying? If you do have the one-two-three blues, put something in it, make it stand out. You might do a certain solo, a twelve-bar solo, and—God *damn*—not just your regular basic blues lovers, but *everybody* would listen. I'm talking about that feel which just hits you. I think I can do that."

On stage, Lurrie's guitar solos had a choked and sometimes crippling inten-sity. Few guitarists attempted to express such depth of feeling, and fewer still were prepared to take the risks he took. I saw him at the Kingston Mines one evening, down in front of the stage, sitting in on guitar with the Junior Wells band. The great harp player was in full flight, jerking and jiving and contorting his face, carried along with the music like some electrical conductor. Suddenly, as if Lurrie's mind was moving too fast for his fingers, his solo lost its momen-tum. He stumbled, and stopped, leaving Wells suspended in mid-pirouette. Barely creasing his immaculate cream suit, the diminutive blues legend leaned forward and had a word in the young guitarist's ear.

• • •

The New Living Room was a comfortable little neighborhood bar in the far South Side, a long way past the dividing line where intimidating ghetto gave way to settled suburbia. The SoB band had regular dates there, Fridays and Saturdays, and the place was pretty full. The audience was smartly dressed, middle-aged, and entirely black. Eli wasn't a full member of the band, but at gigs he would borrow Lurrie's guitar and sit in for a couple of numbers, enduring a ribbing as he did so from the rhythm section, drummer Mose Rutues and J. W. Williams on bass: "I ain't doing none of that Hendrix shit, now!" Eli's style, it was true, did stray more toward rock than blues.

Lurrie was fascinating to watch in much the same way as Hubert Sumlin was. He thought hard about every note he played, crouching over his guitar and genuinely improvising. Every now and then—which was a lot more often than most guitarists in Chicago—he would come up with something new and unexpected. He traded solos with Billy Branch and stepped off the stage, still playing, to dance among the audience. The two of them shared the singing, their repertoire a mix of crowd pleasers like "Sweet Home Chicago," some of their own material, and occasional surprises like War's jazz-rock "The World Is a Ghetto," which the sardonic Branch introduced to the audience as "Latino blues." The evening came to a cacophonous finale with the SoBs' own particular version of "Mystery Train," sung by Lurrie and driven hard by the thunderous rhythm section, with not just the harp doing the moan of the train but Lurrie's guitar as well.

It was an excellent gig. Afterward the band stood around on the street in the early hours, talking and laughing, slightly amazed with themselves. I arranged to do an interview with Billy Branch at their next one, at Biddy Mulligan's on Wednesday, and Lurrie offered me a ride to the Racine L stop in his big Ford LTD coupé. Eli sat in the passenger seat while I was folded into the space behind them, puzzled not for the first time by the way in which American cars could be the best part of twenty feet long and still have no room in the back. As we cruised along dark and deserted South Side streets, a song came on the radio that was fast becoming the soundtrack to the summer of 1982:

> Broken glass everywhere
> People pissing on the stairs, you know they just don't care

It was "The Message," by Grandmaster Flash.[10] The chorus went:

> Don't push me, 'cos I'm close to the edge
> I'm trying not to lose my head

Eli said he liked it. Lurrie seemed less convinced. As the two young musicians discussed the merits of the song, I wondered what message they were getting from it. It didn't sound like the blues to me, but it was surely a member of the same family: perhaps a delinquent cousin. And I was no expert, but from what I had seen, that edgy, defiant chorus seemed a far more relevant reflection of South Side life than "Sweet Home Chicago."

At the L station, Eli came in with me to act as bodyguard. It was deserted except for the man in the ticket booth, who was practicing on an alto saxophone. Eli started teaching him "Cold Women with Warm Hearts." As a guitarist Eli was, naturally, an Albert King fan.

• • •

Wednesday came, and I arrived at Biddy Mulligan's just gone midnight, after an hour and a half at the mercy of the Chicago Transit Authority. The place was almost empty, but the band was sounding good. Eli, on stage, glanced up and greeted me like an old friend. J. W. and Mose propelled the music forward as Lurrie focused on backing Billy Branch's harmonica with his guitar, not just note-for-note but tonally: hunched and frowning, brushing the strings with the pads of his fingers, tongue pinched between his teeth in concentration.

In the set break, true to his word, Branch came over and sat down. Light-skinned, bearded, articulate, the thirty-one-year-old was born in Chicago but brought up in Los Angeles. It wasn't the only thing about him that was far from typical for a Chicago bluesman: he had a politics degree. So was he a political animal? "Yeah, I am a political animal, to a degree," he shot back. Then perhaps he could expand on the politics of the blues and tell me why the music had fallen so far out of favor with its traditional audience?

"Everybody got their own theory. My theory is that after the sixties, after demands were made, and riots, we did receive some compensation. We got civil rights programs, a lot of us went to college under the scholarships, and different special programs under Kennedy and Johnson. So there was a feeling of content, maybe a feeling like, 'We don't have the blues any more.' So it kind of disappeared from the airwaves."

A feeling of content. Really? "You know in the fifties—and this is only thirty years later—black people couldn't even sit at the front of the bus," Branch explained. "In the United States, not just South Africa. And even still, you don't have the signs, but there's plenty of places black folks can't go, right here in Illinois, right here in the city of Chicago. Like Cicero, like Mayor Daley's neighborhood, Bridgeport. I wouldn't walk out there after dark."[11]

I had to point out that there were plenty of places I wouldn't go either. "Contrary to popular belief, black people aren't naturally inborn violent against white people," Branch said evenly. "How could they be, when . . ." He stopped and smiled, leaning on the table. "Don't start me to talking. We live in Mayor Byrne's city, and that's Mayor Byrne's city from the North Side to downtown to the South Side, to the West Side. These are the politicians that run the city, and they gotta get their money, and we have to get favors in order to eat. So you don't bite the hand that feeds you. That's the way it is. Times are hard."

I had read in *Boss*,[12] the veteran journalist Mike Royko's merciless dissection of Chicago politics, how Mayor Daley's infamous, corrupt Democratic machine in the 1960s was propped up by the black vote. "It was like, Daley or who else?" Branch explained. "It was one or the other, and at least Daley would send some turkeys around Thanksgiving time, maybe a few hams around Christmas. At least you might make five or ten dollars if you pulled the right lever in the voting machine. What other candidate was going to do that? Something beats nothing, you know."

William Earl Branch returned to Chicago from California at age eighteen to study political science at the University of Illinois. He had already taught himself the harp and would cite Little Walter and Sonny Boy Williamson as influences. He toured with Arvella Gray, did occasional session work, played with the Jimmy Walker Trio at Bill Gilmore's club Elsewhere, and in 1975 sat in with Muddy Waters at the four-hundred-seat Quiet Knight on West Belmont Avenue. His politicization in the blues began after graduation, with a series of music residencies in Chicago public schools. Funded by the Illinois Arts Council, he was in partnership first with a piano player, Shelley Fisher, and then a guitarist, Martin Dumas. "We actually taught the kids how to play the instruments, make up their own songs," he explained. "We'd bring in blues artists like Willie Dixon and Big Walter, and the kids would put on their own blues show. It went good."

For the past three years, however, Branch had been working with Lurrie Bell on a more ambitious program of blues education. "That's under Urban Gateways: like a private donor, and a state-funded agency. It hires artists, all kinds of artists. Magicians, dancers, singers, you know," he said. "We deal a little bit with the history of the blues and incorporate it into a performance: take it back to slavery and try to work it up to date. We've had 'em as young as three and four years old, all the way up to high school. Me and Lurrie, we travel all over, white suburban schools, black ghetto schools, Mexican schools, all over."

Chipping away at a wall of ignorance, it must have seemed especially galling for the young duo that they had to work so hard to make their music relevant to black children who had never encountered it before: whose parents, even, might never have owned a blues record.

"We come from a cultural basis, and let them realize that the blues is the foundation of every American music," said Branch. "We tell them, 'This is your music. Black people created this music, and it's something to be proud of.' A lot of times the kids, they don't know anything about the blues, but after it's brought to them in such a way that they find out that everything is the blues, it's one of the few times a child would actually, in a group, air his problem. We make a song about, 'I didn't do my homework today, and I can't go out and play, I feel so bad, just like a ball game on a rainy day.' And there's like five or six hundred kids singing this all together: well, they feel good."

But the serious young harmonica player was under no illusions. Radio and television were the doors to recognition, and you had to listen pretty hard to find the blues on the airwaves. It was unheard, unappreciated, and unloved, lost among the background noise of popular culture, and virtually ignored by its own people.

"With the advent of rock and rhythm and blues and then finally funk, it disappeared so bad that right now the main reason they don't identify with it is they don't hear it," he said. "They refuse to play it. They claim they refuse to play it because nobody wants to hear it—I'm talking about the media people in control of the radio stations—but actually it's a Catch-22, because the reason it's not in demand is because they don't play it. If they don't hear it, how can they buy it?"

• • •

Branch had also been playing in Willie Dixon's Chicago Blues All Stars since 1976, and Dixon had made a big impression on the young harmonica player. He did that to everybody. He was a huge man, an ex-professional boxer and bass player who was steeped in show business, with a music career reaching back to 1930s vocal harmony groups that played Chicago lounges like Cafe Society and The Pink Poodle.[13] He first recorded with the Five Breezes, on the Bluebird label, back in 1940, but he was best known for his years spent at Chess Records as a producer, songwriter and organizer in the 1950s and 1960s.

Since the demise of Chess, the king-sized bassist had carved out a solo career of his own, mining virtually the entire Chess blues catalog for his performances. It was true that many of the songs were credited to him, and how many Dixon actually wrote was a subject for discussion among musicians, although not while he was within earshot. There was no dispute about "Wang Dang Doodle," at least. Surely the most irritating song ever recorded, except possibly for "29 Ways," no one else claimed to have written it. Even Dixon, it was said, agreed that its charms quickly faded.

He put on a great show and commanded the stage. He would bring a double bass along—as much as a prop as an instrument, although he was a competent player—but would mostly leave the playing to his band and simply stand at the microphone like a preacher or, as he would have it, a storyteller. I had seen him perform several times, in 1979 and 1982, sometimes with Billy Branch on harp and sometimes with Sugar Blue, and usually also with one or two of his sons, Freddie and Arthur, on electric bass and piano. It was fun to hear him rattle through classics like "Spoonful" and "Little Red Rooster," and when he introduced "I'm Your Hoochie Coochie Man," he was careful to point out that its hoodoo paraphernalia of black cat bones, mojos, and John the Conqueroos were primitive superstitions, and not what blues singers really believed. His more interesting performances were often of more recent material. The chorus of one new song went: "It don't make sense—you can't make peace." Another I hadn't heard before railed against religion: "Get you a straight or get you a gay, get a man or a woman, but have it your way. I'll tell you why, it could be a lie— there might be no pie in the sky when you die." It wasn't often that you heard a new song in a Chicago blues club. He sang these with real commitment, and they always went down well.

Lately, just as Billy Branch had become engaged with thinking about the future of the blues, Willie Dixon, at age sixty-seven, had begun to think about his legacy. Blues Heaven was a foundation whose purposes sounded noble, but my grasp of its actual function was a little vague. I knew its headquarters were to be at 2120 South Michigan Avenue, the old Chess studios, but I wanted to find out more. Unfortunately, access to the great man was strictly controlled by his manager, Scott Cameron, who never returned my calls and seemingly guarded his client as if he were a prize porker at a county show. I was bemoaning my lot in the Kingston Mines one night when someone said, "You need Willie Dixon's phone number? Here."

I picked up the phone on a Saturday afternoon at about five o'clock. I had given up trying to obtain permission from Scott Cameron, and in phoning out of the blue I felt like an intruder. Dixon was a little surprised to get my call, but courteous. I asked if he could tell me about his foundation. "Yes, I can tell you a little bit about it," said the big man slowly. It was an organization intended to promote the blues, he explained. And also to protect the heritage of the music and to propagate it around the world. It would fund college scholarships for promising underprivileged young people. It would help blues artists gain financial recognition for their work. It was coming together: its nonprofit status was just being legally finalized. "Now you see we know that there's a lot of the underprivileged people that get involved in the blues," Dixon said. "These people don't have no protection. Me knowing quite a bit about the blues, and being involved with the blues, why I feel like it's necessary for the blues artists to be protected. Because nobody has no respect for the average blues artist. They think the average blues artist is just somebody that go around drinking and getting lonesome because he's drinking and getting drunk, and be ridiculed by other people. So that's what the Blues Heaven organization is all about."

This laudable aim seemed motivated more by paternal than fraternal feelings. Dixon didn't sound like he was including himself among those underprivileged and ridiculed unfortunates, which was understandable given that in his Chess Records days he probably wielded more power and influence than any other black person in the blues business. It wouldn't be surprising if there were an element of poacher-turned-gamekeeper in his attitude: as if, after a long period of working closely with the Chess brothers, he regarded himself as more management than musician, more boss than bluesman.

And then of course there were the songs. He did churn out a lot of glib, gimmicky, formulaic pop and rock 'n' roll, but as far as I was concerned those sins were easily absolved by listening to Sonny Boy Williamson sing Dixon's "Bring

It on Home." He also made important contributions to the repertoires of Muddy Waters and Howlin' Wolf, which, as Robert Palmer observed in *Rolling Stone*,[14] helped to define them as artists, and which they performed throughout their careers. Many of these songs—such as "Hoochie Coochie Man," "Got My Mojo Working," "Little Red Rooster"—were self-consciously "country" in outlook, laden with rural imagery and hoodoo themes, and they contrasted markedly with the kind of thing Dixon wrote for himself. So markedly, in fact, that when performing them in later years, he would feel the need to distance himself from their primitive superstitions, just as I had seen him do.

For Dixon was a sophisticated urbanite. He arrived in Chicago years before the great 1940s influx of migratory Mississippians who supplied Chess with both their artists and their record buyers. It was hard to imagine a song like "I Got My Brand on You" coming naturally to a man who wore a suit and played string bass in a vocal harmony group down at the Capitol Lounge.[15] He wrote such songs "in character," without irony, from the point of view of a superstitious, ignorant country dweller. And if that was the target market he saw for the songs, what did it say about his attitudes to the artists he wrote them for? Did he regard Muddy Waters as a hick, Howlin' Wolf as a primitive? Now there was a question.

But I felt like I was on borrowed time, half expecting a tap on the shoulder from Dixon's management at any moment. If a question like that were to elicit any answer at all, it was unlikely to be a short one. And there were so many others I wanted to ask. I was interested in the American Folk Blues Festival tours, which Dixon organized with Memphis Slim and the German promoters Rau and Lippmann. I wanted to know about the internal politics at Chess Records: How was it possible to persuade a colossus like Howlin' Wolf to do a song like "Wang Dang Doodle"? And what kind of record company allowed Leonard Chess to play the bass drum, badly, on Muddy's "She Moves Me"?[16]

I just told him how much I enjoyed his new songs. "Thank you," he said. "I have one I sent to the president: 'It Don't Make Sense, You Can't Make Peace.'" I wondered what Ronald Reagan made of it. "I always have new songs," said Dixon. "It's all pertaining to the facts of life, the things that's going on as of now. The blues features the past, the present, and the future."

Then he paused. "Excuse me, I got Scott on the other line right now. So call back later, will you?"

Caught in the act. When I called back I managed to get Dixon talking, briefly, about those early tours to Europe, but then he said: "Listen, I appreciate it very much, but my manager tells me that a lot of the people that's writing books and things like that want the information pertaining to Blues Heaven, but the other information, you'll have to get permission from him. If he give you permission, then I can go further."

And Willie Dixon hung up.

• • •

In Lurrie's car after the Biddy Mulligan's gig, Eli was fishing for compliments. He had brought his own ruby-red Gibson SG along, the band had given him plenty of opportunities to shine, and he had played superbly. His "Crosscut Saw," in particular, had been dazzling: rock inflected, fast and rough edged. But he still wasn't happy. He complained about poor technique, fumbling on the frets.

"Well," said Lurrie soothingly. "That's some intense music you're playing there. You can't expect everything to go smoothly all the time." It was a cool evening. A gentle breeze was making its way inland from the lake as Lurrie, one-handed, steered us south on Sheridan Road, left at the Hollywood Avenue lights, and out onto the spectacular six-lane freeway of Lake Shore Drive, between the lights of the city on the right-hand side and the blackness of the lake on the left. Lurrie seemed a little weary of the band. There was some friction between him and Branch, and he admitted that he was looking forward to performing in Japan in a couple of weeks without him. I complimented him on his playing. I particularly admired the way he backed Branch's harp so skillfully. Eli agreed: it came, he suggested, from the years Lurrie had spent accompanying his father. That was probably true. From the first flurrying cascades of notes on "Ballbuster," the opening track of their new album *Son of a Gun*, it was clear that theirs was a special relationship: guitar and harmonica, father and son, in perfect harmony. It was a dynamic instrumental to kick off a pretty good record.

"Yeah, me and the old man," mused Lurrie. "Man, sometimes playing with him I get this feeling: I'm going at a hundred miles an hour, I'm in a world of my own." Orange street lamps flashed overhead as the white lights of the Loop loomed on the horizon. I told him how lucky that made him: very few people got to feel like that. "Yeah," he conceded. "I'm blessed, man. And to think I nearly gave it up."

They dropped me off at North Avenue. It was four in the morning. At the bus stop by the vast vacant lot on the corner of Halsted an old black man in threadbare clothes sat patiently, looking at the ground, tired. Standing over him was a ragged, gap-toothed woman, drunk, who punctuated a rambling and incoherent monologue with dismissive gestures in his general direction. The old man didn't look up, or speak. After a few minutes he got slowly to his feet and walked away, and she followed. I sat down to wait for the bus.

5

Turning the Tables at WXOL

We're trying to open up everybody's ears—white blues
taste in Chicago is about fifteen or twenty years behind
what is legitimately happening in the blues world.

—Amy O'Neal

It was seared on my memory like the octave-leaping Otis Rush guitar riff in "All Your Love" or Skip James's haunting falsetto on "Killing Floor": the introduction on B. B. King's album *Live at the Regal*.

"Ladies and gentlemen, how about a nice, warm round of
applause to welcome the world's greatest blues singer,
the King of the Blues—B! B! King!"

Cue horns. Cue drums. Cue audience hysteria.

The emcee who introduced that sublime live set, recorded in 1964 in Chicago, wasn't credited on my late-1970s copy of the record, but everyone knew it was Pervis Spann. The "Blues Man" was a manager, booking agent, club owner and promoter who had been associated over the years with Junior Parker, Aretha Franklin, Chaka Khan, The Jackson Five. and B. B. King himself. But he was best known as a disc jockey. So one humid Tuesday lunchtime I made my way over to radio station WXOL[1] at 3350 South Kedzie Avenue, across the ship canal from Interstate 55. Behind the modest low-rise a tall, latticed transmitter mast ventured upward into a dun-coloured sky. I knew about radio, or thought I did, having hosted a late-night show on my university station. It was low-wattage in every sense, but it gave me an opportunity to play blues records as loud as I liked and occasionally—very occasionally—I might hear, second- or third-hand, that someone had tuned in and enjoyed it.

Mr. Spann was busy when I arrived. Not only was he on the air, but it was also "record day." "They come in around one o'clock and bring the records, and I take 'em and look at 'em," he explained, with one eye on the clock. "I review the records. If it sounds good enough, if it meets what I'm trying to do, I'll put 'em on. Some of them come through the mail, but most of them they bring, and today is the day."

Spann was wearing a dark grey suit, white shirt, a striped tie, and headphones; he sat facing two turntables, one set to 33 rpm and one to 45. There were stacks of records behind them, notices and memos pinned to the walls, and towers of eight-track tapes piled up precariously. He barely had room to turn around. A handwritten sign above the console read: "WXOL-1450—The *Soul* of the 80s, with Blues & More!!" I had arrived to interview him, but while I was getting myself organized in the crowded studio he swung the microphone over and started interviewing me. What was I doing in Chicago? Was blues popular over in England? Who was my favorite singer? It was a bigger audience than I was used to.

The laconic DJ had been in radio for nearly twenty-five years, since leaving the army and using his G.I. Bill[2] money to study electronics and radio at college. He started out on WOPA—named for the Oak Park Arms hotel where the studios and transmitter were sited—and in 1963 moved to WVON, "Voice of the Negro," a twenty-four-hour blues station that was part of the Chess Records empire. "It was fun," said Spann. "I guess the salary was in line with those years—no problems with that. I wish all the bosses were like the Chess brothers." Now age fifty, Spann had been co-owner of Midway Broadcasting Corporation, WXOL's parent company, for the past three years: "I am the operations manager, and I'm one of the owners, and I guess maybe I'm the program director," he explained. "And I'm the announcer, and ... whatever it takes to make the program go." WXOL was on air from 10:00 P.M. until 1:00 P.M. the next day, offering "blues, news, and contemporary," with a daily lunchtime gospel music show, and news and headlines every half-hour. "Even though we're a shared-time station—we only have fifteen hours a day—we made a tremendous impact as far as the marketplace is concerned, because we specialize in blues," he claimed.

As "Chicago's Only Blues Station," according to the media pack, WXOL broadcast blues "not only to Chicago's 1,600,000 Blacks but also to those blues lovers of many other racial and ethnic groups." The enclosed map showed a circle with a forty-mile radius around the station, indicating broadcast coverage from Lake View in the northern suburbs, out west to Aurora, and south as far as Gary, Indiana. A sixty-second advertising spot cost sixty-five dollars.

Musicians I spoke to in Chicago about the state of the blues often blamed its decline in popularity with black audiences on a lack of radio airplay. I was pretty sure it was more a matter of changing fashions: if a station wanted younger listeners, it had to play younger music. Up to a point, Spann agreed: "I've never known young people to be too much in love with the blues, first place," he observed. "Most of the black stations hire young programmers, and young programmers don't relate to the blues, they program what they relate, the Bootsy Collins, the Leroy James, you know, the up-tempo beat thing," he said. "You can brainwash people with records, and so they brainwashed them with the Funk-adelics." This could work both ways, according to Spann: "If you are a program director, and you picking a pop tune, and every once in a while you sticking a blues in, then your young audience will become exposed to some of the blues records. That is one way of creating new blues listeners," he said. At WXOL they used the same strategy, sort of, but in reverse: "We program the blues and institute a few of the other contemporary records into our programming." The station's ratings were healthy, although Spann did feel that the parlous state of the U.S. economy in 1982 might deserve some of the credit for that: "Right now, the economical hard times have hit a lot of black folks, and we're more popular now, I guess, than any time since we've been on the air." It seemed that the Blues Man's listeners actually had the blues.

But blues—the music—meant different things to different people. Anyone who listened to my own radio show—and I never really knew for sure whether anyone did—would have concluded that I liked guitars, mainly. A typical play-list aimed at my fellow students one Saturday night in May 1979 included songs from Jimmy Johnson, Lightning Slim, T-Bone Walker, Left-Hand Frank, all three Kings, of course, and Buddy Guy and Jimi Hendrix. To leaven the dough a little I threw in a couple of piano players, Memphis Slim and Roosevelt Sykes, plus the sax-led scurrility of Eddie Shaw.[3] Prewar acoustic blues was represented solely by 1960s "folk blues" discovery Robert Pete Williams. Out of twenty-six selections, only three, by Little Milton, Israel Tolbert, and Freddy Robinson, suggested that I had been doing any research in the library: in this case, by the looks of things, into the Stax record label. It was a fairly blinkered outlook, but it reflected, I hoped, the tastes of my hypothetical legions of blues-loving fol-lowers, who were all, virtually without exception, young, British, and white. It dwelt closely on the styles that influenced the white blues and rock bands of the 1960s—the Delta bluesmen, the Chicago sound, and the guitar virtuosos—and the focus was on instruments rather than the voice.

Black blues taste still drew on a much richer, vocal blues tradition. Little Milton, for example, was a wonderful guitar player, but his fame was founded on a beautiful voice. He was a virtual unknown to white fans. Likewise Bobby Bland, one of the most successful of all blues stars, who commanded the stage like Frank Sinatra and needed no prop but a microphone. And for me one of the most extraordinary things about B. B. King's *Live at the Regal* album was that for one entire track he didn't play his guitar at all. He just sang. He was every white blues fan's favorite guitar player, but for him the song was the thing, not the solo. Pervis Spann did introduce him on the record, after all, as "the world's greatest blues singer."

• • •

The most popular blues song of 1982 was Z. Z. Hill's "Down Home Blues." It came from his *Down Home* album, released by Malaco Records out of Jackson, Mississippi, and it was everywhere: on the radio, blaring from the cassette players of passing cars, and happily absorbed into the repertoires of Chicago's jobbing blues bands. For a while that summer, whatever band you were listening to, in whatever club, you could be pretty sure of hearing the song played most nights. It became a standard, like "Hoochie Coochie Man" or "Sweet Home Chicago."[4]

The song, and its success, revealed certain crucial truths about black attitudes to the blues.

I hadn't even heard of Z. Z. Hill. He was a forty-six-year-old, Southern, "soul-blues" star whose singing career stretched back to the late 1950s and who, like most of his contemporaries, worked the so-called "chitlin circuit" of urban theaters. He was therefore all but invisible to white audiences. "Down Home Blues" was a memorable song, beautifully produced, with keyboards, a funk-laden bass, and some incisive guitar playing. Hill's vocal was as committed and honeydripping as Bobby Bland's, but smoother, and he was backed by some fabulous gospel singers. They sang like angels, but didn't sound like good little girls.

It wasn't anything like Muddy Waters or Howlin' Wolf or any of the other acts central to "white" blues taste. The song had a conventional blues chord structure and the loping rhythmic vibe of a Jimmy Reed tune but the feel of a soul ballad: Barry White, not Bukka White. The lyrics hinted at the hitherto unsuspected seductive possibilities of old blues songs:

> She said "Your party's jumpin' and everybody's having a good time . . .
> Do you mind if I get comfortable and kick off these shoes
> While you're fixin' me a drink
> Play me some o' them down home blues"

What could she possibly mean? If I had a girl on my sofa kicking off her shoes, I don't think I'd risk putting "I Can't Be Satisfied" on the turntable, or "Black Snake Moan."[5] Not unless she had a pretty good sense of humor. How about Bo Carter's "Please Warm My Weiner"? What this lady meant when she asked for some "down home" music was smooth and urbane blues, possibly with horns and strings: the sort of stuff that was way too slick for most white "blues purists," but which, in a world of black music now dominated by newer forms, she clearly regarded as quaintly old-fashioned. Whack anything on the record player that a white fan regarded as "down home" and she'd be gone before you'd stuck an umbrella in her pina colada.

As far as white blues taste was concerned, "Down Home Blues" was the polar opposite of down home blues. The song's narrator was in control, with a pretty woman on his sofa, getting comfortable. This song owed no debt to the Romantic, hobo-savant mythology exemplified by the cult of Robert Johnson. Neither was it a cultural anachronism like the Chess Records catalog, revived and revered by white rock bands and record buyers. This song was black music that had not been expropriated by whites and therefore could not be patronized. It was smart, sophisticated and upwardly mobile.

When "Down Home Blues" was set alongside those whiskery staples of the North Side clubs like "Hoochie Coochie Man" and "Sweet Home Chicago," it also revealed certain crucial truths about white attitudes to the blues.

With little cultural context for their love of the music, the early white fans of the 1950s could hardly be blamed for regarding the blues as a discrete musical style: more macho than Dixieland jazz, more "real" than skiffle, earthier than rock 'n' roll. But the blues had never existed in that sort of vacuum. Even in its heyday it was just one of many types of popular music played at parties, pubs and street corners. Robert Johnson's twenty-nine sides for Columbia pointed to a repertoire that included ragtime numbers and gospel songs, as well as blues: anything he could do that would get a juke joint jumping or persuade a passer-by to throw a coin in his hat. He wasn't atypical. The great musical polymath Lonnie Johnson confessed that he never intended to be a blues musician, but his big break was winning a recording contract in a singing competition: "It just happened to be a blues contest, so I sang blues," he said.[6] One of the original rock 'n' roll singles, Chuck Berry's "Maybellene," which was itself a country dance tune given the R&B treatment, had a blues song on the B side.[7] And when the musicologist Alan Lomax went blues hunting in the Mississippi Delta in 1941—the same trip on which he found Muddy Waters—he was surprised to find people in juke joints jitterbugging to Fats Waller.[8]

The blinkered white notion of blues left little room for this sort of diversity, either in musical styles or in the songs themselves. Encouraged by the blues-focused writings of Paul Oliver, Samuel Charters and other researchers, and guiltily aware of the blues-engendering nature of black American history, white fans were also misled by how the blues craze of the 1920s and 1930s had encouraged record labels to ignore the wider repertoires of their rural troubadours and night-club entertainers and insist on cutting nothing but blues. The result was a tendency to imagine that blues was the principal black music, and that blues singers belonged to a distinct species, when in reality many, or possibly most, were just entertainers who happened to know a lot of blues songs. As black audiences for the blues dwindled in the 1960s and whites became the main market, this distorted view tended to isolate the blues from its musical hinterland, like a specimen in a jar. And this isolation not only fed the idea that the blues was something separate but also allowed the narrow white notion of the blues to define it.

The barriers between blues, jazz, soul, pop and rock 'n' roll were a lot lower and more porous than my university radio audience might have realized. For Pervis Spann and his audience these barriers barely seemed to exist. The WXOL playlist was nothing if not eclectic: "I run from the top of the contemporary all through the blues," Spann explained, laying an Albert King album on the left-hand turntable. "There are those old standards anyway, the B. B. Kings, the Bobby Bland, Albert King, Little Milton, Muddy Waters, folks of this nature. The Johnny Taylors, Z. Z. Hill—now he's very popular—you just got to go with these particular people anyway. And there are newcomers—Guitar Junior Johnson," he remembered. "I play the top of the contemporary, the Stevie Wonder, the Smokey Robinson, the Isley Brothers, if they got a hit record. But I also don't get too far from my B. B. King, my Howlin' Wolf, stuff of that nature. All the blues and the top contemporary."

It hardly seemed to matter how the music was categorized. If the jump and jive of Louis Jordan, the stone-age boogie of John Lee Hooker, the soulful crooning of Bobby Bland and the troubled spirituality of Skip James were all blues, then so was the mellow schmoozic of Z. Z. Hill. Indeed, you had to question whether the word "blues" meant much at all. But it was nearly one o'clock. For Pervis Spann, the Blues Man, things were about to get busy. I had to go.

"I've answered the phone over the course of my career in radio," Spann said as I packed up my stuff. "You can get a general feel about what the listeners want to hear just by answering that telephone."

• • •

Lee Shot Williams was backstage at the Regal Theater[9] on that night in 1964 when Pervis Spann introduced B. B. King and the great live set got under way. Back then Williams was a young singer recently arrived in Chicago from Mississippi via Detroit, finding work with various bands in the city's clubs. He enjoyed some success, cutting a few singles and scoring a handful of local hits, and he even performed on the stage of the Regal itself: "Pervis Spann introduced me one time."

We were sitting with cups of coffee in the Town and Country, a diner at the junction of Interstate 94 and North Avenue, with Williams's agent, WOPA producer Ruth Young. The young waitress, on discovering Lee Shot was a singer, asked about musicians she used to know: "What happened to Chuck Smith, is he still around?"

"Chuck Smith? Did he blow tenor?"

"Tenor sax, yes."

"Tenor saxophone," mused Lee Shot, frowning. "Yeah, I know who you mean. I haven't saw him."

Ruth had secured Lee Shot a run of three Thursday-night engagements at the Kingston Mines, which would be the first time he had performed before a white, North Side audience. The first gig was tomorrow. But what Williams really wanted to do, it seemed, was reminisce.

"I was there, backstage," he said, animated by the memory of that B. B. King show nearly twenty years ago. "It was a great LP. He had to work, man. B. B. told me, he said, 'I'm afraid to go out to them kids out there, they probably won't like the blues.' It was five or six-thirty in the evening, there were kids still in there. He tore them kids up, man. You hear the audience, how they's howling? I was there." Lee Shot explained that a Regal show was an all-day affair, starting in the early afternoon and going through until late at night: "They had twelve or fourteen stars, everybody who was anybody: Duke Ellington, Count Basie, anybody you could name played at the Regal. A dollar and eighty cents to go in, and see a movie and five shows a day. You could stay all day and all night. You could tell when there was a superstar there: they had lines from the middle of the block all the way back round Forty-Seventh, down to Vincennes, three deep. B. B. would draw them like that, Temptations, Jackie Wilson."

Chubby, friendly and talkative, the forty-four-year-old singer was upbeat about his work. He had a new single out, on the Tchula label: a soul-blues cover of "I've Got a Problem," with "Times are Tough" on the B-side. But just as B. B. King had concerns about his audience's expectations that night in 1964, Williams was, in fact, a little worried about his forthcoming gigs on the North Side. "I don't know it's going to be at the peak," he said doubtfully, "but I'm going to do my best. Because I haven't rehearsed it with the band."

I tried to reassure him that the house band at the Mines were about as good as bands got. I knew about Doc Pellegrino's week-night policy of insisting that artists were backed by the All Stars, and Lee Shot would clearly have been happier to bring with him musicians who knew his repertoire. Although I didn't say so, I feared that his problem would not be the band but the audience. With his sharp suits and smooth patter, Lee Shot's stage act was in the Bobby Bland or Junior Parker mold. He was simply not the kind of blues singer they were used to up there: they'd probably wonder what he'd done with his guitar. It was true that I had recently seen Jimmy Witherspoon at Stages on North Clark Street, but Jimmy Witherspoon was a jazz and blues legend. To a Kingston Mines crowd,

Lee Shot Williams was an unknown with an unfamiliar repertoire who might easily be taken for a soul singer.

Our waitress came over again to see if we wanted more coffee. Ruth asked for a glass of water. "Water?" the girl repeated. "Whatcha gonna do, take a bath?"

• • •

Amy O'Neal sighed heavily. "I hate doing interviews," she groaned. "I've done this so often! I keep trying to think of some new angle to talk about." The thirty-three-year-old co-editor of *Living Blues* magazine was sitting in a small and phenomenally untidy basement office in the house on North Wilton that she shared with her husband, the magazine's co-founder, Jim O'Neal. It was a pleasant North Side neighborhood, just around the corner from B.L.U.E.S and the Kingston Mines.

"We've been here about six years," she told me. "I'm glad we came into this neighborhood when we did now, because prices have gotten just ridiculous."

Living Blues had just come out with its latest issue, number 52, a densely packed maze of minuscule type and black-and-white pictures, which had Johnny Copeland on the cover, a long feature inside about Sylvester Weaver, several pages of record reviews, and a letter to the editor that began, "Siggy's a motherfuckin' liar!"[10] This was signed: "X (his mark) Big Joe Williams."

The O'Neals founded the magazine in 1970 while they were students at Northwestern University, with the help of like-minded friends who included the writer Paul Garon and future Alligator Records boss Bruce Iglauer. Although Amy was from the Chicago suburbs and Jim was brought up in Mississippi, they discovered the music in the time-honored way of most white people: "The Animals, the Rolling Stones, the Beatles—the great British invasion opened our eyes up to the American music that we didn't know existed," she confessed. "And we noticed that what little information there was about blues was coming from Europe: and that didn't make any sense!"

There had been a complete, bound collection of the British magazine *Blues Unlimited*[11] in my university library, dating back to its first crudely stapled edition of 1963. This was an undoubted treasure trove for any blues researcher, full of record-company news and discographies. The very earliest issues conveyed a real sense that the editors were hacking out facts from the coal face of blues research, picking up whatever nuggets they could from trade papers, record shops and collectors, and from the occasional rushed and informal conversation with a touring musician. But as a magazine for fans like myself, who liked listening to the records and might occasionally read the liner notes, it was not an especially appetizing prospect. It was a bit like those old same-sounding 78s that I only listened to out of a sense of duty.

"We always thought *Blues Unlimited* was kind of a bizarre magazine," agreed Amy. "They concentrated on old records, and we wanted to concentrate on the live club scene. It's sort of a different viewpoint over in England, how they examine the music, as to what we see because we're smack in the middle of it. There are different sides to the story, and they're both right."

So *Living Blues* featured plenty of reviews of live performances at clubs and festivals, and because the magazine had ready access to actual blues musicians, it was able to run regular profiles and interviews. It was also different from its British counterpart in other ways. Two of the latest issue's fifty-eight pages were devoted to obituaries of Big Walter Horton, who died a pauper's death the previous winter of heart disease and alcoholism at age sixty-three. These pieces contained some good anecdotes, much useful information, and a lot of sentimental gloop that would never have made it past the sub's desk in a British editorial office: "Walter's many friends and admirers knew that his heart had not merely stopped; it had been broken too many times," mourned one of the authors. Another brought his piece to a saccharine-soaked conclusion: "If that Judgment Day ever does come, and if Gabriel is still in the mood to blow one final swinging solo before it all comes down, rest assured we'll be hearing a harmonica somewhere in the choir. And if I know Walter, Gabriel is going to have to share that solo." The third piece ended simply: "So long, Grandpa." For anyone seeking examples of how well-meaning white fans unwittingly patronized the old black musicians they purported to admire, this sticky mess was priceless.[12]

The magazine was nevertheless taken seriously. Jimmy Johnson's song "Twelve Bar Blues"[13] even contained the line, "Cover of the *Living Blues* is where I hope to be." The O'Neals granted his wish with issue 47, but Johnson was one of the lucky few: there were many more musicians vying for the honor than there would ever be cover slots available. "They think it will make them instantly famous and rich!" Amy fretted. "And they don't understand how we pick who goes on the cover—they want to pay a hundred dollars. You can talk till you're blue in the face and they can't understand why they can't be on the cover if they pay the money."

She sighed and went on: "Of course we won't take the money. The thing that's so pathetic about it is that we can't make anybody a star. We don't have the power. They just think we do." The magazine sold about six thousand copies per issue worldwide, all by subscription, she explained. They had tried newstrade distribution, but it turned out to be an expensive mistake: "It was naive. Since then we've learned not to be too sensitive about the fact that it doesn't sell, and it doesn't make money," she admitted. "The business end is God-awful: we pay ten thousand dollars a year postage! We have a cheap printer, and we can barely afford to pay him issue by issue. Incredible."

So just as Bob Koester used the Jazz Record Mart to subsidize his record label, the O'Neals cast around for other ways of making money to keep the magazine afloat. Booking bands was one such venture: "That's a whole other ball game," Amy groaned. "You don't want to know about booking blues: it's just horrible. It's an even worse way of trying to make money than publishing a magazine." But they also had Rooster Records, a label set up with backing from partners in England. It had so far put out three albums, starting in 1980 with *The Chief* by singer and guitarist Eddie Clearwater.[14]

"We'd wanted to cut Eddie Clearwater for years and been trying to get Koester to do it and Iglauer to do it. He's a West Side Chicago rock 'n' roller. They never took him seriously, but we knew he was a damn good songwriter and performer," said Amy. "We pretty much let Clearwater do it himself, because he knew what he wanted and he knew what we wanted, which was a fairly solid Chicago blues album. He picked the sidemen, wrote all the songs but one, rehearsed them, went into the studios, lovely session." Rooster had also recorded an album with Magic Slim, which went equally smoothly, according to Amy.[15] Carey and Lurrie Bell's *Son of a Gun* album, however, had offered more of a challenge: "Carey and Lurrie are a whole different ball game," she said. "Their record was a bitch to produce. Carey and Lurrie and Eli are all brilliant musicians, but their heads are not on very straight. They don't rehearse. They get in there and wait for the lightning bolt to strike. In the studio. You know what studio time costs? The session was just bizarre. I wanted to kill them."

If you had to guess what kind of albums a pair of young white fans like the O'Neals might produce, then you'd probably go for rocking, guitar-led Chicago blues, with maybe a little harmonica for added bluesiness. This was the kind of thing white people liked. But Rooster's fourth venture was different. "Larry Davis is not the type of blues artist that your average Chicago blues fan will go nuts over," Amy explained. "He's very much a more Southern-style, contemporary blues artist, in the B. B., Albert King, Little Milton school, and that is not fashionable here in Chicago in the white market. We're trying to open up everybody's ears to that variety of blues: white blues taste in Chicago is about fifteen or twenty years behind what is legitimately happening in the blues world."

Larry Davis was a forty-five-year-old singer and guitar player from Kansas City who had worked the South since the late 1950s and cut a few singles for labels like Duke and Kent in Houston and Los Angeles. His Rooster album *Funny Stuff*[16] was recorded not in Chicago but St. Louis, and to oversee the sessions the O'Neals brought in a new producer, the saxophonist and bandleader Oliver Sain. "Oliver knows about how to manufacture a more commercial, black, blues-oriented record," Amy explained. The differences were subtle—a funky flavor to the bass, little hints of synthesizer here and there—but *Funny*

Stuff was clearly the kind of record many white fans would regard as somehow inauthentic, like Howlin' Wolf with backing singers or Muddy Waters recording with a horn section. Not "real" blues, in other words, but a manufactured confection designed to sell records. Perish the thought.

Where white fans celebrated the raw, rough edges of improvised performance, the black market enjoyed smooth urbanity and control. White fans liked their blues to sound as if it was wrestled into shape in some edgy tavern, even if they had never been to one. Black listeners, it seemed, preferred to imagine a cool, modernist apartment overlooking the lake, where Z. Z. Hill had a pretty girl on his sofa kicking off her shoes and the only thing white was the shag pile. "The twain don't meet, they really don't," said Amy.

This gap between the chitlin circuit and white blues venues was seldom bridged. B. B. King had managed it, but it puzzled me that a great artist like Little Milton had not. "He is wonderful," Amy agreed. "But he's a very black act. He will not go up and do four sets in some little joint paying four hundred dollars a night. To many blues artists that represents success, because they've crossed over the fence into white, honky appreciation, and they think they've made it. But they know, deep in their hearts, another way to make it is like Little Milton has: work on the chitlin circuit for a million years. It's something queer, it really is, and it's one way we can tell the country's not integrated. It never will be until all those barriers are broken down."

Rooster's gamble on Larry Davis seemed to have paid off: the record was selling. But to Amy there was a more important indicator of success than mere sales: "We have got some airplay on black radio stations, which is very gratifying. Pervis Spann likes it," she beamed. "Spann plays it! That's such a trip, to hear him play a record that we produced. On black radio."

• • •

Pervis Spann wasn't the only blues man on Chicago's late-night airwaves. There was Big Bill Collins on WNIB, whose one-hour *Blues Before Breakfast* show started at four in the morning. And from midnight on Saturday night to five o'clock on Sunday morning, the soft-spoken Steve Cushing took the microphone at WBEZ. Thirty years old, bearded and bespectacled, Cushing was a musician as well as a blues fan who played drums as a member of Smokey Smothers's band, the Ice Cream Men. He had recently produced a single for them, in the WBEZ studios, which had been put out by Rooster Records. It wasn't very good, but I bought my copy from Smokey himself, and he had signed it for me.

As a keen young fan who discovered the blues in his teens through rock 'n' roll and Fleetwood Mac, Cushing studied for a broadcasting degree and got a slot as a blues DJ on a suburban college radio station while working as a telephone clerk. Then he joined WBEZ as an engineer. WBEZ was a public-service station, Cushing explained to me when we met to talk in the Jazz Record Mart. It was run by the Chicago Board of Education and therefore had strict racial quotas for its programming, a fact which—ironically, since he was white—helped Cushing to get his program. "There was a woman there who was their consultant for black programming," he said, "and when she found out that I actually knew what I was talking about, she went to the station manager. They thought it was something they could use, even though they had a white host."

Cushing's show was called *Blues Before Sunrise*.[17] It could easily have been called *Blues Before 1965*, because he didn't play anything recorded after that date. I wondered if he knew who his listeners were. "Well, it surprises me," he said. "It seems like it's split down the middle between young white folks and old black folks." His black audience, he surmised, had grown up with Louis Jordan and the postwar Chicago blues bands, and they had probably heard the classic blues singers and the country blues when they were small. The white audience—well, that would be people like me.

"I get a pretty good reaction, as much from the jazz-influenced things that I do as from the postwar and Mississippi blues, because the station is basically a jazz station," said Cushing. So you could hear Jimmy Rushing and Billy Eckstine on his show, or Joe Williams and Helen Humes—the kind of big-band performers that jazz aficionados tend to regard as blues singers, and blues fans think of as jazz—but only for the first hour or two. "The first time I play a harmonica, I lose all the jazz fans," he said. "That's one thing I found out right away: if I put Little Walter on in the first hour, all the jazz fans are gone. There's something about people who like horns, they won't listen to harmonicas." In the first part of the show he might also risk some of the more polished urban blues acts, like T-Bone Walker, Big Maceo Merriweather, or Tampa Red: "They'll sit through that. The first, say, Elmore James: they're gone."

As WBEZ was a public-service broadcaster, Cushing was under less commercial pressure than his rivals and could play exactly what he wanted to. And there were no advertisements, entertaining as Spann and Collins often made them, to interrupt the music. "I'm conscious of trying to preserve an art form," said Cushing. "The idea of my show is to expose people to as many tunes by as many people as I can."

In two-and-a-half years, *Blues Before Sunrise* had become something of a broadcasting phenomenon, lifting WBEZ to second in the Chicago radio rankings during its time slot, according to Cushing, when the rest of the time the station languished down in seventeenth or eighteenth place. Pervis Spann and Big Bill Collins were strong radio personalities, and their full-on presentation style was fun to listen to, but if you wanted the old blues, Cushing was the man.

"This will sound sort of egotistical," he said, "but Pervis wouldn't touch a postwar Chicago blues record till I got on the air." He meant postwar in the sense that white fans understood: 1950s Chicago blues. "They started that station of his, WXOL, a couple of years ago, billed it as the blues station, and all he was playing was soul and disco. And when he found out that I had a following, about six months later he started digging out his Little Walter records."

• • •

I need not have worried about Lee Shot Williams's first Kingston Mines gig. The house band, the All-Stars, were tight, attentive and professional, and there was a pretty good crowd. Among them was Irish rocker Rory Gallagher, and during the set break I noticed him wander over to compliment Bob Levis, the guitarist. Lee Shot put on a lively, crowd-pleasing performance with charm and good humor. The band didn't know any of his songs, but they backed him capably through a selection of soul classics, some blues and gospel, "If I had a Hammer," a refrain from "Blowing in the Wind"—seemingly anything Lee Shot could think of. He had power and range, and while he didn't sing "Hoochie Coochie Man" or "Sweet Home Chicago" he did do "How Blue Can You Get" and "Mannish Boy," and the audience seemed happy enough with the show.

The second gig, the following Thursday, went just as well, but the crowd was noticeably thinner. Williams remained upbeat and spoke to me about the need to build up a following, which he knew could be a long process. Doc had booked him for at least one more gig.

When I arrived the next week, Lavelle White was on the bandstand. Lee Shot wasn't there: he hadn't shown up. Doc Pellegrino, whom I had earlier quizzed about his insistence on week-night acts using his house band, had the satisfied air of a man who had been proved right: the Kingston Mines All Stars had ridden to the rescue. He said there had been "some sort of screw-up. Ordinarily it would have just knocked us on our head and we'd have been without anything," he told me. "I called Lavelle White to come in, so I have Robert Covington singing, Lavelle White singing, Bobby Anderson singing, the music is great, the people are having a good time, and they don't voice any feeling that they have been cheated. As soon as we found out he wasn't coming in, we took the sign down and put up the All Stars sign. I have a solid group."[18]

• • •

The blues and religion always trod parallel paths, a cultural yin and yang that saw the music—highly emotional, self-obsessed and, quite often, lyrically filthy—regarded as the antithesis of God-fearing Christian values. It was "the

Devil's music," a construct sardonically embraced by numerous singers, perhaps most famously Robert Johnson, and chillingly evoked by Lonnie Johnson:

> Blues and the devil is your two closest friends
> The blues will leave you with murder in your mind,
> That's when the devil out of hell steps in

Many a young singer was lured away from the sacred music of the church by the prospect of fame and fortune in the blues. But while this might have dismayed their mothers, it didn't necessarily mean that the musicians and singers regarded blues and religion as mutually exclusive. Hip Linkchain and Jimmy Dawkins were two musicians I knew who were practicing Christians. Dawkins asked me straight out if I was a believer, and he countered my reply with all the seriousness of my old headmaster: "Well, it doesn't matter, God won't fall out of the sky. He's your God whether you believe in him or not." Fenton Robinson converted to Islam in 1969 and reckoned "quite a few" of his fellow bluesmen shared the faith.

So although I had read about superstitious country folk who regarded the blues as the Devil's music, I never thought I would meet anyone who professed to believe it. But Big Bill Hill came close. A legendary figure in the Chicago blues and radio scene, he had not presented a blues show since 1976, but he hadn't so much retired as banished himself from the blues world. He was a promoter, manager, and club owner, and in a long career as a blues disc jockey had not only pioneered outside broadcasting but hosted one of the first black dance shows on television. Now he was a preacher. He broadcast gospel music every night, from midnight to two in the morning on WTAQ.

We arranged to meet at his church and studio late one afternoon in the heart of Chicago's West Side, at 2853 West Madison Street. Or at least that's what he said on the phone. I couldn't see any church. When I tentatively pulled open the door of what looked like a boarded-up store, I found him waiting for me in the gloom among rows of steel chairs: a tall man with a stoop, wearing a grey suit. A pair of kindly eyes gazed at me from behind horn-rimmed glasses as he extended an enormous hand in greeting.

"I'll never play no more blues, because you don't continue to lie to God," he told me, settling himself behind his console, an L-shaped desk that supported some remarkably ancient-looking broadcasting equipment. "A wise man will change. The Bible said, 'What gain is it for man to win the world and lose his soul?'"

Sixty-eight years old, Big Bill Hill had been in Chicago since moving up from the South as a teenager in the early 1930s. "I started in 1949 on WLDY, on FM radio, and I promoted blues locally with Muddy Waters, Howlin' Wolf, and later on Elmore James," he said. "I'm the first man to bring B. B. King to Chicago, I'm the first man to bring Albert King to Chicago, and Little Milton, which I work with Little Walter, Homesick James, Ike and Tina Turner, Lightning Hopkins . . ." He went on. When the time came to transcribe the tape of our interview, this list covered more than half a page. It contained names I didn't know, like Sugar Pie Desanto, and names I never expected to hear anyone mention, like Memphis Minnie. It seemed that at one time or another Hill had managed, booked, or in some way been associated with pretty much everybody. He found fame on WOPA in the 1960s with his "Shopping Bag Show," in which he would play soul and blues records, read advertisements for local grocery stores and car dealerships, and promote his own events. "Back in those days we were independent radio announcers," he explained. "We didn't get a salary, we worked as brokers. We bought our time and we sold it, and we could do anything that was legal." With a successful formula, the rewards could be great. Hill remained a man of means: his modest storefront church was paid for, he informed me, and he owned several other buildings, both in Chicago and in his home town of England, Arkansas.

Hill's big thing was outside broadcasting. "Oh, I was all over Chicago, with Muddy Waters, Howlin' Wolf, Little Walter, any number of places," he said. He put on shows in West Side blues clubs and even broadcast from a drive-in hot-dog stand: "We had a band out there. Hundreds of people would come and eat hot dogs and listen to the blues." He filled major venues like the Ashland Boulevard Auditorium.[19]

He was a successful promoter and entrepreneur, but his upbringing had been fiercely religious. It didn't seem that he regarded the blues as the Devil's music, more that making money out of it was the Devil's work. "I knew the Lord before I went into the blues," he said. "I went out into the world and I made a lot of money, and there's no way you're going to keep it: once you know the Lord and you backslide, there's no way." Haunted by the fear that he was betraying his religion, when things started to go wrong he became convinced that he was being judged—or if not judged, at least tapped on the shoulder. "The Lord gives you your choice," he told me. "I enjoyed the fame. I made a lot of money, but I lost much more. I booked bands, and there come a big snow or a big rain, you lose fifteen or twenty or thirty thousand dollars in a night: I've had that to happen. See, that's when you're being whipped by the almighty God, just like when you was a kid, when your father told you he was going to give you a spanking, and you knew what he was whipping you for. It's because you promised to do something and you reneged on it. That start turning something in your head: 'Why, why, why?'"

After five years hosting his *Red Hot and Blues* TV show, he fell out with the television station in 1973 and lost his night-time slot. With it went his audience and his advertisers. "I wasn't drawing flies," he said. "You see a lot of guys that live big—you know, big cars, lotta clothes—I didn't do that. But it still went. I just couldn't stand the pressure, got tired of losing. And broke ain't but broke," he added wearily. "Lawyers. Lawyers. Marriages. Everybody you marry want to sue you. Anybody who got money can borrow money, but when you don't have it, that's the time you can find out who's your true friend."

So Big Bill Hill got out of the blues, and into religion: not to atone for a misspent youth but, as he saw it, a misspent adulthood. But he still liked talking about the old days. He remembered how great bluesmen like Elmore James and Howlin' Wolf could work a crowd, alternating fast dance tunes with slower, deeper blues: "And everybody would sit real quiet, and they wouldn't even drink, because they were listening, they was concentrating. The blues tells a story, same as gospel," he said.

Asking after the blues people he used to know, the old man struggled to remember some of their names, and I filled him in as best I could. He wondered how Jim and Amy O'Neal were doing: "Are they still around? Oh, I knowed them for years. He kept up with the blues. I know his magazine went all over the world. He used to send it to me, but he don't send it no more. When you get with the Lord, all the people that you know, they don't associate with you."

There was a flash of sunlight as the door swung open, and three small children burst in—two vivacious little girls and a slightly more circumspect boy of about ten years old. "Hello. How are you?" Big Bill enquired politely. "Have a seat. I'm busy right now, I'm doing an interview." Seeing him in his gloomy little church on West Madison, it was difficult to imagine this placid and slightly melancholy man as Big Bill Hill, the blues DJ, friend and fixer to the stars. It was impossible to hear him now as Chicago's premier blues radio jock: all his shows had evaporated the instant they were broadcast. I wondered how he would be remembered. Or if.

But there was one place where you could get a sense of the man as the larger-than-life emcee. In July 1963 Chess Records recorded an album at Big Bill's club, the Copa Cabana on West Roosevelt. It was released the following year as *Folk Festival of the Blues*[20]—a misleading title, but the folk fad was in full spate—featuring a lineup that included Muddy Waters, Howlin' Wolf, Willie Dixon, Buddy Guy and Otis Spann. Doing the introductions was the man himself, Big Bill Hill, his voice revving like a racecar.

As a slice of live, contemporary blues, the record wasn't intended as a museum piece or an archive recording, but that is what *Folk Festival of the Blues* quickly became. At the time, Muddy Waters and his fellow Chess artists were near their considerable peak as live performers, although their days as hitmakers were long past. Buddy Guy, on the other hand, was a twenty-seven-year-old club and session musician, plugged into the creative zeitgeist and clearly intent on pushing the music forward. The horn and rhythm sections were essentially his regular band: James Brown himself never had a tighter crew. Guy was thoroughly steeped in the old blues of the South, fully in tune with the emergence of soul and funk, and also beginning to find his own instrumental voice. The record provided an intriguing synthesis of old and new: the deep mud of Mississippi, nuggets of diamond-hard soul, and startling outbursts of electric guitar. This was the Chicago blues, in Big Bill Hill's club, in 1963: a living thing, adapting and evolving.

The date was significant. In 1963 the Chicago blues still belonged to its black audience: the same audience who, as Big Bill remembered, used to sit quietly and listen to the words whenever Elmore James or Howlin' Wolf did a slow one. And that was exactly how they reacted on the record, when Muddy Waters began the haunting "Sitting and Thinking," his voice soaring over the crowd like an ancient field holler:[21]

Well, my home is in the Delta, way out on that farmer's road

But that audience was aging, and their children were growing up in a different world, listening to different sounds. From 1964 a new, white audience started to appear, turned on to this venerable music by the Rolling Stones, the Blues-breakers, Paul Butterfield and the rest, and heralded by the arrival at JFK of four chirpy young Scousers who quipped, "Don't you know who your own famous people are?" when reporters asked where—not who—Muddy Waters was.[22]

These new fans had less sense of the blues as an essentially vocal music. Not for them the smooth, gospel tenor of Little Milton or Bobby Bland, nor even the bright, modern, and funky sound of Guy's young gunslingers, who seemed intent on moving the music into the present. Their fascination was for the styles that inspired the white bands—Delta bluesmen, the Chess sound, and the guitar virtuosos—and theirs was the narrow focus that would, eventually, seal the fate of the blues. By 1982 you could see how it was turning into a museum exhibit. Some of the city's clubs seemed stuck in an endless loop of old favorites like "Hoochie Coochie Man," "Sweet Home Chicago," "Baby Please Don't Go," and half a dozen other cobwebbed standards. It was what the people wanted—the white people. They were loving the blues to death.

No one could have foreseen that in 1963, when *Folk Festival of the Blues* came out. Looking back, the record was like a post stuck in the sand at the high water mark of the music's development. It was the future that the blues never had. Perhaps that made it a fitting memorial to Big Bill Hill.

B.L.U.E.S, 1979: Left Hand Frank on the bandstand, with Little Joe Berson (harp), Frank Bandy (bass) and, almost invisible to the left, Jimmy Rogers (rhythm guitar).

"People give me credit for that willpower." Smokey Smothers in B.L.U.E.S, with Mad Dog Lester Davenport on harmonica, while his brother Abe "Little Smokey" Smothers looks on.

(above) "You get more money with the white peoples: it's just a very earthly thing, you got to live." Sunnyland Slim in B.L.U.E.S, 1982.

(right) "Most white guys cannot sing the blues. If I tried to do it, or if you tried to do it, it would sound vaguely ludicrous." Bill Gilmore, co-owner, outside B.L.U.E.S.

(above) Going down slow: Floyd Jones and Homesick James in B.L.U.E.S, 1979.

(left) "He's supposed to be a big deal, but to me he's no big deal. This is my gig, man!" Jimmy Johnson plays the Kingston Mines.

(right) "I don't know nothing about no color. I look at you as a man, and I try to treat you that way. It's just that easy." Jimmy Walker at home.

(below) "When I first met them it was a great big kick because it was the Rolling Stones. But after I got to know them . . ." Sugar Blue at Stages.

"If you making money out of me, I want some of it. Ten percent." Junior Wells on the blues stage, ChicagoFest, 1979.

"I don't have time to look for colors, I look for good musicians." Jimmy Dawkins (right) plays B.L.U.E.S. with Rich Kirch (rhythm) and Willie Kent (bass).

(above) Hip Linkchain and band: Rich Kirch (guitar), Frank Bandy (bass) and drummer Fred Grady.

(right) "Everything the black man created, the white man taken. If they could sing, we'd be out of the blues." Johnny Littlejohn at B.L.U.E.S, with bass player Harlan Terson.

(left) "I will not go with Alligator. I can't discuss it, but I just don't see nothing he could do for me." Luther Allison on stage at the Kingston Mines.

(below) "There was always a fight, somebody shooting. They throw chairs at each other. It just got that I didn't want to play for black people." Hip Linkchain in concert at ChicagoFest.

"Me and the old man—sometimes playing with him I get this feeling: I'm going at a hundred miles an hour, I'm in a world of my own." Carey and Lurrie Bell, Kingston Mines, 1979.

"You don't bite the hand that feeds you. That's the way it is. Times are hard." Billy Branch at Biddy Mulligan's.

(left) "We've been playing for black clubs four nights a week, and the crowd seem to be getting off into it real tough." Lurrie Bell at Biddy Mulligan's, 1982.

(below) "Nobody has no respect for the average blues artist." Willie Dixon, the storyteller, at Stages.

"You can get a general feel about what the listeners want to hear just by answering that telephone." Pervis Spann, the Blues Man, on air at WXOL.

"You hear the audience, how they's howling? I was there." Lee Shot Williams on stage at the Kingston Mines.

"The Animals, the Stones, the Beatles—the British invasion opened our eyes to American music we didn't know existed." Amy O'Neal at *Living Blues* magazine.

"I made a lot of money, but I lost much more." Big Bill Hill and admirers, in his church and broadcast studio at 2853 West Madison Street, 1982.

"At that time, Lefty used to smoke Buddy fairly regularly." Lefty Dizz at Buddy Guy's Checkerboard Lounge, 1982.

"I've approached the last three mayors about the need for a blues museum. The response has been lukewarm." Ralph Metcalfe Jr. (right) at the Delta Fish Market.

(left) Theresa's Tavern, 4801 South Indiana Avenue, 1982.

(below) "I'm from Greenville, Mississippi, home of Eddie Shaw, Hound Dog Taylor, and I don't know how many more blues players." Oliver Davis in his office at the Delta Fish Market.

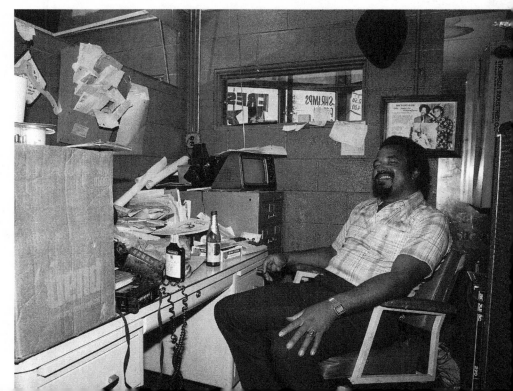

(right) Delta Fish Market, 1982.

(below) Playboy Venson and band, Maxwell Street flea market, 1979.

"For the white audience I think blues is essentially interpreted as a branch of rock 'n' roll."
Bruce Iglauer in his office and bedroom, Alligator Records, 1982.

"I was raised on a cotton farm, and every day we would go to the cotton field, me and my
brothers and sisters. We was singing blues." Koko Taylor with Son Seals in performance at
Stages.

Albert Collins, "master of the Telecaster," with the phenomenal Emmett "Maestro" Sanders, Stages, 1982.

The author with drummer Fred Grady outside B.L.U.E.S.

(above) "Blues is jazz, and jazz is blues. You don't have to play that same thing all the time." The enigmatic virtuoso Fenton Robinson at the Wise Fools Pub.

(left) "And that's when the knife came out." Left Hand Frank at B.L.U.E.S, 1979.

(right) "I ain't making no money, but I'm working. I hope pretty soon things'll break, you know." Magic Slim at Florence's.

(below) The Checkerboard Lounge, 423 East Forty-Third Street, 1979.

A young French musician named Cody gets a harmonica lesson from
Good Rockin' Charles, outside B.L.U.E.S, 1982.

(left) East Forty-Third
Street, 1982: Johnny
Twist's shop, just
across the street from
the Checkerboard
Lounge.

Theresa Needham in her club, 1982.

Buddy Guy at ChicagoFest, 1979.

(left) Buddy Guy at ChicagoFest, 1979.

(below) "Being a white musician back in Chicago in that black blues world, you're basically being judged by other white people." Steve Freund in B.L.U.E.S, 1982.

(above) "I'm not going to sell myself cheap, man. I don't know when I'm going back." Eli Murray, "Elisha Blue," in England, 1985.

(right) "I can't get a gig at a blues festival in the UK for love nor money. They just want rock musicians." Thomas Ford, 2014.

6

Fried Mississippi Catfish Blues

You're saying that I don't exist. This is the truly
American black music, in the purest form. You're
saying my culture ain't shit – and I am not amused.

—Lefty Dizz

One hot July evening I met a man carrying a guitar outside the Kingston
Mines. He was wearing a cowboy hat, a shiny red suit, a yellow shirt and a blue
tie. I asked if I could do an interview with him sometime. "Sure," he replied.
"Checkerboard, Monday." He went by the name of Lefty Dizz, and I mentioned
that I'd seen him perform in Paris in 1979, which seemed to please him. I had
also seen him in the Checkerboard Lounge that year, drunk, playing the guitar
with his foot. "I've been drunk since I got back from Korea," he retorted. "I'm
forty-seven, not thirty-seven. I killed a lot of people."

There had been nothing by Lefty Dizz in the university library's music collection, and he wasn't mentioned either by Paul Oliver or in my dog-eared copy
of Mike Rowe's *Chicago Blues*. There was no entry for him in the *Blues Who's
Who*, not even in the index, under D for Dizz or W for Walter Williams, his
given name. I knew nothing about him except what I had seen and heard, and
what I had seen and heard was far from straightforward.

I had one record of his, an album on the French label Black & Blue, which
I bought at Dobell's in Rathbone Place: ten tracks featuring great personnel,
including Moose Walker, Willie James Lyons on second guitar, and Elmore
James's drummer Odie Payne Jr.[1] It was recorded in Chicago in June 1979 and
was hugely disappointing. It might not have seemed so bad if my expectations
had not been so high, having seen the man perform.

And yet even in performance there were no guarantees with Lefty Dizz. He
was a superb player but an inveterate showman. He liked teasing the audience
by launching into a song and then abruptly stopping, as if snatching away a
treat. But then he might forget to carry on. He would dangle the guitar at arm's

length and play with one hand—with one finger, really, hammering away at the D string—or lean the unfortunate instrument against the amplifier and play it with his shoe, scowling at the audience. It could seem more like performance art than music, and from an artist drowning in conceptual angst. He didn't seem to care about what he was doing. He certainly didn't care what his audience thought. I once saw him do a version of "Baby Please Don't Go" that went on for twenty minutes: it was no wonder she wanted to leave. He had a special verse he inserted into Z. Z. Hill's "Down Home Blues":

> You tell me you don't like my sound
> You don't like my guitar because I play it upside down
> Well I don't care, I'll do it any way I choose
> I'm just playing these down home blues.

He appeared to regard his immense talent as valueless, or even as a burden.

Of medium height, his slight build made him seem lanky, and he could never quite fill the sharp suits he wore on stage. His face was mobile and expressive and could exude a childlike charm. His ancient, battered Stratocaster wouldn't stay in tune, but I once saw him lose his temper during a set break at the Kingston Mines when someone picked it up without permission, as if they could possibly have inflicted any more damage to it. At the Checkerboard Lounge one night Louis Myers got up from the bar and confided: "I'm going to play Lefty's guitar." He was back after one number: the instrument was an untamable beast. The only time I saw behind the mask of existential invulnerability Dizz wore on stage was when he lost his grip during one of his one-handed routines and the guitar went crashing to the floor. He looked utterly mortified.

Ralph Metcalfe Jr. was a man with first-hand experience of the baffling set of contradictions that was Lefty Dizz. A local politico, black activist and evangelical blues fan, he first worked with the enigmatic guitarist in 1973, when as a twenty-four-year-old graduate he agreed to help out some friends by providing a blues act for a black cultural festival at Kalamazoo College in Michigan.

"Junior and Buddy's career was going pretty good, and their price was up," recalled Metcalfe, "so I asked Lefty, and he said yeah. I picked up fifty bucks for emceeing the show and I was officially into the music business. Lefty asked me to look for more gigs for him, and we started working together." The arrangement lasted about four years. At one gig some video was recorded: "It turned out to be the videotape that circulated through all the European rock stars, and he was the mystery guitarist, because on the tape he had introduced everybody in the band except himself: so they didn't know who he was, but they knew he was smokin'. When the Stones got through here in seventy-nine, they found him at the Kingston Mines and went all three nights at the weekend to jam with him." Then Metcalfe said something that stuck in my mind: "At that time, Lefty used to smoke Buddy fairly regularly."

We were talking in a comfortable room on the ground floor of his impos-ing family house on Michigan Avenue, on Chicago's South Side. The athletic-looking Metcalfe had recently set up regular Blue Monday shows at the Taste Entertainment Center, he told me. "We started with a kick-off for Lefty Dizz's birthday, which Lefty didn't attend himself," he recalled drily. "He claims that they owed him nine thousand dollars at the Checkerboard, and he had to stay there." Dizz had long had the Monday gig at the famous Forty-Third Street bar. Metcalfe was dismissive. "About all the Checkerboard is surviving on is those Blue Mondays, where they've been able to assemble a nice definitive collection of talent. It's just not set up to cater for a modern quality clientele. Who wants to go down there and there's all kinds of dust on the floor, and you get your battery stolen, and you've got ignorant greasy motherfuckers hitting on your woman? Nobody want to go through that. It's very distasteful."

The urbane promoter must have known it was risky to book Dizz, even to play at his own birthday party. The guitarist had missed bigger gigs. "Lefty blew a quarter-of-a-million-dollar recording deal that I had set up with Columbia Records," pronounced Metcalfe. This was in 1979 and must have been shortly before I saw Dizz perform in Paris. "We had a video demo I was going to take to New York, but he was so up in the air about going to Europe that he spent the day before fucking some bitch, man. We were all in the studio, and we had all the technical deal cleared, and the bass player had carried his big bass amplifier down from the third floor, and they had a suit and tie on for the show, and I was there, and all we needed was for Lefty to show up with his brother Woody, the drums and guitar and amp in their car, and we could have cut a beautiful video demo with some original material. But he got the pussy, and now he has no record out on Columbia. So that," concluded Metcalfe grimly, "plus his disappearance at his own birthday party, has limited my involvement with Mr. Dizz. He is one of the greatest, but he keep drinking all that Grand-Dad 100, man, and he doesn't seem like he wants to help himself. The saddest part is all of his talent that's going down the drain. Lefty fears success. He's had success knock at his door several times, but he's turned his back."

I mentioned my disappointing Black & Blue album. "He did a recording for Victoria Spivey before she died, just one or two tracks on one of her anthology albums," Metcalfe recalled.[2] "I don't know if he got any money for it at all, but I know they got very drunk before they did it, and the tapes are just terrible. Alcohol is a problem. It rots these guys' brains out after so many years of use, and it makes them real assholes. Lefty and a lot of the other guys are weakened from fighting their cause and even from seeing it properly through the haze of all that alcohol. It's heavy. I drink some myself, but I'm not a drinker, and I can't keep up with them at all. And I don't want to learn."

In spite of his discouraging dealings with Dizz, Metcalfe was determined to remain optimistic: "There's some young guys coming up into the blues now, like Billy Branch and Ron Abrams, who offer great promise for the future, if they could just manage to capture the secrets from the great masters." He invited me down to Taste to sample his Blue Monday evenings. The next one, he said, would kick off with Johnny Dollar and his tight and funky Scan'lous Band, while the star attraction would be none other than Junior Wells.

· · ·

What Hip Linkchain told me about Junior Wells not wanting to play at Theresa's because they didn't pay him enough sounded plausible to me. Whenever I went down to Theresa's it was because the ad in *The Reader* said the harmonica maestro would be there. I didn't go down very often because although it was only one L stop farther south than the Checkerboard Lounge, it was a scarier walk to the club once you got off the train. I never saw Junior Wells anywhere near the place.

But I saw him in plenty of other places. You could hardly miss him. There were a lot of snappy dressers among Chicago's blues musicians, but none scaled the heights of sartorial perfection as triumphantly as Junior. Everyone said he carried a gun, but such was the immaculate line of his well-cut three-piece suits that nobody could say for sure where he kept it. The small of his back seemed to be the best guess. He was a short, handsome man of forty-five, with a trim physique, a steady gaze, and a liking for big hats. And gladly or otherwise, he didn't suffer fools.

We first met at the Checkerboard Lounge one Tuesday night, introduced by Dion Payton, the young singer and guitarist who led the house band. Wells was complaining about ChicagoFest, the city's summer music festival organized by the mayor's office, which had offered him fifteen hundred dollars for two sets. According to Wells, bands from outside Chicago were getting paid twenty-five hundred, so he felt they were trying to rip him off. "Fuck 'em," he said.[3] His pale suit was so perfect, it looked like he had never sat down in it, and in his crisp white shirt and pastel tie he stood there like a miniature mannequin from a Savile Row shop window. I knew I probably looked like I had slept in my clothes, but I took a deep breath and asked if he would give me an interview. Junior Wells regarded me through narrowed eyes, friendly enough, but with a lack of interest that did not appear to be feigned.

"How much you gonna pay me?" he demanded. I had been warned he might say that. "If you making money out of me, I want some of it. Ten per cent." He wasn't joking. I briefly toyed with the idea of telling him that being in a book would repay him by making him famous, but it was pretty obvious to everyone, not least himself, that he was famous already. I admitted that I couldn't pay him anything.

Not long afterward I saw him play a Friday and Saturday at the Kingston Mines. It was a strange weekend. He made no attempt to put on a show, stopping after each song, conferring off-mike with the band, and asking the audience, with heavy sarcasm, what he should sing next. One drunk at the back kept offering suggestions, and Junior looked out through the smoke with half-closed eyes and murmured into the microphone, "I wish you'd go home." He seemed not so much arrogant as bored, but beneath his boredom I thought I could detect an acrid dose of contempt. And it wasn't just one off-night for the miniature harp wizard, it was two off-nights in succession: on Friday the place was half full, but although on Saturday the Mines was a little more crowded, and Wells did seem to try a little harder, it was still an oddly disengaged performance.

I could understand if Junior Wells couldn't summon up the enthusiasm to play at Theresa's for a mere forty dollars, as Hip Linkchain said, but the Kingston Mines was probably paying him four hundred or more. It obviously still wasn't enough. Something was not to the man's liking, and whether it was the audience, the Mines, or the North Side generally, I couldn't figure it out. He definitely wanted to be somewhere else. I needed to ask him about it, but further attempts to get him to talk led to further rebuffs. Then, finally, he told me that if I was prepared to sign some sort of contract, drafted by his and Buddy Guy's lawyer, he would give me an interview. It was a Tuesday. He told me to meet him at the Checkerboard on Thursday night.

I got there early. Eventually Junior arrived. He talked to some friends at the bar and then shot a glance across. He seemed surprised to see me there. I waited expectantly. Junior turned back to his friends, and after a few minutes, he left. My questions remained unanswered.

• • •

Taste Entertainment Center was lively. The men wore suits, the ladies party frocks, and the atmosphere was polite and middle class. With its carpets, mood lighting and beer garden, the comfortable venue at 6331 South Lowe Avenue was a world away from the grime of traditional South Side blues joints like the Checkerboard and a good deal more sanitary than the mannered grunginess of the North Side clubs. Mine was the only white face in the place, and in such swish surroundings a jacket and jeans which passed muster in the Kingston Mines made me feel grubby and rumpled. When Metcalfe called for a round of applause "for my man Alan Harper, come all the way from Great Britain to write a book about the blues!" I wasn't sure where to look.

Metcalfe initiated the Blue Mondays as a personal crusade to reintroduce the blues to Chicago's black community. Or that was part of the reason, at least. "I started them off in late April as a fundraiser because I was in political debt," he conceded during our interview. "My political debts have been paid from other sources, but we've lost money on Taste, we're just not getting to the point where we're breaking even. But we believe in paying the musicians at least half-way properly for what they're doing, and that's what I like about Taste: the people make sure everybody get theirs."

With political fundraising no longer a priority, Metcalfe was focused on promotion. "What I'd really like to do is just build the blues, do the things necessary for the tradition to grow, and share it with more people, and provide for the financial stability of the artists," he explained. "I've approached the last three mayors about the need for a blues museum: Daley, Bilandic, and Byrne. The response has been lukewarm in all three cases. The deck is stacked against us in the business realm because the major labels are insensitive to the blues." Not just the labels, but the people too, Metcalfe suggested: "Because it reminds them of their heritage and background, of which they're ashamed. LeRoi Jones speaks of it in *Blues People*,[4] right after the rise of the bourgeoisie."

I had picked up every book with "blues" in the title at either Kroch's and Brentano's on Wabash or in the Bookseller's Row secondhand shop on North Lincoln, and what LeRoi Jones said was: "Rhythm & blues also became more of an anathema to the Negro middle class, perhaps, than the earlier blues forms because it was contemporary and existed as a legitimate expression of a great many Negroes and as a gaudy reminder of the real origins of Negro music."

Jones wrote that in 1963. The author went on to admit that he wasn't a particular fan of the new urban blues: "It seems a less personal music than the older blues forms if only because the constant hammering of the overwhelming rhythm sections often subverts the verse, the lyrics, and the lyric content." He also worried that "it seems more easily *faked* . . . one gets the idea that a man falling down on his back screaming is doing so, even though he might be genuinely moved to do so, more from a sense of performance than from any unalterable emotional requirement. But again, the opposite idea also seems true—that for the Negro who found his most complete statement in rhythm & blues, the dramatic or *burlesqued* part of the performance might be as integral a part of the expression as the blues itself, since it made the departure, the separation, from the social implications of the white popular song complete."

In other words, Howlin' Wolf wasn't just the opposite of say, Frank Sinatra; he was an anti-Sinatra, and aspirational, black, middle-class audiences, Jones felt, were uncomfortable with that. Writing a year or two later in *Urban Blues*, Charles Keil, a Chicago academic who could sometimes have difficulty summoning up enough faint praise with which to damn LeRoi Jones's literary efforts, asked a young black fan at a concert what he liked about B. B. King and Bobby Bland: "B. B.'s cleaned up the blues—no harps, moaning, shit like that," came the reply. "Those guys have brought the blues up to date—made it modern." For most black Chicago blues fans, Keil concluded, "the distinction between clean and dirty (or new and old) is the only criterion of any importance. There exists a minority group—usually middle-aged women and older people generally—who still like the dirtier down-and-out styles of Muddy Waters and Howlin' Wolf. For the most part, however, the audience at an Ashland Auditorium blues festival or at one of the Regal Theater's blues shows favors singers that bring back memories of the 'old country' (the South) without forcing their listeners to identify themselves as lower-class, farmer types, or recent migrants from the South."

Ralph Metcalfe Jr., crusader for down-and-dirty Chicago blues, had no worries on that score. With an impeccable family background as a member of black American aristocracy—his father studied at university, won gold and silver alongside Jesse Owens at the Berlin Olympics, and served with distinction in Congress—he was sent to an expensive and dazzlingly white boarding school in Connecticut.

"It's funny how I got hip to the blues," Metcalfe said as he recalled his schooldays. "I took all my records: the Drifters, stuff like that. I used to sit around with the guys and turn them on to my music, which they weren't aware of, and they would do me the same favor. I guess my favorites were the Beatles and the Rolling Stones. And then one guy came back and he had a Paul Butterfield record, and I said 'My, that's a very intense sound, them guys sound really soul.' I went home for Thanksgiving, and went to a store on Fifty-Eighth Street to get some records, and among them was this Paul Butterfield record. But right next to it on the shelf was this record called *Hoodoo Man Blues*, by Junior Wells, which had just been released. I said, well, this is Chicago blues and *this* is Chicago blues. These guys are white, and these guys are black—let me try his album too. So I take Junior's album home, and it's really smoking—I liked it tremendously, I fell in love with the record. And I was reading the liner notes, and I noticed that Junior worked at Theresa's Tavern, which was on Forty-Eighth and Indiana. Here I've lived on Forty-Fifth and Michigan all my life and I say, 'My goodness, all these good blues are right around the corner from me.'"

So although brought up within a stone's throw of Theresa's, in the heart of Chicago's black South Side, Metcalfe's conversion to the blues in 1965 mirrored that of countless hormone-charged white boys, from Boston Lincs to Boston Mass, in search of artistic authenticity and an emotional fix. Not too many other young black men in the South Side of Chicago at that time shared the same epiphany. But at least having discovered the music, he was able to see it performed regularly, although still just seventeen: "I was kind of big for my age."

Metcalfe's Blue Mondays at Taste had begun in April. The attempt to recreate the ambience of a down home blues club, complete with fried Mississippi catfish, had got off to slow start: the place was busy, but it wasn't full. Looking around, I couldn't help thinking that all these well-dressed, middle-class people would have been happier at a Tyrone Davis concert or sitting in a supper club listening to Bobby Bland. I was pretty sure that their idea of down home blues would have been Z. Z. Hill, not Junior Wells. And if Junior wasn't their kind of bluesman, they weren't his usual kind of audience, either. He didn't know these people, and they didn't know him.

But that was Metcalfe's point. This was his personal crusade to convince black people not to turn their backs on their cultural roots. It wasn't going that well. "People are just intimidated," Metcalfe insisted. "There's a dress code, you have to be fairly neat and clean. The drinks don't cost any more than they do at the Checkerboard or Theresa's. We've got free food for folks now. Two blues bands. We're fighting, man." I had a feeling he already knew it was a losing battle.

At the end of Johnny Dollar's set, Metcalfe walked to the microphone, thanked Dollar and his Scan'lous Band, and then called conspiratorially down to Junior Wells, standing at the bar, to check whether he'd had "any of that good fried catfish." But Junior wasn't playing Metcalfe's game. He excused himself with icy disdain: "No thanks," he replied. "I just had some neckbones and black-eyed peas."

Irony dripped from his words like battery acid. It seemed it wasn't just audiences who were reluctant to identify themselves as "lower-class, farmer types, or recent migrants from the South."[5]

· · ·

The Sunday before my interview with Lefty Dizz, there was an afternoon street fair on the North Side where Lefty and his band, Shock Treatment, took to the stage. As always, it was impossible to know what to expect of him. Strolling under a bright blue summer sky, eating a roast beef sandwich and drinking Pabst out of a plastic cup seemed an odd way to listen to blues: so odd that it almost felt as if I were seeing him for the first time, like most of the young crowd. But I knew what he was capable of on a good day, and I found myself hoping he would do himself justice.

He did. High on stage with the L tracks behind him and a long view south down Lincoln Avenue, Dizz took complete possession of the situation for a masterful forty minutes, one moment seducing the crowd with jokes and smiles, the next unleashing guitar solos through the huge sound system of such seismic intensity that the asphalt trembled and aftershocks echoed off the buildings. The air crackled. His fingers were a high-speed blur on the fretboard, his frown of concentration like death itself. He was charismatic, unpredictable, anarchic, unnerving: as alien in his scarlet suit and Stetson as an emissary from the court of Genghis Khan. He constructed towering monuments of sound, only to bring them crashing down again. The earth shook. He went down a storm.

Arriving at the Checkerboard Lounge for our interview the following evening, I found him hanging out by the door. He took leave of his friends—a little ostentatiously, I thought, as if rather enjoying the attention—and directed me out to his car. Knowing so little about him, I had no choice but to start, like some folk researcher standing in a ditch in Mississippi, by asking him to tell me about himself.

"I'm from right here in Chicago," he said, settling himself behind the steering wheel. "When did I start playing music professionally? Well, 1958 really. Actually I was doing it in fifty-six, because I was working with Sonny Thompson, and we toured all over the country—we was down in Florida, up in Seattle. We were playing rock 'n' roll, rhythm and blues. Sonny Thompson was the director of King recording company, Chicago branch, on North Michigan Avenue. We played behind Lulu Reed, Esther Phillips, Wayne Fleming, Dee Clark, on 'Raindrops' and all that stuff. We were a show band, ten pieces, we had the whole bit." He reckoned he started playing blues in about 1960. "You grow older, and you get into the blues. When you hear the blues all your life, up and down Forty-Third Street, up and down Thirty-Ninth, up and down Twenty-Fourth Street, Fifty-First, you take it for granted. I could play it, but it's not that easy. Because blues is really not written, it's felt."

As a guitarist Dizz had few peers. Although he learned his trade in the rigorous academy of Sonny Thompson's show band, his powerfully individual playing style came straight out of the febrile club atmosphere of 1950s Chicago. One of his show-stopping tunes was an electrifying rendition of Magic Sam's tectonic boogie "I Feel So Good."[6] But the man who Ralph Metcalfe said had once been capable of blowing Buddy Guy off the stage didn't acknowledge any one guitarist as a major influence. "I had no special person. I liked everything everybody done. Everybody is special, that's what I mean: Earl Hooker, John Lee Hooker, old man Muddy, the Wolf, everybody in the business I had to listen to, because I love music. I'm still learning my music. Every time I pick up my instrument, I learn something new. It's the only approach."

He was stationed with the U.S. Army[7] in Europe from 1954 to 1956, and the first time he went there as a musician was in 1964, with Junior Wells. "I was his bandleader. I worked with Junior until 1970, and then him and Buddy teamed up. We did Africa, and Southeast Asia, whole bit." There was an urgency about Dizz. He listened carefully, spoke fast, and fired back his answers with a spiky intelligence. I was ill-prepared, and when I started generalizing about white audiences and black audiences, he shot me down: "Are you kidding? You're assuming. You don't know. Three-fourths of the University of Chicago will be here between now and eleven o'clock. Don't assume anything. Ask questions if you're going to do this interview, otherwise I'll interview you." That seemed to give him an idea. "When did you start in this business?" he demanded. "I'd like to know that." Sheepishly, I gave him a date: not very long ago. "All right. And what brought you to this?" That one was easier: I really liked the music. "You have a feeling for the blues. When did you first feel the blues?" But his eyes were full of mischief. He couldn't keep it up, and the car filled with laughter. "You're a big boy now! Here, have a sip of this Grandaddy," he offered, producing a slim bottle of bourbon from his jacket pocket. "All right. Anything you write about me, just write the truth."

I told him about finding my one Lefty Dizz LP and wondered how long he had been recording under his own name. "Wow—it hasn't been too long." He pondered for a moment. "Seventy-two, I did a thing for CJ, Carl Jones Productions,[8] a single, a forty-five. And I did four things with Spivey Records, Victoria, before she passed away—I was in New York at the time. I wouldn't mind recording in the States, but why record, waste all that time, if your records are not going to be played?"

The absence of blues on the radio was a common complaint among Chicago's musicians. The commercial imperatives of advertising and demographics were simple enough, but for many musicians, nostalgia for the heyday of blues radio was hard to shake. "There was a station down in Nashville, Tennessee, which was WLAC, that was playing the blues," Dizz explained. "The station reached all over. But now the blues has no airplay at all." The famous fifty-thousand-watt AM station was aimed at black American listeners in the northern cities and the rural South, but it could be heard from Canada to the Caribbean. From the 1950s through to the 1970s its influence was enormous. It was credited with kick-starting the careers of James Brown, Ray Charles, and B. B. King, among others. WLAC was even said to have made possible the development of ska, and ultimately reggae.

"I don't know why," Dizz continued, lamenting the loss of blues airplay. "But I talked to people that are disc jockeys, and their producers, so then they say, 'We don't have a spot for it.' Why don't you have a spot for blues? You got a ten-minute spot once a week for blues, you got a twenty-three-hour show for rock: what are you saying, that the blues don't exist? Then you're saying that I don't exist," he snapped. As he warmed to his theme, the demon guitarist worked himself up to a pitch of righteous indignation. "This is the truly American black music, in the purest form. You're saying my culture ain't shit, and I am not amused. Yesterday afternoon on Lincoln Avenue, from Wrightwood to Fullerton, wall-to-wall people: so don't tell me there's no market for the blues. You can't tell me that the blues is dead, that the blues is underground. The blues is as alive as I am."

And that, it seemed, was that. Dizz had said what he wanted to say, and was now bored with being interviewed. "Have a little taste with me," he said, proffering his bottle of Old Grand-Dad one more time. "That's enough!" he laughed. "Well, I've got to get back inside and take care of my business . . ."

• • •

Just as Ralph Metcalfe was using fried Mississippi catfish to sell the blues at the Taste Entertainment Center in Chicago's deep south, over on the West Side there was a man from the Deep South using the blues to sell fried Mississippi catfish. At the Delta Fish Market, some of Chicago's best musicians would congregate and play outdoor gigs in the afternoons. It really was a fish market, on the busy intersection of Jackson Boulevard and Kedzie Avenue, and it was here that Oliver Davis, the proprietor, hit upon the idea of putting on blues shows in his parking lot as an obvious marketing accompaniment to the truckloads of fish he was bringing up from Mississippi.

As a blues venue it seemed even stranger than watching Lefty Dizz play on a sunny afternoon on Lincoln Avenue. Showing up sharp at the advertised start time of one o'clock was not usually necessary. The music was free, and it started whenever the musicians were ready. The stage was a simple wooden structure decorated with Delta signs that looked like they might have once belonged to the airline of the same name. But the sound system was pretty good. The whole thing had a ramshackle air, but it was popular, and it worked, because Davis was a serious blues fan who booked excellent bands. They played on Fridays and Saturdays.

"I'm from the Delta, and we named the fish market after the Delta because we go there to get ninety percent of our fish," he told me in his office one afternoon. "I'm from Greenville, Mississippi, home of Eddie Shaw, Hound Dog Taylor and I don't know how many more blues players." On the stage outside, Johnny Littlejohn, from Lake, Mississippi, was playing screaming slide guitar, while Sunnyland Slim, from Quitman County, sipped from a bottle of Crown Royal and waited to go on. It was early, and the crowd was a little on the thin side, but the air was thick with the smell of frying fish. Davis was relaxed, leaning back in his executive chair, surrounded by boxes. "This is not for making money for me," Davis explained. "It only employs the guys that's playing in the band, and I pay each and every one of them that play there, out of my own pocket. And I have it as a service to the community."

The weather was warm and bright, the atmosphere festive, and Johnny Littlejohn was accompanied by a piano player named Bob, who brought his young children up on stage. Bob's son Eric was introduced as the "Blues Baby" and proceeded to play guitar reasonably well for an eleven-year-old before moving on to the drums, where he seemed more confident. His singing was slightly off-key, although not as much as his younger sister's. But she was so cute, it seemed churlish to criticize. Later, Bob came over to tell me where I could see his children play again—Willie's Place, 107th and State Streets—and suggested that I might be interested in helping him with publicity. I was on the point of making my excuses when I noticed he had a thick scar running from the right-hand corner of his mouth, across his throat, and up to the lobe of his left ear. I said I'd try to make it.[9]

Once they got going, on a good day the bands at the Delta Fish Market would play through until about nine o'clock at night. It was the nearest thing to a Southern fish fry that most of Davis's customers had seen for years. "They feel at home when they come here," he said. "It's a like a nostalgia, because you think of the old times, you can hear the old-time songs the musicians play."

• • •

A black person's nostalgia for the South sounded to me like an East Ender's nostalgia for the London Blitz. It didn't make sense. But I was no expert. One afternoon at the Fish Market I met Jim O'Neal, who was standing in the background, watching the band's preparations with cool detachment. The slim, long-haired co-founder and co-editor of *Living Blues* magazine, thirty-three years old, was intending the next day to drive down south to the Mississippi Delta Blues Festival, at Greenville: the heart of Delta blues country. He asked if I wanted to come along. It was a generous offer, which I ought to have accepted without hesitation. But I felt that I had unfinished business in Chicago and should be focusing on that. Also, I was obscurely aware that however fun and fascinating it might be, to make a trip like that in the company of such an eminent blues scholar would be to run the risk of seeing and hearing everything through his eyes and ears, not my own. And that would probably dissolve what little belief I had in my own blues credentials.

My only experience of the South, three years before, really wasn't great. After two months in Chicago in 1979 mopping floors, trying to sell newspaper subscriptions and hanging out in blues clubs, I carried on hitchhiking westward to California, and there I met up with a couple of English friends who were headed in the opposite direction. We agreed to rendezvous in New Orleans and travel back to New York together. Hitchhiking[10] as a threesome in Europe would have been a non-starter, but American vehicles were big. On a dusty, rural roadside somewhere in Alabama, a pickup truck drew alongside, driven by a slight, young, white man with a pair of crutches propped up against his seat. We threw our rucksacks in the back and climbed in, sitting four abreast, glad to get out of the sun. It was tight, but OK.

"I guess you boys are all right," said our driver, after a few minutes of chat. He reached down beside his seat, pulled out a pistol and slotted it back into place behind the sun visor. He had to be careful, he explained to his startled passengers: a friend had recently picked up a hitchhiker who became aggressive. Had to shoot him.

"What?" we said. "Dead?"

"He was a nigra. He had mental problems," he explained. Not any more, apparently.

Grateful as we were to have been judged "all right," this additional information was unsettling, and an awkwardness descended. We were unwilling to exhibit any behavior that might lead to the reappearance of the gun, so we sat quite still. This, it seemed, implied tacit approval, so the young man began to regale his wide-eyed British audience with tales of the Ku Klux Klan. There were no further stories of extrajudicial killings and no murders or lynchings, but violent intimidation was a recurring theme. One black family who were moved into a white neighborhood as part of some well-meaning affirmative-action program were persuaded to move out again, he said, after a gang armed with machine guns lined up outside and loosed off their weapons in a waist-high fusillade. "Practically sawed that house in half," remarked our host approvingly.

Squeezed across the cab of the pickup, it wasn't easy for the three of us to make eye contact, but I sensed a certain stiffening of shoulders. As the poisonous monologue wore on, our polite interjections of "Gosh" and "Really?" were gradually supplanted by a heavy silence.

By inviting us into his confidence merely because we had the same color skin, our young driver was clearly possessed of the fathomless ignorance required by all who hold strong and irrational opinions. That was disturbing enough, but worse was the fact that every minute we remained silent, we were sucked deeper into a shabby complicity with his worldview. But we weren't going to argue with the little bastard. He had a gun.

After that, being run out of Cartersville, Georgia, before we even arrived in the town was merely a comic interlude. Following a long and welcome ride in the high cab of a truck, we fell out onto the roadside and began relieving ourselves into the bushes: one of us, possibly me, doing so within sight of passing traffic. A few minutes later, a police car skidded to a halt on the dusty verge, and out stepped Sheriff J. W. Pepper, or at least someone very like the law enforcement officer from *Live and Let Die*, with his short stature and waddling gait, gun and handcuffs jangling around an ample waist. The resemblance was total. We gazed at him admiringly.

"One o' you boys been urinatin' in public?"

It was tempting simply to explain that "in England, we piss anywhere," as Bill Wyman once said in a similar situation.[11] But we succeeded in appearing contrite and abashed, and the sheriff was mollified. Our punishment was to stay on the highway. Just keep moving. Don't even think about entering town.

Later on, trudging about in a rural backwater looking for somewhere to bed down for the night, we came upon some old shipping containers in a wood, which seemed to fit the bill, and climbed inside. In the twilight I caught a glimpse of a solitary figure standing in the trees, looking us over. It was an uneasy night. We were up and out before the sun rose.

I have little doubt that every white person in that district knew of our arrival within minutes of our run-in with the caricature cop, and that our cards had probably been marked: three fag English hippy types, degenerate but harmless, to be kept an eye on and helped, if necessary, to move on. I also have little doubt that had we been black, we could have disappeared into that dismal swamp of suspicion and prejudice and never been heard from again.

So I was in no hurry to go back to the South. But a trip with Jim O'Neal to Greenville, Mississippi, to see the likes of Hammie Nixon and Sam Chatmon, might have been a welcome corrective. I should probably have said yes.

· · ·

One Friday I heard a rumor that James Cotton was going to play at the Delta Fish Market, and I turned up to discover that the show was being filmed by an ABC crew for a one-hour television show. Vans circled like wagons as the parking lot filled with cameras and cables. The producer was standing wryly on the sidelines. Along with Cotton, he told me, the film would include Erwin Helfer, Koko Taylor, Buddy Guy, Little Milton, and a host of other luminaries. There were even plans to shoot on Sunday at Maxwell Street. That surprised me: the legendary flea market where many older Chicago musicians had served their musical apprenticeships barely even seemed to be a shadow of its former self. My dutiful visits had unearthed no music of note. I had always felt that the least plausible scene in *The Blues Brothers*, including the car chases and John Belushi doing backflips up the aisle of James Brown's church, was the Maxwell Street sequence, because it featured John Lee Hooker and Big Walter Horton.[12] But the television producer explained that their focus in the street market would be the future, not the past. The cameras would be following Billy Branch and Lurrie Bell, who were taking one of their school classes to Maxwell Street on a field trip.

There was a good crowd at the Delta Fish Market, attracted as much by the commotion as by the reputation of the great harp player, who cut his teeth in the Muddy Waters band and had been a successful solo star since the 1970s. "A long time ago they didn't want to hear the blues," said Oliver Davis. "But nowadays, most youngsters that's in a band, a little rock 'n' roll band or rock band or disco band or whatever they got, they like the blues because they found out, most of them, that it's easy to play disco, but it's hard to play blues. When they first listen to the blues and don't even practice, they say oh, I can play that. But they really can't do it, because it's harder than the disco, and rock. And we try to keep it alive, right here at the Delta Fish Market."

James Cotton was bouncing around on stage to "Boogie Thing." His backing band were phenomenal. After one particularly cunning breakdown, orchestrated with a few vague hand signals from the genial harp virtuoso, Cotton laughed and said: "Ladies and gentlemen, please give my band a round of applause for being so intelligent!"

7

Comparing Hangovers at Alligator

> When they say, "We can't play this—our audience can't identify with this kind of music," what they're saying is, "Our audience doesn't want to hear niggers."
>
> —Bruce Iglauer

Alligator Records' global headquarters on North Magnolia Avenue, a couple of blocks from the Granville L stop, appeared to be a modest, wood-framed house in a shady suburban street. The label's owner, Bruce Iglauer, met me at the door. It was a Saturday morning, and he confessed to being tired and hungover and anxiously awaiting a phone call from one of his artists, Albert Collins, who was touring in California. This more or less mirrored my own condition, as I was naturally a little anxious about interviewing one of the most important men in Chicago blues, and was also, after a late night at the Kingston Mines listening to Jimmy Johnson, tired and hungover. It seemed that the Albert Collins tour bus had suffered a gearbox problem between Los Angeles and San Francisco. The band was due on stage at a blues festival in an hour and a half.

"Albert, rather than calling me to report this, has attempted to get it fixed," Iglauer said. "And his excuse will be that he's 'booking'—that is, attempting to move as quickly as possible—when actually I could cover for him much more effectively were I to call the promoter, so that Albert looks more professional. He instead will say that he wanted to look professional, and therefore he didn't call, because he was hurrying. As you may have noticed," he concluded wearily, "we've had this conversation before. I almost went out to California last night to beat my head against the wall in person."

We arranged ourselves in the sitting room, the company boss close to the telephone and Grace the cat prowling suspiciously. Mentally filing away this explanation of what "booking" meant, which shed useful light on the Robert Johnson line, "I'm booked and I got to go,"[1] I fired off an opening question. Then Iglauer talked almost without pause for two hours.

Thirty-five years old, bearded, bespectacled, articulate and amusing, Iglauer proved capable of spinning his narrative thread long after most listeners would have been tempted to give up on it, on the assumption that after so many digressions, sub-clauses, parenthetical observations and seemingly blind alleyways, the point of the story must have long been mislaid. Following Iglauer's train of thought required effort, especially by a slightly hungover mind. But it was not without reward. He was very entertaining.

He never intended to start his own label, he explained, and like many others in the Chicago blues business started out working for Bob Koester, on the Delmark label and in the Jazz Record Mart, hoping to be given the chance to produce. "I wanted to produce Luther Allison. He was with the label. I came to Delmark because of Luther," he said. "Then he and I had a falling out, which has continued to this day."[2]

Luther Allison was no longer with Delmark. In our interview the guitarist had alluded to some sort of rift with Alligator but refused to explain. Yet he seemed to me to be a perfect, tailor-made blues-rock act for the younger label, and I wondered why Iglauer hadn't signed him up. "Yeah, a lot of people have asked that," said Iglauer. "It's because he's a jerk—and you can print that—and he's a liar, and he's a hypocrite, and I don't trust him. He made a very important promise to me and shook my hand on it when he knew that he was not going to keep it, and it almost cost me my job at Delmark, which he knew was terribly important to me. And I have never forgiven him that, and believe me I have forgiven a lot, of a lot of musicians." He glanced at the still-silent telephone. "And I may be forgiving Albert Collins very shortly, if he doesn't call."

Alligator eventually came into being to record another of his favorite artists, with the help of a financial backer, Wesley Race. Iglauer hadn't been able to persuade Koester to record Hound Dog Taylor. "I was working behind the counter at the Jazz Record Mart, back when Delmark was in the basement with the world's biggest roaches," he explained. "Wes said, 'I've got a thousand dollars: I'd invest in that Hound Dog record if I could eventually make the money back.' It was a Tuesday night. I said, 'I'm your man.'"

That conversation took place in late 1970, and *Hound Dog Taylor and the Houserockers* came out in September 1971.[3] Iglauer stayed on at Delmark for the next nine months or so, until eventually Bob Koester noticed that Alligator Records was staking more of a claim on his young sales assistant's time than Delmark was: "Bob and I had a head-to-head, and he said, 'You're going to have to make a decision.' And he was right, absolutely."

Koester had faced the problem before. For years Delmark had been a kind of kindergarten for white blues people,[4] and a fair few had launched careers as musicians, writers, editors, producers, and label owners while working there. Iglauer reeled off a list of well-known names he had worked with and who had gone on, as he had, to make their own mark on the blues business. He described Koester as a father figure. "The real rivalry was between myself and Steve Tomashefsky," he remembered. "He had the same job I had for a number of years. I have nothing against Steve, but he can't tolerate me at all. Part of it has to do with what most people perceive as Alligator's intense pushiness, which is true, we are very, very pushy people when it comes to sales, our artists, our media image. We're 'on' all the time, because we're operating with no capital, we have nothing to fall back on. There is nothing in the bank. Everything that is made is spent. This company makes no money. Some of the employees make money. I'm not one of them."

From the outside the headquarters of Chicago's most successful blues record label looked like an ordinary house, and it was. When Iglauer said his office was his bedroom, he wasn't joking: there was his bed, and there, in a corner by the window, his desk, covered with paper. Of Alligator's three other employees, two worked upstairs and the third was based in a back room on the ground floor. "We had a total of five at one time, but early this year I let the other guy go, because of money," said Iglauer.

Unlike Bob Koester, who came to the blues via jazz, or the O'Neals of *Living Blues* magazine, who discovered the music through British rock, Iglauer arrived at the blues via folk music, catching many of the great country blues singers at 1960s festivals, as well as a few Chicago musicians like Sunnyland Slim, Johnny Young and Big Walter Horton. He heard *Hoodoo Man Blues* and didn't like it, then bought the Muddy Waters compilation LP *The Real Folk Blues*[5] and the first Paul Butterfield record, which impressed him much more than the Blues-breakers' *Beano* album. "Much more so than Mayall, the Butterfield band was a real crucial band in the white blues boom, probably because they were actually a good band," Iglauer suggested. "Although," he conceded, "everybody I knew owned that Mayall album."

· · ·

Lonnie, Albert, Koko and Son sounded like a children's television show, or perhaps an unusually progressive legal practice, but in fact these were four of the most successful blues artists of the day, and they were all signed to Alligator Records. Lonnie Brooks was a youthful-looking and dynamic singer and guitar-ist from Louisiana who had scored a few local hits in the late 1950s under the name Guitar Junior. He moved to Chicago in 1959, and I knew him as a regular on the North Side, particularly at the Kingston Mines. As a female vocalist, Koko Taylor was practically unique in the Chicago blues, but she was extremely popular and in 1982 already too expensive for the city's small blues clubs. But she wasn't as successful as Alligator's star attraction, Texas singer and guitarist Albert Collins. The "master of the Telecaster" recorded a well-regarded instrumental single in 1958, "The Freeze," and in the 1960s enjoyed some crossover success into the rock market, recording several albums on Imperial in California after an introduction from blues-rockers Canned Heat. His signing by Alligator in 1978 was the latest and most successful step so far in a long blues career.

The Alligator artist whose music I knew best was the youngest of the foursome. Son Seals was an Alligator discovery, picked up by the label in 1972 after he took over Hound Dog Taylor's residency at the Expressway Lounge on Fifty-Fifth Street, and Wesley Race called Bruce Iglauer and held the phone out so he could hear this new band play. Seals had recorded before, a couple of 45s in 1963, but they hardly counted, as even he seemed unable to remember anything about them. There had been two Seals LPs in my university library. *Live and Burning*, recorded at the Wise Fools Pub on Lincoln Avenue in 1978, was a favorite, of mine, anyway, on my late-night radio show, which was piped to a handful of drunks and insomniacs in the student halls of residence.

At age forty Seals had been based in Chicago for more than ten years but originally came from Osceola in Arkansas, an hour north of Memphis, and so naturally fell under the spell of local hero Albert King. Guitar virtuoso Earl Hooker was another influence. His father was a bar-owning musician, and the young Seals grew up in the music business. He sat in on the drums for visiting acts, learned guitar by osmosis through his bedroom wall, turned professional while still a teenager, and even played drums on tour with Albert King. The great Flying Vee pilot's influence was clear in Seals's guitar playing, which was no bad thing in my book, but whereas King strove for a velvety texture to his angular instrument's endless sustain, Seals was more of a fuzz man, which was also OK with me. Seals's guitar sound was as smooth as broken glass and his vocal was gruff. He and his guitar sparked off each other: it was like listening to an angry bear. But along with most blues guitarists, he played more notes than Albert King and ended up saying less. He had technique, but lacked soul.

Therefore he was best live. His studio work seldom caught fire, but *Live and Burning*, his third album, certainly had its moments. More than once I used its opening track, a punchy reinterpretation of Elmore James's "I Can't Hold Out," to kick off my radio show. It helped that it was short. Seals was no great ideas man, and when his guitar solos ran out of steam, time could hang heavy. But his growling vocals and often unsimulated air of moodiness made him a formidable presence on stage, and he had learned enough from Albert King to know how to time an attack.

The Wise Fools Pub was his usual haunt when he was in Chicago. It was different from the other North Side blues bars: slightly more expensive, better decorated, more grown-up and less bacterial. They booked jazz as well as blues and had a logo that looked like it might have been designed by a designer, as opposed to a nine-year-old. So it attracted a different kind of clientele from B.L.U.E.S or the Kingston Mines, even on blues nights. Smartly dressed young white men, young urban professionals, packed the place out to see Son Seals, and they howled and screamed at every solo. This seemed odd at first, then it became annoying, and after a while it was unbearable. An alien peering through the window would have seen a weird inverted zoo, in which musicians were caged in by a yelling mob of besuited apes. You got the feeling that in apartments all over the North Side, the hapless wives and girlfriends of these beered-up blues fans sat awaiting their return with a sense of dread.

But if there was one thing worse than being appreciated by a noisy and enthusiastic bunch of fans, it was not being appreciated by a noisy and enthusiastic bunch of fans. By blues standards, Son Seals's success had been meteoric. He had made four albums for Alligator. He played regular club dates, toured all over the United States, and had traveled overseas. His career seemed in great shape at a time when most bluesmen hardly had a career at all.

Bruce Iglauer gave me tickets for a show at a big concert venue called Stages,[6] headlined by Albert Collins, Koko Taylor and Son Seals, which was being filmed for a television special. It was the only time I saw Seals share a stage with another star. After Koko went off, he seemed content to play second fiddle not only to Collins, whose musicianship and stage presence were in another league, but also to Koko's guitarist Emmett Sanders, known as Maestro, who was an instrumental phenomenon and easily my favorite guitar player of the night. The battle laid Seals's limitations bare, and after a while he surrendered the stage to Maestro and Albert Collins. But he really didn't seem to mind. He looked a lot more cheerful than he generally did at the Wise Fools. It was a great show.

An interview was arranged at Alligator. The bearded bluesman sat down affably at the kitchen table and remembered his first meeting with Iglauer back in 1971, at the Expressway: "He came up and introduced himself, told us that his friend had let him listen to us over the phone, so he asked me if I did any writing, was I interested in making a record, and all this sort of jive. I said, well, you know, go along with it. I thought it was just a bunch of crap," he chuckled. But Iglauer was serious. The Hound Dog Taylor album was doing well. Alligator's second record was out already,[7] and the young music mogul had the bit between his teeth. He told Seals that if he was interested he should get rehearsing and call when he was ready.

"We rehearsed, I guess—heck, man, every day for about two weeks—and finally we told him we're ready," said Seals. "He listened and say he liked what he heard, and we did that first album. I been with Alligator ever since. He put the record out and started to book us. They do the whole thing, and they do a darned good job." Iglauer was bustling in and out of the kitchen, but I didn't get the impression that the singer was being at all insincere. Theirs seemed to be a pretty adult and collaborative working relationship: "We'll sit down and listen to things together and make suggestions together: this need changing, or that need changing, what do you think, what do I think," Seals said. "It's a thing where we work together, and I like that. It seem like to me it works out better."

Seals was a blues man, but growing up near Memphis he enjoyed everything from Count Basie to country and western. When I wondered whether the blues would ever achieve the kind of mainstream success then being enjoyed by country music, he smiled at the thought: "Oh, man. And they're so closely related, man. I grew up around country and western and blues, and I played with the country and western guys. The music seemed to have so much of the same meaning, lyric-wise especially. And it was country music just like our blues is country music."

• • •

The first Son Seals album, *The Son Seals Blues Band*, was fascinating. Not musically—musically it was remarkably ordinary—but for what it revealed about Iglauer's priorities. The Hound Dog album's success with the young college crowd encouraged him to try the same formula again, with a small band, a mix of covers and originals, and a charismatic front man who played guitar. Iglauer just needed to find the right artist: and suddenly there was Son Seals, an exciting, unknown but undeniably "authentic" young blues singer and guitarist. Iglauer's liner notes on the back of the album underlined Seals's appeal as an original. Unlike most young bluesmen, he wrote, the new Alligator signing was his own man: "Seals has been writing his own personal blues and developing his biting, 'scuffling' guitar sound for thirteen years."

Leaving aside the question of whether thirteen years had been long enough, it was obvious that despite Seals's Memphis roots and eclectic tastes, Iglauer wanted him for his ability to front a hard-driving Chicago blues band. "In 1971," Iglauer explained to me, "when John Mayall was still a name to conjure with"— he caught my look and interjected: "hard to believe, isn't it?—there was a large, untapped white market for blues." And not just any blues, but blues designed to cater to rock fans: hard and gritty electric guitar music. "For the white audience I think blues is essentially interpreted as a branch of rock 'n' roll."

But almost as soon as the first Seals album hit the racks in 1973, the market began to change. The 1970s was the decade of disco, and the backlash against it had unforeseen side effects. The grassroots "disco sucks" movement came to a head in 1979, during my first stay in Chicago, when in a well-publicized stunt, the white rock jock Steve Dahl blew up a pile of disco records in the outfield of Comiskey Park after a White Sox baseball game. It was reported at the time as a harmless bit of fun, but for Iglauer it was more serious than that: "I hated disco, but I have to believe that one of the reasons that happened is that disco had such a strong identification with being black music. There was a real anti-black undercurrent in the anti-disco thing."[8]

Then an all-important conduit for marketing Alligator's artists, "progressive rock radio," went bad. When Iglauer started taking the first Hound Dog Taylor album around in 1971, he recalled, "I was walking into stations, and meeting each jock individually as they went on air, saying, 'Hi, I'm from Chicago, and I'm a blues fan, and I started a record company and produced a record by my favorite band. Here it is.' And the jocks would say something like, 'Oh wow, far out, heavy.' I remember the first time I was in Detroit, with the first record, somebody played the whole record on his show. Just said, 'Oh yeah, I like blues,' and put it on and played it. The whole LP."

By 1982 it wasn't like that. "Album-oriented rock radio has become lily-white," Iglauer said. "The only acceptable [black] artists are oldies artists. You can play an old Motown cut, that's fine, and Hendrix. Nobody else allowed, not even Stevie Wonder. It's the most lily-white form of radio. When I walk into a station, and they look at the cover, and without even breaking the shrink-wrap, say 'We can't play this record—our audience can't identify with this kind of music,' what they're saying is, 'We think our audience doesn't want to hear niggers.'"

This was a problem for a label whose slogan was "genuine houserockin' music" and whose acts were all black. "If you don't get your records played on the radio, you don't sell records," said Iglauer. "It's very discouraging right this minute. I feel that the black market is where the real future of the blues is going to lie." Maybe because he was looking for them, he had noticed encouraging signs to back up this view: a couple of years before, to everybody's surprise, a black radio station in Oklahoma City had started playing Koko Taylor's second album. "We sold three or four thousand LPs and eight-tracks, a supposedly obsolete tape form, in Oklahoma." Then in early 1982 a black station in Memphis started playing the eight-minute slow blues "Conversation with Collins" from Albert Collins's *Ice Pickin'* album. "We sold a thousand LPs in Memphis in the period of a month," said Iglauer. "Of a three-and-a-half-year-old record."

If white rock radio had pulled down the shutters, the label would have to try and get more airplay on black stations. This change in approach could be traced in Son Seals's albums.[9] His second, in 1976, was a notably more polished effort than the first, with tighter arrangements and jazzy horn parts, which wouldn't have sounded out of place at the Regal Theater backing up B. B. King. It seemed like much more the kind of record that a musician of Seals's eclecticism might have wanted to make. The third Seals album was that straight-ahead 1978 live set from the Wise Fools, but the fourth, 1980's *Chicago Fire*, both looked and sounded like it was made with the black record-buyer in mind. Compared with his earlier output, it had more interesting melodies and more complex scoring. It had horns, funky bass, and superior production values. There were still blues-rock elements, but they were competing with some solid R&B. And where all the previous cover photos played up Seals's image as a dangerous blues-rock axe-man, there on the front of *Chicago Fire* was a well-groomed guitarist wearing a pinstripe suit. There was even a song entitled "Gentleman from the Windy City.'"

But for all its slick presentation, *Chicago Fire* didn't convince as an attempt to position Seals as a rival to Little Milton or Z. Z. Hill. I wasn't sure that Seals's vocal style was right for a self-consciously sophisticated soul-blues audience, where smoothly expressed passion seemed to carry more weight than raw emotion. And his guitar playing was still pretty limited: it rocked, but it didn't swing. Iglauer admitted, "Right now, he's not really selling significant numbers of records, although he has in the past." I found myself wondering if, as far as black blues fans were concerned, the weakest component of the Son Seals proposition was Son Seals himself.

It reminded me of Amy O'Neal's point about white-versus-black blues taste: "the twain don't meet." And if they did, like when "Conversation with Collins" suddenly got airplay on black Memphis radio, it didn't take long to work out why. Albert Collins might have been marketed by Alligator as a guitar hero for young white rockers, but he also had deep roots as a performer and decades of experience playing for Southern black audiences. That particular song, a witty, talking blues about having to babysit while his wife was out partying, could hardly have been targeted more accurately at a mature black blues demographic. And yet it was still a great guitar track. It ticked all the boxes. Of course, none of this would have mattered if it had not also been a work of superlative quality.

Iglauer might have been right about the black market being the future of the blues, but it seemed unlikely that Son Seals would be breaking into the chitlin circuit anytime soon. His career was built on the fascination white boys had for black men with guitars, and it was going pretty well: according to Iglauer, he had plenty of bookings. The college kids and their older brothers—those howling young urban professionals in the Wise Fools—all knew that Son Seals was great live.

• • •

Bruce Iglauer was generous with his time, and with much else. Among the record racks in his basement, he handed me sample albums until I told him to stop: I couldn't carry any more. In an office upstairs—the one with his bed in it—he thrust pieces of paper at me that he thought I might find useful or interesting. Later, sorting through these record catalogs, gig posters, photocopied articles and promotional leaflets, I found some old sheets of typed notes. One of these was headed "Some Ideas for the New Album":

"I want to try to do an album that shows the different sides of your talent," it began. "I want to avoid sounding like any other blues album, or sounding like any other musician. Here are some things I had thought of:

1) no more than two shuffles.
2) no more than two slow blues.
3) a lot of modern rhythms and funky beats.
4) some tunes that don't have regular blues chord changes.
5) at least one instrumental song (and I'd like it to be *very* unusual).
6) I'd like each song to sound different from each other song. That means I don't want to hear the same riffs, the same turnarounds, the same feeling on two different songs. I want each song to be as important as the whole album.
7) Do you have any songs that aren't about women? (Like 'Cotton Pickin' Blues' or 'Now That I'm Down'). There are a lot of things to write about. I don't want you trying to write something you don't feel. But this album should tell people more about what you think and feel than just your feelings about women. I'd like to hear your ideas about this.
8) We can use different instruments on different songs. Maybe a tenor solo on one or two, maybe use both organ and piano on some, maybe one with just three pieces—what are your ideas? If we can rehearse it, we might try two instruments playing lead together, maybe in harmony.
9) I'm very interested in dynamics. By this I mean a lot of variation between quiet and loud parts in songs, and I also mean building a tune and 'breaking it down,' maybe even dropping out the band like in 'Hot Sauce' and bringing them back in. Maybe an introduction where the guitar starts the song by itself (or the bass, or the organ, or your voice), and the rest of the band comes in. Maybe some songs, or parts of songs, that have a more mellow, relaxed feel, so that when you really come on strong, it has even more power.

I've seen and heard you do all of these different things on the bandstand. But they must be planned and rehearsed, or they don't work right. And if they are sloppy, they sound worse than if you didn't try them.

I hope this gives you some ideas. This is an important album for both of us. It should make a lot of people take notice and also should be able to bring your gig price up a little, and get you more gigs. We need an album that is *you*.

I'm looking forward to talking more with you next week about it."

It was signed "B. I."

The old image of the label boss hauling a singer in off the street, putting a bottle of whisky on the piano, setting the tape running and fabricating a writing credit was no doubt an oversimplification, but it must have held a kernel of truth. Bruce Iglauer clearly wasn't like that. This short note, perhaps the first recorded sighting of a management memo addressed to a blues musician, was obviously intended for Seals. But it spoke volumes about Iglauer's attitude to all his artists.

"I wouldn't take nothing from Alligator," said Koko Taylor. "The years I've been with them they've been fantastic. When you record a record for Alligator, they do their best to promote it, see to it getting played, see to it to the artist's working, you know, and I just love them for that."

We were sitting on the sofa together in the comfortably furnished front room of Taylor's bungalow, way down on South Ada Street. Grammy nominations adorned the mantelpiece alongside pictures of her grandchildren. Somewhere in the background her husband of nearly thirty years, Robert "Pops" Taylor, was keeping out of the way and possibly, by the sound of it, doing the washing-up. At age fifty-four, the matronly, soft-spoken and fastidiously courteous singer was at the top of her game. She had three Alligator albums out, but well before signing to Iglauer's label she had a long recording career at Chess, which included a top-ten single. She had toured Europe with the American Folk Blues Festival in the mid-1960s, performed at the Ann Arbor Blues Festival, and sung alongside Muddy Waters at Montreux.

"I been singing all my life, singing and dancing, and I grew up going to church every Sunday, singing gospel with the rest of the family. I was raised on a cotton farm, and every day we would go to the cotton field, me and my brothers and sisters. We was singing blues." One brother made a guitar by nailing baling wire to the side of the house.[10] Another made a harmonica out of a corncob. Taylor sang. "We had a real band going—you shoulda heard us," she smiled. The first songs she learned were Memphis Minnie numbers, "Black Rat Swing" and "Me and My Chauffeur Blues." There was no electricity, but they owned a wind-up Grafonola: "That was probably before you were born," she said, surveying her interviewer skeptically. "They wasn't even making 45 records then, all of the records were 78s."

Perhaps because of her experience of keeping her brothers in line, on stage Taylor was more of a bandleader in the Chicago club mold than a traditional blues diva, and she had recently turned down an engagement in Germany because they didn't want to bring her band over. By the time she moved to Chicago at age twenty-five, she was a fan not of Bessie Smith or Ma Rainey but of Howlin' Wolf, Muddy Waters, Jimmy Reed, Sonny Boy Williamson, and Magic Sam: "Those was peoples that just really stuck with me, I just fell in love with them," she said. "And when I got to Chicago, I heard about all these people that I'd been listening to, that they lived right here. My husband and I, we would travel round the different clubs and they would let me sit in."

There was a passage in Peter Guralnick's *Feel Like Going Home*[11] in which he described seeing Koko Taylor, whose version of "Wang Dang Doodle" sold a reputed million copies, being kept waiting in the Chess Records foyer. She was taking a day off from her job as a maid. "The whole time I was with Chess Records I was under the jurisdiction of Willie Dixon," she told me briskly. "He was the one who would select the tunes that I would record, and he would also do the writing of the tunes, and the arranging and everything, so I didn't have no say-so about how something should go. My job was to sing, and that was it." It was different at Alligator: Taylor had a writer's credit on five songs from her three Alligator albums[12] and clearly felt that her new label was helping her develop as an artist: "Now that I have more experience in singing and how things go, and more experience at writing tunes, you know, I execute this talent with Alligator, because they give me a chance to do it," she confirmed. "You never know what a person can do until you give them a chance to do it."

When I clarified this with Iglauer, he said: "I helped a little."

As a female Chicago blues artist, Koko Taylor was possibly unique. She certainly had no direct rivals in the city, as far as I could tell. I saw Bonnie Lee, a terrific jazz singer, perform at B.L.U.E.S with Sunnyland Slim. Big Time Sarah, a singer who worked behind the bar at both B.L.U.E.S and the Checkerboard, was as likely to be found sitting in with a West Side gunslinger like Hip Linkchain as contributing to a cool jazzy set with Erwin Helfer and Fred Below. There was Queen Sylvia Embry, but she also played bass, which was more of a tomboy vibe, while Lavelle White, a Kingston Mines habituée and a singer of quality, came from a more soul-blues, Texas tradition.

But then there was Valerie Wellington, a classically trained, twenty-three-year-old blues belter who impacted the North Side clubs in 1982 like an outrageously sexy earthquake. She was obviously a big fan of Koko Taylor, which was something that clearly irked Alligator's boss: "When I [first] saw Valerie, she was in her Aretha Franklin period, and I liked that a lot more," Iglauer had told me with a wry look. "I'm encouraging Valerie to get into her post-Koko period."

I asked Koko Taylor if she'd heard of her young imitator. "The girl who be up at the Kingston Mines? Everybody tells me that I am one of her admires, that she idols me," the singer gushed. "Valerie goes on the bandstand and she thinks she Koko Taylor! One night we was out, and so sho nuff we stopped at the Kingston Mines and I got a chance to see and hear Valerie." As far as the older woman was concerned, imitation really was the sincerest form of flattery: "It was amazing. I felt good about it because I would like to see more womens, and younger people, follow in my footsteps. I wish there was a lotta other Koko Taylors that's really into the blues."

• • •

You couldn't have a boring conversation with Bruce Iglauer. Standing in the street outside a club late one night, he started telling me stuff that made me reach for my notebook: there were just six hours of studio tape for the first Hound Dog album, for instance, against thirty-six hours for the first Albert Collins.[13] On that album "Ice Cold" was done in one take and "Mastercharge" was intercut from four, during which Iglauer was prancing around in front of the artist, miming with his hands on his hips as Collins vamped the female part. The recording of "Voodoo Daddy" saw Lonnie Brooks driving his band through the song for fifteen frenetic minutes, which ended with the guitarist lying full-stretch on the studio floor, stopping them dead, keeping the rhythm going with his foot, and then launching into the twelve-minute version from which the album track was cut: all on a thirty-minute reel of tape, while Iglauer sweated in the control room. That very morning Lonnie Brooks had woken him up to play a cassette of a new song down the phone. The songs on the Brooks album *Bayou Lightning* were largely written late at night, on the phone, between the two of them. Iglauer had said of Koko Taylor's songwriting, "I helped a little." I began to wonder exactly what that meant.

Everyone understood that the blues was a mode of personal, emotional expression. A good singer could inhabit the song, express the emotions contained within it, and use the lyrics to relate to his audience without having lived through the exact experiences described. An artist choosing to perform "Hard Time Killing Floor Blues" was not absolutely expected to have actual, firsthand abattoir experience. When Roosevelt Sykes sang "All My Money Gone," not even the most swivel-eyed blues purist would feel the need to organize a whip-round in the bar. Big Bill Hill said the blues tells a story. Willie Dixon liked to style himself on stage as a storyteller.

Nevertheless, I did feel a line was crossed when, in the song "Inflation," Lonnie Brooks sang: "I've got four years of college, and I can't find a decent job." When I first heard it, I actually looked at the record player in disbelief. I dutifully checked my *Blues Who's Who* and the album liner notes, but I knew before I started that I wasn't going to unearth any reference to a hitherto unsuspected university degree. Like most of his contemporaries, Brooks went into music because he didn't want to be a farm laborer, not because it sounded more fun than working in daddy's bank. If this lame lyric was an effort to push him toward the college crowd or secure airplay on white rock radio, Iglauer had not only made his artist appear ridiculous but also seemed to have lost sight of one of the main reasons blues and rock artists appealed to white teenagers: that they were cooler, more virile, less inhibited versions of themselves (or in the case of elder statesmen like Muddy Waters, cooler, more virile and less inhibited versions of their fathers). Young white fans wanted to be like their bluesmen, they didn't want their bluesmen to be like them. Academic qualifications were not a requirement. As an attempt to align the artist with his target audience and encourage them to identify with him, this lyric was not only transparently clumsy but also unnecessary.

Still, if I had caught Iglauer trying a little too hard with Lonnie Brooks, perhaps it was understandable. To me, in the Kingston Mines, Brooks was a great singer, an entertaining performer and a virtuoso guitarist who invariably put on a tight, professional show. But to Alligator he was a worry. I went down to see him one afternoon at his family house on South Union Avenue, in a pleasant, leafy neighborhood four stops south of the Forty-Third Street L.

Lonnie Brooks did not grow up singing the blues: "You would hear country and western, and zydeco music," he explained of his Louisiana childhood in the 1930s and 1940s. In his teens, he remembered ice-cream sellers playing Lightning Hopkins, John Lee Hooker, and Muddy Waters. There was also WLAC radio out of Nashville, which broadcast blues on Saturday nights, but his first personal contact with the music had to wait until 1952, when at age nineteen he moved from rural Louisiana to Port Arthur, Texas. There he was able to see the likes of B. B. King, T-Bone Walker, Gatemouth Brown and Guitar Slim: "A lot of blues acts came to that area, and I went to see them all," he told me. The young guitar player's first professional position was as a sideman in the accordionist Clifton Chenier's band, the Zydeco Ramblers, in the mid-1950s.

He characterized his first records, when he called himself Guitar Junior, as "a kind of Louisiana rock 'n' roll sound." The Lake Charles label Goldband recorded him in 1957, and songs like "Family Rules" were an intriguing take on popular R&B, with a Cajun flavoring. "I did about two or three of them. Went real good," he recalled. "But all my feeling was I wanted to be a blues player." Arriving in Chicago at age twenty-six, he was dismayed to discover that local success in Louisiana didn't automatically translate into contracts and club bookings, especially as the name Guitar Junior was already taken by Luther Johnson. "It was kind of messin' up, you know. I was playing on the South Side most of the time, and he was playing on the West Side, and a lot of people didn't know which of the Guitar Juniors to go see," he told me. Born Lee Baker Jr., he adopted the stage name of Lonnie Brooks.

"It was kind of hard for a young blues player to get a break," he admitted. "I came to Chicago, and it didn't happen like I dreamed it would happen. I had to just hang here for a while, and keep hanging. I thought since I had made records it would be easy for me, but after changing into a different type of music, it took a while to get a foothold. I was sitting in with a lot of guys, and I got to learning blues tunes. But I was mixing it up. I was doing a little soul, rock, and blues." As a capable professional, Brooks was able to keep working, even if he couldn't find work as a blues singer: "I played a lot of rock 'n' roll clubs." He recorded a 45 for Chess in 1967—soul on the A side, blues on the B side—and an album in 1969 for Capitol,[14] but neither of them led anywhere.

A European blues festival tour in 1975—and another album, opportunistically recorded during the tour by Black & Blue[15]—boosted his confidence and, he felt, the confidence of industry suitors: "After I went there, the people started knowing I can play the blues. I guess a lot of blues recording companies were kind of scared, saying well, he plays too much rock 'n' roll. But after I went to Europe and they started writing about me and proved that I can play the blues all night, then a few companies got interested."

Meanwhile, Bruce Iglauer was beginning to realize that there were too many artists he wanted to record, and too little time. His *Living Chicago Blues* series, inspired by Vanguard's three *Chicago/The Blues/Today!* session albums from the 1960s, was a way of recording acts he admired who had either not recorded before or, he felt, not been recorded well enough: among them Jimmy Johnson, Left Hand Frank, Magic Slim, Carey Bell and, of course, Lonnie Brooks. "I'd been hearing this journeyman musician for years," Iglauer told me, "and all of a sudden I found somebody real creative hiding underneath, somebody who was not a jukebox copycat. And that was very exciting." When Alligator picked him up in 1978, Brooks was working in a die-casting plant for a sympathetic boss who would give him time off to play out-of-town gigs.

The Brooks session, on the second disc, was among the highlights of the *Living Chicago Blues* series, and Iglauer moved quickly to clear studio time for a complete album. *Bayou Lightning* came out the following year, and a second album followed, *Turn on the Night*, in 1981.[16] Brooks was happy: "I think I should have met him a long a time ago," he told me. "He can see things that you don't see in yourself, and get it out of you. I've been trying a long time with blues. With rock 'n' roll I guess it was a little bit different, in that it was a natural thing. But for blues, I guess it took some of his ideas to bring out the realness in me."

But along with Son Seals, Lonnie Brooks was proving a tough sell for Alligator. Iglauer had signed a four-artist booking contract with Variety Artists in Minneapolis, which had worked out well enough for Koko Taylor and Albert Collins, but at the beginning of 1982 Alligator had to take Seals and Brooks back. "We didn't want to, we hate booking, it's a drudgery job, but we did it," he said. "So they didn't work as much for a period of about eight months. Both their careers suffered and are now being rebuilt."

Iglauer wasn't too worried about Son Seals: the bearded bluesman had four albums out, and in nine years with Alligator he had become a well-known name in the United States. But the Louisiana guitarist was a concern. Not only had white rock radio become less accommodating, but Brooks's debut album coincided with the onset of three years of double-digit inflation: "It got much more expensive real quickly to be out on the road," said Iglauer. "We never built the touring base for Lonnie that we were able to for our other artists." In the meantime, clubs were losing money and starting to prefer bands who would play for the door money rather than a fixed fee. This was not an option for Brooks, who was a family man and a professional, with a band to pay.

"Lonnie has been our most frustrating project," Iglauer admitted. "Well, not as frustrating as Fenton Robinson. But I've never been able to take Lonnie's career as far as his talent would indicate it should go."

· · ·

"There was a small town down where I live, in Leflore County, Mississippi," said Fenton Robinson. "I used to go down and shine shoes on Saturday and Sunday, and I would listen to the jukebox, you know. There was John Lee Hooker, Lightning Hopkins, T-Bone Walker—well, you can name many, but T-Bone was my favorite because he had the smooth style."

We were backstage at ChicagoFest. I was talking over the music—shouting, really—to the one man who, in Bruce Iglauer's words, "came to the label and, by mutual agreement, left the label." He recorded a much-praised album called *Somebody Loan Me a Dime* on Alligator in 1974 and followed it up with another in 1977, *I Hear Some Blues Downstairs*,[17] which was nominated for a Grammy Award. And then label and artist parted company.[18]

"I haven't had an improvement for a while," Robinson admitted mildly, just about making himself heard above the raucous, rocking blues of Hip Linkchain's band, up on stage. "I seem to have a problem getting with the right company." At age forty-six he was one of the most respected blues musicians in Chicago. He had a soulful tenor voice and played guitar in a clean, jazzy style of a kind which wouldn't normally have appealed to me, but he did so with such authority that when I first heard his music, in a record shop in London, I had to ask the snooty youth behind the counter who it was. The record sleeve was pointed out to me with lofty hauteur.

Robinson was a connoisseur's bluesman: "When you go to the Checkerboard and Fenton shows up on a Blue Monday, he gets announced in a different way: literally a little hush falls over the room," said Iglauer. "He gets respect as being a guitar player of quality beyond that normally found in the blues, in terms of technical ability, and I think an ability to express a real subtlety of feeling in his playing."

There was the rub, as far as Alligator was concerned. Respect didn't necessarily translate into sales, and a label that prided itself on its "genuine house-rocking music" perhaps wasn't the natural home of such a sensitive and well-read musician. When I jokingly accused Robinson of knowing more than three chords, he laughed: "Blues is jazz, and jazz is blues. If you want to play that form"—indicating Hip, who was just launching into "Baby Please Don't Go"—"that's cool. There's different forms, there's different chord progressions that you can use, and it sounds great. You don't have to play that same thing all the time." Maybe not, but I doubted whether a well-lubricated ChicagoFest crowd would notice particularly if he did. It seemed ironic that such a gifted and technically accomplished musician would probably be more successful if he dumbed down his act to please the blues crowd. Not that I could imagine him doing such a thing.

"In many respects I feel Fenton would be happier in a lounge situation, where he was perched on a stool and wearing a suit, and people would listen to him like they'd listen to Kenny Burrell," Bruce Iglauer said. "But I don't book such places, and those places don't know who Fenton is. Places I would book Fenton, he would not always be as well received as my other acts. People would say, 'Gee, the music was real good, people didn't buy very much booze, not a lot of people danced, people left after the second set.' So we had a hard time booking him."

There were other difficulties. Just as the first album came out, the singer found himself in court on involuntary manslaughter charges after a road accident. "So we released an album with an artist who couldn't tour: he was in jail for nine months. It pretty much killed the album," said Iglauer. Then there was money. According to Iglauer, Robinson was quietly convinced of his worth and simply wouldn't play for the kind of money Alligator could generally get for him.

"I wasn't pleasing Fenton: I wasn't getting the work he wanted, I wasn't getting the money he wanted. He wasn't pleasing me in that he wasn't really giving me what I wanted to sell, as far as gigs, and I wasn't selling records. We just reached a point of mutual frustration. Not anger, just resignation."

Iglauer pondered, briefly. "I probably could have sold Fenton black, now," he said. "But I didn't know at that time how to do so."

• • •

I had arranged to talk to Magic Slim at his Sunday afternoon gig at Florence's, and Bruce Iglauer said he'd drive me down there. This was a welcome offer, because the club was at 5443 South Shields Avenue, between the Dan Ryan

Expressway and some huge rail freight yard, and didn't look easy to get to on the bus. I was beginning to wish I'd suggested B.L.U.E.S instead.

"The fact that you're getting to clubs on public transport is amazing to me," Iglauer said. This wasn't a topic I cared very much to pursue with people like Iglauer, whose experiences over the years with angry drunks waving guns and knives around in various impoverished parts of Chicago could make your hair stand on end. I hadn't, so far, been mugged or murdered or even seriously alarmed, but I did feel I had been fairly fortunate, and if that was true, I didn't really want to be reminded of the fact. But already the Alligator boss had told me how Magic Slim had been shot at Porter's, an innocent victim of someone else's argument, which put the guitarist out of commission for eight months just when Iglauer had been hoping to record him for the *Living Chicago Blues* series. Then there was the Hound Dog Taylor story. He shot his own rhythm guitar player. "Oh yeah," said Iglauer. "Shot Brewer Phillips the week I released Koko's album, and the week I got married. Three times, in the leg. When Hound Dog died, he was involved in an attempted murder case. He was probably mad at me because Son Seals played my wedding reception."

Iglauer had also been on the receiving end himself several times, or nearly. "Have you seen Youngblood, B. B. Jones, the B. B. King clone?" he asked. "He's amazing, I mean he studies in the mirror, and it is an amazing imitation. His name is Alvin Nichols, and I like him because he saved my life once." It was at the Sportsman's Lounge on West Roosevelt Road in 1970, when someone came at him with a broken bottle: purely, according to Iglauer, because he was in the wrong place at the wrong time, and the wrong color. "Interceding doesn't always mean you've got to pull out your gun and jump between Mr. Bruce and the offending party. Sometimes it just means saying something like, 'Hey, cool out, he's OK.' Youngblood got this guy to cool out, which I appreciated, because I was in the back of the club and there was no back door." On another occasion, in a club called the One Step Beyond, someone else stepped in to extricate Iglauer from a sticky situation, saying, "This isn't Mississippi." "Which is interesting," said Iglauer, laughing, "because the fact that the guy was willing to go after me was an indication that, indeed, it wasn't Mississippi."

Such examples of racial hostility were rarer now, he said. It was some years since he had been picked on by a stranger for being white. But there was one story he told me that was closer to home and still carried with it an air of unfinished business. "A musician tried to stab me on a street corner last year, fairly seriously," he said. "I wouldn't embarrass the musician, who was sort of flipped out at that particular time, by mentioning the name, but it was an interesting situation. I'll paraphrase: the musician admitted that yes, I'd recorded the musician. Yes, I had paid the musician for the session exactly what I said I would.

Yes, I had paid the musician's royalties. Yes, although I had not agreed to do so, I had assisted the musician in getting other work. But: 'I hadn't done as much for him as I had for some of those other niggers.' And that's when the knife came out."

Iglauer shook his head. I had heard about this one, and I knew who he was talking about. Left Hand Frank was one of the star turns on the *Living Chicago Blues* records, and I had seen him play regularly at B.L.U.E.S during my 1979 trip. He was a strong singer and played the guitar upside down, Albert King style, with a distinctive finger-picking lead technique I really liked. He always seemed to be having a good time, and between songs would do pretty fair Donald Duck impressions. "If I hadn't done anything he would have been my best friend!" exclaimed Iglauer. "But I only made him a few thousand dollars instead of hundreds of thousands of dollars, so he's my enemy. Anyway, it was pretty scary."

As we pulled up outside Florence's in the warm summer sunshine, he remembered one more episode, which took place at that very spot, when Brewer Philips saved him from a knife-wielding drunk. Whether this was before or after the guitarist was shot by his own bandleader, I didn't ask.

Magic Slim's real name was Morris Holt, and he was a massive, gentle, solidly built man with a round face and boyish smile, one finger missing on his right hand,[19] and a permanent bump on the side of his head, as if he had just walked into a lamp post. He got the Florence's gig direct from Hound Dog, who died in 1975, as a kind of bequest: "We was real good friends," Slim told me. We were standing in the barbecue smoke on scrubby grass outside the club, between sets, as musicians and customers milled around in the sunshine. Taylor offered Slim a place in the Houserockers, after he once fired Brewer Philips—or possibly fired at him—but the big guitarist turned him down: "I was just getting started, see, and I had a pretty good thing going for myself. I couldn't stop, I couldn't let my fellows down, because see I had worked hard with them, worked so hard to get 'em started." Slim's band included his brother Nick on bass.

Magic Slim struggled to establish a career as a musician, arriving in Chicago for the first time in 1955, age eighteen, and starting out by sitting in as a bass player with the likes of Shakey Jake on the West Side and his old school friend from Mississippi, Magic Sam. Sam also helped him learn guitar: "Magic Sam, the onliest man," Slim said affectionately. "The only guy that really gave me a chance. And here's another guy that really speaks up for me, real highly, and I love him for it, and that's Son. Son Seals. He's a dirty motherfucker, but he's all right with me."

In a city full of imitators, Slim stood out as a man with his own way of doing things. His guitar style was entirely his own: unhurried and soulful, tonally unmistakable, and seemingly rooted in the Mississippi soil. Such was the strength in his left hand that he could generate vibrato at the same time as bending the string through a full tone, with complete control, simulating a slide sound. His band, the Teardrops, were loud and tight. They had a habit of speeding songs up until by the end they were noticeably faster, which Iglauer reckoned was rhythm guitarist Daddy Rabbit Pettis's doing, but Slim said was Nate Applewhite: "He's a good drummer, but he will speed a song. I think the motherfucker crazy."

Slim was forty-five, married with six children, and one of the city's most successful bluesmen. He had a strong following and regular North Side gigs, as well as his Sunday residency at Florence's. He had played in Europe three times and recently recorded two albums: one a French production licensed by Alligator, and the other on Rooster, due out soon.[20] By Chicago blues standards he was riding high. But he wasn't satisfied. "I hope pretty soon things'll break, you know. I ain't making no money, but I'm working."

As we stood there, a man strolled past who looked familiar. Left Hand Frank: I hadn't seen him for three years. When Slim and I finished talking I headed back inside, wondering if things had been patched up between Frank and Iglauer since the knife incident. One glance at the apprehensive record producer told me they hadn't. Iglauer had seen him walk past. We kept our eyes on the door for the rest of the afternoon.

8

Louis Myers's White Eldorado

I didn't have any intention of doing this.
I was helping a friend out. Caught myself
doing somebody a favor and got stuck.

—Theresa Needham

   The Checkerboard Lounge was the second-best blues club on the South Side. A single-story building at 423 East Forty-Third Street, it was a modest affair when I first saw it in 1979, but by 1982 it had been knocked through into the room next door and almost doubled in size. The music area was off to the left—a jumble of steel chairs and plastic-topped tables illuminated by bright strip lights, facing a low stage—while down the right-hand side there was a poorly stocked bar. At the back, the toilet's scarlet-painted walls added an apocalyptic edge to squalor so breathtaking that the very bacteria's survival seemed to hang in the balance. A can of Old Style was a dollar, rising to one-seventy-five once the music started.
   The Checkerboard Lounge was the most famous blues club in Chicago or possibly in the world. In November 1981 it hosted the Rolling Stones. In town for three shows at the eighteen-thousand-capacity Rosemont Horizon, the fragrant Englishmen—their tour was sponsored by the Jovan perfume company—took to the club's cramped stage while Mick Jagger gurned through a set of blues standards alongside a gracious and beaming Muddy Waters, who wrote most of them. This unannounced gig had become part of Chicago blues legend.[1] Its memory even long afterward could set the rumor mill grinding into action at the merest hint of an English accent in a blues club. In the Kingston Mines one evening about eight months later I was politely accosted by a young black drummer with a knowing smile. "I know you. Will you sign this for me?" he asked, proffering a scrap of paper in the face of my bemused denial. "Use your real name, not your stage name." Trying not to dwell on who he thought I might be, I obliged. Meanwhile an actual rock star, Rory Gallagher, was sitting at the back of the room in blissful anonymity.[2]

The glory of the Stones gig reflected well on the Checkerboard, but the main reason the club was so famous was that it was owned by Buddy Guy himself. With a business partner, L. C. Thurman, Guy had set the place up in 1972 to host local and visiting blues acts, with his own name as the principal draw. Every Friday in *The Reader*, Chicago's essential free weekly, there was the promise of regular appearances by the legendary axe-man in his own domain. In the edition of September 24, 1982, to pick a random example, the club's listing read:

> CHECKERBOARD LOUNGE, 423 E. 43rd: Tonight and Saturday, Buddy Guy, Little Oscar. Sunday, Syl Johnson, Buddy Guy, Junior Wells, Big Time Sarah, Lefty Dizz, Magic Slim, Muddy Waters Jr., 43rd Street Blues Band, Little Oscar, Johnny Dollar, Jimmy Johnson. Monday afternoon, Lefty Dizz & Shock Treatment. Tuesday, Junior Wells, Magic Slim & the Teardrops. Thursday, Magic Slim & the Teardrops. 373–5948.

This was some of the finest blues talent in the city, augmented by a chart-topping soul artist, Syl Johnson, plus—on four nights out of the seven—two actual living legends, Buddy Guy and Junior Wells. Such a line-up would appear to make the Checkerboard as essential as it was unmissable.

Behind the advertising, the reality could be rather different.

· · ·

Forty-Third Street was Chicago's version of Beale Street or Route 66: a cultural epicenter. Muddy Waters and Howlin' Wolf were regulars at Pepper's Lounge, just down the street from the Checkerboard at number 503, with the White Elephant a few doors past that. The 708 Club was four blocks south, Theresa's five, and within a one-mile radius—eight Chicago blocks—blues fans in the 1950s and 1960s could choose from more than a dozen other venues, with names like Smitty's (on the corner of Thirty-Fifth Street and Indiana Avenue), Club Claremont (Thirty-Ninth and Indiana), the Cosy Inn (Forty-Third and State), Cadillac Baby's (Forty-Ninth and Dearborn) and the Barrelhouse (Fifty-First and Michigan Avenue). The Regal Theater, immortalized in B. B. King's seminal 1964 live album, was at Forty-Seventh Street and South Parkway. Those screaming kids on that record were some of the best-informed blues connoisseurs in the world.

With the solitary exception of Theresa's, none of this remained. The neighborhood was dubbed Bronzeville in the 1930s in a kind of patronizing civic salute to the color of its inhabitants, but nobody called it that any more, and in 1982 parts of it looked more like war-ravaged Brazzaville, with empty buildings, abandoned cars, and an air of desolation that could seem threatening, especially after dark.[3] Sometimes when getting off the train or emerging into the street from a club

I imagined the atmosphere to be so alien and hostile I had an urge to hold my breath. The nearest L station to the Checkerboard was on Forty-Third Street itself, just two blocks from the club. Eyes straight ahead, walking not too fast but not too slow, past blank windows and dimly lit doorways, it always seemed farther than that. At 4801 South Indiana, Theresa's was a slightly longer walk from the Forty-Seventh Street stop. I went down there less often. Once, from maybe a block away, I heard a gunshot.

The Checkerboard was a friendly place, and it was always a relief to arrive, plunge into its welcoming brightness, and breathe again. The club was often all but empty, apart from a couple of vague drinkers slumped on stools, an unceasing card game going on by the door, and a couple of awestruck Swedes or Italians[4] in the music area, sitting on their hands with anticipation, awaiting the promised performance by the legendary Buddy Guy. There might also be a gaggle of students from the nearby University of Chicago campus, who, although slightly wiser to the ways of the place, would still drop by for the Blue Monday sessions and at the weekend to wait out a set or two by the house band, just in case they were lucky and Guy got up to play. Occasionally, the excitement of these invariably young and white men would be stoked by the sight of the man himself, sitting at the bar with his film-star looks and winning smile. He was always courteous and approachable but sometimes seemed rooted to that stool. You could wait a long time for Buddy Guy.

However, there were worse ways to spend an evening than sitting in the Checkerboard listening to the house musicians. The 43rd Street Blues Band, as they styled themselves, were led by Dion Payton on guitar and vocals, who was the perfect front man: tall and good-looking, with a Stetson and an unflappably cool demeanor, he was in his early thirties and originally from Mississippi. He had reputedly worked with Albert King. His solos wove an endless thread around the band's solid rhythms and went on so long they ought to have become tedious and repetitive, but they never quite did so. King's "Cadillac Assembly Line" was one of their signature songs.

As one of the most reliable bands in Chicago, the 43rd Street Blues Band had gigs all over town. I first saw them at Sports Corner, a bar across the road from Wrigley Field, which was full of Chicago Cubs supporters. Among the white track suits and trainers was the formidable Lady Blues, a platinum blonde of indeterminate age with a pronounced squint. What she lacked in height—and that was plenty—she made up for in width and volume, clad in flared white nylon slacks and a tight, red chiffon blouse that strained to contain a pair of enormous breasts. She was obviously a regular. She also seemed to be the kind of woman who got what she wanted. I stood at the bar trying to be unobtrusive, but she made straight for me and demanded a dance. I would like to say I granted her wish out of chivalry, but it was fear.

. . .

I arrived at the Checkerboard one evening to find Smokey Smothers and Louis Myers standing outside. The sleepy-eyed guitar player had recently returned from touring Holland, France and Belgium with the American Living Blues Festival and was comparing road stories with the well-traveled Myers. Smokey said he couldn't believe how well he was treated over there: "Everyone was so nice to me." Smartly turned out in a jacket and tie, Louis had some copies of an album with him, *I'm a Southern Man*, recorded in Hollywood in 1978, on Advent.[5] Seven dollars: I bought one and got him to sign it. Sitting at the bar, guitarist Buddy Scott, of Scotty and the Rib Tips, studied my purchase with interest, peering closely at the band photos on the back. "Freddy Robinson? One of the baddest in Chicago," he remarked, tapping the record sleeve approvingly. Beers were one-ninety because, apparently, Buddy Guy was going to play, although he hadn't yet arrived. That evening's Swedes or Italians were hunched over their drinks in anticipation.

By eleven o'clock there was still no sign of Buddy Guy. Dion and the band were into their second set and halfway through a lilting version of "Nobody Wants to Lose" when Louis came in and said he was going to Theresa's, if I wanted a ride. His car was just around the corner. It was a huge, white convertible with red leather upholstery. I just stood there. "It's a 1973 Cadillac Eldorado," Myers explained. "It's got the biggest engine ever fitted to a production car—eight-point-two liters. It's a real gas glutter."

Glowing in the dim street lighting like a sensuously carved slab of Carrara marble, it was the most outrageously beautiful automobile I had ever seen. And it was my ride between the Checkerboard Lounge and Theresa's, with Louis Myers at the wheel. "Wow," I said. "Thanks."

Louis Myers was the quintessential Chicago bluesman. His entry in the *Blues Who's Who* spanned three pages. He was born in Mississippi and arrived in Chicago at age twelve, in 1941, on the crest of the second great wave of black migration from the South. Equally adept at guitar and harmonica, he worked with Muddy Waters and Little Walter. With drummer Fred Below and his older brother Dave on bass, he formed one of the classic Chicago blues bands, The Aces, which became The Four Aces when joined by Junior Wells. He had toured the world, played all the clubs, and worked and recorded with just about everyone. As his Cadillac cruised silently among the potholes in the darkness, he wasn't just at home in those stark, warm South Side streets, he was a part of them.

. . .

Theresa's regular listing in the *Reader* was just as hyperbolic as the Checkerboard's.

THERESA'S LOUNGE, 4801 S. Indiana: Wednesdays through Mondays, Tuff
Enuff House Band with Phil Guy, John Primer, Junior Wells, Foree Montgomery, Johnny Dollar, Michael Robinson, Ernest Johnson and others. 285–2744.

This all sounded great: a blues legend, six nights out of seven, backed up by some
serious talent. Anyone hoping to see Junior in this, his regular South Side haunt,
would generally learn to deal with disappointment, but Phil Guy was Buddy's
brother and an excellent guitar player in the B. B. King mold. John Primer was
making a name for himself as a bandleader. Foree "Superstar" Montgomery was
a fine singer, Ernest Johnson had played bass for Elmore James and Magic Sam,
and the superb and studious young guitarist Michael Robinson was still only
twenty-five years old, with a style that encompassed the entire modern blues
idiom from Freddie King and Southern white slide to Jimi Hendrix.

Then there was Johnny Dollar. With his tight, professional Scan'lous Band,
the singer and guitarist played gigs all over the city, and if he wasn't playing, you
would often find him at the bar in B.L.U.E.S or the Kingston Mines drinking
Wild Turkey: a big man with a big personality and a big hat.

He also happened to be Lefty Dizz's kid brother, and like his brother he had
a magnetic stage presence and knew how to put on a show. But while there was
an appealing vulnerability to Dizz that suggested hidden depths behind his on-
stage antics, Dollar's character seemed less complex: he wasn't laughing to keep
from crying, he was just laughing. His brand of blues was bright, modern and
funky: perhaps too bright, modern and funky for some of the more traditionally po-faced blues fans in the North Side bars.

He was a good singer and a charismatic bandleader, and his considerable
instrumental skills suggested an apprenticeship in something more technically
demanding than the Chicago blues. His playing had a polished competence
and reminded me of those shining little Buddy Guy vignettes that punctuated
the *Folk Festival of the Blues* album, recorded live at Big Bill Hill's club. I came
to feel that Johnny Dollar would have fit right in with Guy's band of young
gunslingers in 1963, because back then the future of the Chicago blues looked
bright, modern and funky. But then came the British invasion, which made
an evolutionary blind alley of that particular musical path, and Johnny Dollar
and many like him were left stranded. He could have probably made a living
anywhere in Chicago playing rock, soul or disco, but he had thrown in his lot
with the blues, limiting his options to occasional gigs in black-owned places
like Taste and Theresa's and more regular bookings on the North Side. There
his shows went down well, and his musicianship was appreciated, but few of
the white fans took him seriously as a bluesman.

Yet there was no denying that he was serious about his music. One Monday night when I saw him perform at Taste, opening a Ralph Metcalfe blues show for Junior Wells, a trio of local teenage horn players from the New Testament Band had been recruited to accompany Dollar's Scan'lous crew. But the youngsters were unfamiliar with the material, stricken with nerves, and their playing was ragged and hesitant. Assessing the situation, Dollar stepped over to them and with perfect solemnity and not a glance at the audience began to conduct the youngsters as an orchestra. The effect was immediate: within a few bars they were relaxed and smiling, supplying confident, brassy crescendos and all the blips, twizzles and beeps required of a good R&B horn section. Stepping back to the microphone Dollar raised some applause for the young musicians, introduced his band, and then drew the audience's special attention to his rhythm guitar player, the luminously talented yet still unknown Ronald Abrams. "He's better than me, but I'm better than him, if you understand me," he explained, flashing his gold tooth with a wicked laugh. It was difficult not to like Johnny Dollar.[6]

• • •

Louis Myers moored his sleek white Cadillac across the street, and we walked over to the dour, grey, brick-and-stone apartment building with the best-known basement in Chicago. Perhaps because of the manner of my arrival the man on the door, Herman, simply unhooked the chain and let me in: no cover charge. Theresa's was as empty as the Checkerboard, a long, thin room with a bar opposite the door and no stage, just a clearing among the tables at the far end, where a pair of young but very capable guitarists were playing jazz, accompanied by bass and drums.

It looked set to be a quiet evening. Then a sudden commotion interrupted the smattering of somnolent drinkers as a weird apparition burst through the door and darted down the room, tall and angular with lots of unkempt hair, a white jacket and checked trousers, and eyes that stared in several directions at once. "I'm the Muck Muck Man, I'm Brother Mud, the man from the sun!" he shouted, turning to face his sparse but suddenly alert audience. "When Junior Wells picked me up in the snow, he thought I was a monster!"

With flailing arms and waving head Brother Mud charged the band up into some driving rock 'n' roll and began to sing, loudly and erratically—jumping up and down, dancing in the aisle, and at one point, in the middle of "Talk to Me Baby," running out into the street. At the door Herman, who looked at least sixty, was dancing like a madman—a slow kind of madman—gyrating at the hip, rocking back and forward, walking on his knees, and finishing one number stretched out full-length on the floor. As doormen go, he was an original. With each succeeding song Mud's act got more frenetic. "I'm a hillbilly, I'm a cowboy, I'm a nigger!" He was yelling. "I'm a nigger, nigger, nigger!"

And then he was gone. It was an unforgettable and necessarily short performance. The young band, left to their own devices once more, launched into a rocking, Hendrix-inflected "Johnny B. Goode," and the barman began to close up.[7]

It was long past midnight, and Louis Myers and his white Eldorado had vanished as completely as Cinderella's coach. Standing in the street, I met a man with a lean and hungry look, wearing a black suit, black shirt, black tie, and matching cowboy hat. This was Johnny Twist, who told me he was "the number-one guitar player in Chicago" and produced a portfolio of cuttings about himself, "otherwise the people won't believe you." He would be using Mud in his shows, he explained, but the Brother wouldn't be allowed to behave like that. "We've got to clean up the acts," Twist urged. "The original acts, Muddy Waters, they were clean: no drinking on stage, no swearing. We've got to get organized."

He gave me a lift back to the Checkerboard Lounge with his drummer. It seemed that Buddy Guy hadn't shown up after all. The Swedes or Italians had gone. I flagged down a taxi, sharing the first part of the journey north with an enormous young woman who had been in the bar for hours and was in a very good mood. "I just felt like some blues," she giggled. She had had a few drinks and was very friendly, and when I found her keys for her in her handbag, I began to wonder if I could handle the waves of flirtatious gratitude. Our driver was young and black and had the air of a student. He was happy to talk. "The old music isn't popular with black people any more," he told me, as we watched the young lady tipsily negotiate the steps to her apartment, "because life is depressing enough all day without going home and listening to the blues." He was in a band himself, he confided, a rock band called The Late News. He sang one of their songs for me. It was a cleverly written lyric about not wasting time, because we were all about to be annihilated in World War III. "What does your band sound like?" I asked.

"It's kind of a mixture of Yes and Jeff Beck," he said.

That I wasn't expecting. Glancing across at this young Chicago cab driver, with his enthusiasm for English rock, I reflected on how music was used to define cultural boundaries, but it was no respecter of them: it seemed to go wherever it wanted. I thought of Ralph Metcalfe Jr. and his efforts to blow some life back into the cold embers of the blues down on the South Side. I thought of Lurrie Bell earnestly discussing "The Message" with Eli but not really getting it. And I thought of Oliver Davis, over at the Delta Fish Market, a businessman with an expensive obsession: "to keep the blues alive." As we cruised north on State Street, it seemed an ever more quixotic quest.

. . .

Theresa's Lounge was famous throughout the world as the oldest blues club in Chicago, but the proprietor was seldom to be seen. I had to make an appointment with Herman to come back another day at six o'clock and catch her before she went home.

Theresa Needham was a plump, gently humorous woman of seventy-one, with silver hair gathered up at the back, spangly spectacles, checkered slacks and a hooped top. She sat patiently on a barstool while I sorted out my notebook and tape recorder. The pipes on the ceiling were wrapped in Christmas tinsel. "I was getting ready to cut it down," she explained, "but they said, 'Leave the wrapping on the pipes, it looks pretty!' That's been about twenty years ago. I change it every year."

Theresa's was a shabby basement that inspired passions and had been home to some of the finest music of the postwar years. Everyone felt they owned it, and its actual owner seemed content with that. Being patronized by uppity Europeans was an occupational hazard. "A lady came here from overseas, and I was talking about doing it over and making it remodernized," said Theresa. "She told me not to. I had to leave it. She told me to keep it clean! I try to do that."

Did it feel strange to be a kind of blues legend? "It does," she said. "James Cotton, he told me a long time ago, he said, 'I don't know how it happen, but everywhere I go I run into your name.' There was a fellow that wanted to come and take the first floor and make a museum out of it," she added. "You might know him: Metcalfe Junior? They were going to build it around me. I told him, 'No, do it on your own, but leave me out. I don't like no publicity.'"

There was an old picture of Lefty Dizz on the wall. "Mm, he started down here. Played right back there. Played here before Buddy. There's old man Muddy over there: he sent me that picture."[8] Theresa was born in Mississippi and came to Chicago in 1933. Did she hear any blues down South as a child? "I wasn't allowed to go in those places, hm-mm. I was raised in the Catholic school. I wanted to be a *nun*." And ended up owning a blues bar. "Mm. I didn't have any intention of doing this. I was helping a friend out. Caught myself doing somebody a favor and got stuck."

The bar opened in 1949, first with a disc jockey as entertainment, then a jazz band, and then in 1957 Junior Wells turned up at the door. "Junior was working for Pepper, and Christmas fell in the middle of the week, and they wanted to play, and Pepper wouldn't let 'em, got another band," Theresa recounted. "So I told him, OK, come on." Did the Theresa's crowd like him? "Oh, they went crazy. He brought all Forty-Third Street down here. When he got through, he asked if I would ever give him a job if he needed one, so I said, any time you feel like it. He came back one Friday night: 'Old Lady, I'm ready for that job, now.'"

Theresa's Tavern became Junior Wells's base when he was in Chicago. "You could always find him here, before he started traveling so much. He was here five nights a week. But after he and Buddy teamed up together, he's between here and the Checkerboard. Have you been able to talk to him?" asked Mrs. Needham. I hadn't, I explained: he wanted money up front for an interview. "That's Junior," she smiled.

It was still light outside, and the club was empty, chairs stacked on the tables. I turned the cassette in the tape recorder. When, I wondered, did she first notice white people among her customers? "It was in about fifty-seven or fifty-eight, kids started coming from Hyde Park," she said. "Junior was working here, and I started the Blue Monday parties. That's what brought them. I used to cook a two-course dinner Mondays and bring it down about eleven o'clock."

She meant eleven o'clock in the morning, when night-shift workers from the steel mills and stockyards would stop in at their favorite bars on the way home. "Mm. Yeah, those were some good old days. I don't think they'll ever come back," said Theresa. "When you try and keep a band together, it's a hard job, 'cos I can't afford to pay 'em no forty or fifty dollars a man," she admitted. "We usually make it on the door there, specially on Fridays and Saturdays. Sometimes when they play Mondays, they have to wait till the following week to get paid."

Fifty dollars a night per man was the going rate in North Side clubs like B.L.U.E.S. "I've been to that one with Cotton; James Cotton worked out of there," said Theresa. "I went over there to see Sammy Longhorn [Lawhorn] working with him. You know Sammy had a tendency to get high and go to sleep on the bandstand? I went over there to see if Sammy was going to stay sober. There's not another man can beat Sammy playing guitar. Not another one in the world. If Sammy would quit drinking, you couldn't touch him. He loves that alcohol."[9]

Junior Wells was an established recording artist and bandleader by the time he got his regular gig at Theresa's, but for Buddy Guy, getting work at the club was a big break. "This the first place Buddy Guy worked when he came here," said Theresa. "He walked up to me and said, 'You look just like my mother to me.'" She laughed at the memory of a handsome, dimpled Buddy Guy, twenty-two years old and fresh out of Louisiana, turning on the charm. "He said, 'Don't put me out—let me play a number, and if the people don't like it, I'll walk out.' At that time there wasn't no youngsters coming here, it was all settled people. Buddy went back there and got the boy's guitar, and I never seen so many old people start to jumping up and dancing! Everybody liked him from the beginning."

Guy worked at Theresa's on Fridays and Saturdays, and on Wednesdays at the 708 Club on Forty-Seventh Street. "They stole his guitar from him down there," Theresa remembered. "I had to buy him a new guitar."

During those early days in the budding young guitarist's career, Theresa remembered a visit to the club by a blues superstar, perhaps after one of his legendary shows at the Regal, four blocks away. "B. B. King came here when Buddy Guy first came here from Louisiana, came in here one Monday, and when Buddy came down off the bandstand, B. B. told him that if he didn't change his style of music, he'd never get anywhere. Him and Buddy went up on the bandstand together, you didn't know one from the other one."

Theresa had to get home, and I started gathering up my notes. "I can't stand too much violent noise," she explained. "I have a ringing in my head, and the doctor said it comes from that band." But it wasn't just the volume that drove her out in the early evenings: she felt that the music had changed too. "They don't play like they used to years ago," she said. "When I was a kid I had to take music; you have it in your soul and body. These fellows, these young ones coming on now, they don't seem to care."

A film crew had recently paid a visit to the Tavern. "From New York," Theresa remembered. "They were filming Buddy's place and came down here. He said, do you know Buddy Guy? I say, 'I should know him, he started out down here.'" It seemed that the crew had managed to film Junior Wells performing in Theresa's but had been less fortunate with Guy at the Checkerboard. "He said Buddy Guy wouldn't even get up on the bandstand and play," said Theresa. "Ain't but one thing I'll tell you about Buddy, I'll tell you now: he's not the person that he used to be."

• • •

The first time I met the name of Buddy Guy was in *The Story of the Blues.*[10] Paul Oliver wrote: "In the playing of Otis Rush, Albert King, Freddie King, Magic Sam Maghett and Buddy Guy may be heard the reverberating echoes of B. B. King and through him, the guitar of T-Bone Walker and Guitar Slim." He went on to describe Guy as "perhaps the best and most flamboyant of these guitarists."

Oliver was writing in 1969. At that time Guy was thirty-three years old and beginning to build a reputation beyond Chicago, but his career had taken a while to get going. He worked initially at the Squeeze Club and the 708, and then at Theresa's. Winning a "Battle of Blues" against Otis Rush, Magic Sam and Junior Wells at the Blue Flame in 1958 led to a recording deal with Cobra, at 2854 West Roosevelt Road: two 45s, one produced by Willie Dixon and the other by Ike Turner, which were released on the short-lived label's Artistic subsidiary.

Otis Rush was Cobra's star bluesman and guitarist of choice, and his playing enlivened the first of two stolidly produced Dixon songs, on which the young Guy's vocals veered in homage between B. B. King and those of Rush himself, a similarity perhaps exaggerated by the acoustic qualities of the Cobra studio. Just twenty-two years old, the youngster showed greater promise under the more sympathetic direction of Turner, contributing accomplished gospel-blues vocals over a full and rich big-band sound. He was also allowed to accompany himself, with some stinging lead guitar that borrowed heavily from the styles of his two main men, Guitar Slim and B. B. King.

These first two singles by Buddy Guy sank without trace, followed in short order by Cobra itself and not long afterward by its proprietor, Eli Toscano, who was discovered in Lake Michigan: the victim, it was said, of a mob hit.

Stardom proved elusive, although Guy was beginning to make his mark. He supported B. B. King at the Trianon Ballroom[11] and was playing regular gigs in clubs as far south as Gary, Indiana, when one day in 1960, reputedly at Muddy Waters's insistence, he was called in to Chess Records at 2120 South Michigan Avenue.

Leonard and Phil Chess obviously had no idea what to do with him. They must have sensed by 1960 that the glory days of their big blues heavyweights, Muddy, Sonny Boy, Little Walter, and the Wolf, were behind them. But folk music was selling, and jazz was looking interesting. The label also had a good line in comedy records, and of course there was still rock 'n' roll: Chuck Berry's first single, "Maybellene"—Chess Records 1604—had sold more than a million copies in 1955, and he and Bo Diddley continued to sell. With Buddy Guy, the Chess brothers could see they had a serious musician on their hands, but he was a blues musician who was still developing his own sound. This sound wasn't a jaunty cocktail of R&B and country like Berry's, which had so effortlessly built a bridge over to the white teenager market, but an intense and emotional synthesis of B. B. King's high, tremulous, wailing gospel and Guitar Slim's dirty, dazzling instrumental virtuosity. At Chess, supervised by Willie Dixon, they gave him songs to sing that came from way down in the dark, superstitious swamplands of his childhood:

> First time I met the blues I was walking down through the woods
> I found my house burnt, blues you know you done me all the harm that
>   you could.
> The blues got after me, people, you know they ride me from tree to tree . . .

Little Brother Montgomery wrote that one, and he played the piano during Guy's first Chess recording session in March 1960. But on the other side of that 45 Guy's own lyrics were also pitched some way wide of the rock 'n' roll market, beyond regular, wholesome sexual suggestiveness into someplace strangely feral:

> You got my nose open, baby, but I got my eyes on you

From his second session, that December, "Ten Years Ago" was a soulful blues full of yearning and regret:

> There's been so many sad, sad years since I had my fun
> Every person I meet now keep telling me, son your life has just begun

But it would be a weird teenager who'd wear that one out on daddy's radiogram. It wasn't exactly rock 'n' roll. Buddy Guy wasn't going to be the new Chuck Berry.

Nevertheless, he was a good-looking kid, and even the Chess brothers could see that their little country boy could play. They just needed to find him the right material. One bizarre and incongruous attempt to pitch the young bluesman into the white youth market was a song called "American Bandstand." Ironically, it was pretty good. Guy's vocals were smooth yet admirably committed, the lyrics were blandly on-message—it was a song about the popular TV show, after all—the session musicians were outstanding, production was top-notch, and the whole marshmallow-cream confection was underpinned by the polished steel of Lacy Gibson's rock 'n' roll guitar. This was music not for the Southern juke joint but for the chrome-trimmed radio of a pink Chevy convertible filled with well-scrubbed white teenagers. It was never released.

Other experimental efforts included "Slop Around," a stab at a novelty dance number that owed more than a little to Ray Charles, although not as much as "My Love Is Real." "Hard but It's Fair" and "Baby" had trilling, all-girl backing vocals that shared the vinyl uncomfortably with Guy's proto-rock axe work. "That's It" was driving, sax-led R&B with slices of guitar brilliance, while "Skippin'" was an instrumental, perhaps intended as Chess's answer to Federal's string of Freddie King hits. As a showcase for the talents of some of the best sidemen in Chicago— Fred Below and Jack Myers, not to mention Jarrett Gibson on tenor sax—it worked well enough, but the inevitable comparison with Freddie King served merely to demonstrate that Guy lacked the spherical Texan's powers of composition.

Most of Guy's Chess output was blues of variable quality, but there were also shining soul numbers, fun pop tunes, the lively dance-band jazz of the unreleased "Buddy's Boogie" in 1963, and even some primal funk in the shape of "Buddy's Groove" from his final recording session for the label in 1967. He could seemingly play anything. But Chess was known as a blues label, Guy was a blues singer from the Louisiana swamps, and the Chess brothers weren't interested in the sharp-suited city stuff he played every night in the clubs: the bright, modern and funky blues he laid down between songs on their own *Folk Festival of the*

Blues LP, for example. Illustrious musicians such as Sonny Boy Williamson, Otis Spann and Robert Nighthawk were brought in as sidemen for some of Guy's sessions—Junior Wells also accompanied on a few sides—but even the efforts of these supreme Chicago bluesmen were too often undermined by poor material, lumpen arrangements and inept post-production that buried the guitar beneath intrusive horns.[12] On some a baritone sax ruminated in a corner of the studio like an absent-minded elephant. The jagged saxes on "Watch Yourself" added nothing but noise. But the brass arrangement and indeed general vibe of "No Lie" were fine—borrowed as they were, pretty much wholesale, from Miles Davis—while the instrumentals "Moanin'" and "Night Flight" also conjured up a cool jazz groove.

Guy's vocals could display impressive range, by turns passionate and urbane, and they drew inspiration not only from B. B. King but also from Bobby Bland, as on "I Cry and Sing the Blues." His guitar playing, sometimes stilted but seldom less than incisive, occasionally surprised with rapid-fire fretwork and shimmering chord vibrato. There was no shortage of support from Chess: Guy was given fourteen recording sessions, resulting in some forty-three sides. But there was a complete lack of vision. The Chess brothers seemed only to know what they *didn't* want. They were clueless.

One studio date on December 7, 1961, had offered them a glimpse into the future. It wasn't edgy soul but elegant blues. Four tracks were laid down, and two of them—the six-minute "I Found a True Love" and the even longer "Stone Crazy"—showed that given time and space, and released from the unforgiving shackles of the jukebox single, Guy could craft structured and meaningful blues performances in the studio. These songs showed clearly that as a blues-man he was more of an album artist than a purveyor of two-minute hits. Those farsighted enough to notice this did not, apparently, include any of the senior management at Chess Records.

The label's lack of direction with regard to their young Louisiana guitar virtuoso was not unusual at a time of such dramatic change in the music business. Even Chuck Berry thought the B-side of "Maybellene" was a surer bet for Chess, because "Wee Wee Hours" was a blues. The way artists like Jerry Lee Lewis and Little Richard had apparently landed from outer space already hardwired into young America's zeitgeist was still fresh in every record executive's mind. The recording studio was no stranger to weirdness and incomprehension on both sides of the glass. Guy's overworked "The Treasure Untold" was odd, but not as odd as Otis Rush's strangely sinister "Violent Love," one of Eli Toscano's more comical misjudgments over at Cobra. Specialty's Art Rupe memorably described Guitar Slim's monster hit, "The Things That I Used to Do," as "the worst piece of shit I ever heard."

Fewer than half of Buddy Guy's Chess cuts were issued as singles. His output under his own name for Chess, from the first recording session in 1960 until the brothers sold up in 1969, comprised just eleven 45s, beginning with "I Got My Eyes on You/First Time I Met the Blues" (Chess 1753) and coming to an end with "She Suits Me to a Tee/Buddy's Groove" (Chess 2067).

The serial numbers tell their own story: Chess was a prolific label, and Guy was virtually sidelined. During the same period there were seventeen Chuck Berry releases, which included "No Particular Place to Go" and "You Never Can Tell." Even Muddy Waters, whose days as a hit-maker were long past, released sixteen singles during that time, although the fact that one of them was called "Muddy Waters Twist" suggests that it wasn't just Buddy Guy's career that was afflicted by a lack of managerial vision.

One big hit would have shown the Chess brothers the way, but it didn't come. A cut-down version of "Stone Crazy" (Chess 1812) came closest, entering the Billboard R&B chart on February 24, 1962, at number 21. With "Skippin'" as the B-side, it spent six weeks in the company of Gene Chandler, Ike and Tina Turner, James Brown and Ray Charles, peaked at number 12, and then slipped out of sight at the end of March. Stardom continued to elude the young Louisiana guitarist.

Meanwhile, in 1964, the Chess brothers released *Two Great Guitars* on their subsidiary Checker label, a self-congratulatory instrumental session album by their international superstars, Chuck Berry and Bo Diddley. Guy couldn't compete with their songwriting, but when it came to guitar playing, he made those rock 'n' rollers sound like tractor drivers. Unfortunately, the only people who knew this were fans and fellow musicians in Chicago's dark and gritty blues clubs.

• • •

Buddy Guy kept busy as a session musician for Chess, laying down solid and professional blues guitar for numerous artists, working unobtrusively but tellingly behind the headliner of the day. Some of his most lauded work from this period was on the acoustic *Muddy Waters Folk Singer* album of 1964, providing sensitive backing to the older man's stentorian vocal and Delta slide guitar.

Since first encountering Guy's name in Paul Oliver's *The Story of the Blues*, glancing up occasionally at the chestnut trees outside the library window, I had noticed him cropping up in unexpected places: playing guitar on three songs on my Sonny Boy Williamson singles album,[13] for example, and there he was again accompanying Poor Bob Woodfork on an obscure compilation LP that I found on a market stall one windswept English Saturday: bootlegged Chess sides, presumably, since Willie Dixon was also credited.[14]

He also played plenty of club dates, appearing not just at Theresa's but at the Club Tay May at 1400 West Roosevelt Road, at Curley's Bar and at Big John's at 1638 North Wells Street. And of course he was a featured artist who provided his own band on that famous live recording session at Big Bill Hill's Copa Cabana nightclub in 1963, alongside Muddy Waters, Howlin' Wolf and Willie Dixon, released as *Folk Festival of the Blues*.

Not yet a star, Buddy Guy was nevertheless respected. Willie Dixon recruited him for the annual American Folk Blues Festival in Europe in 1965. These touring processions of blues royalty took the continent by storm. The expense of a trip to Europe meant that only top musicians got seats on the plane, and the dearth of local session talent meant they had to accompany each other. This provided some dream-ticket line-ups: Big Joe Turner backed by Otis Rush, Roosevelt Sykes and Jack Myers, with the peerless Fred Below in the driving seat, was one particularly felicitous combination.

Still in his twenties, Buddy Guy got to watch from the wings at these concerts as elder statesmen like Skip James and Bukka White held the stage. He accompanied some of the blues Olympians in whose considerable shadow he had grown up as a professional musician, playing alongside artists from Howlin' Wolf and Big Walter Horton to John Lee Hooker and Big Mama Thornton. If there had been any gaps in his blues education at the start of the tour, he was an honors graduate by the end. He was also allowed to perform some of his own Chess material, taking the opportunity to stretch it out beyond the two-minute format. Folkier elements of the audience who had been expecting something more like Sonny Terry and Brownie McGhee objected on occasion to Guy's impassioned soul singing and searing lead guitar—just as, not far away, someone in a Manchester auditorium would soon be shouting "Judas!" at Bob Dylan—but in general, European audiences warmed to the fiery young performer.

Back in the United States, Bob Koester and Samuel Charters demonstrated clearer vision than the Chess brothers as Delmark put out *Hoodoo Man Blues*, and Vanguard's *Chicago/The Blues/Today!* experiment proved successful. Koester engaged Guy and his band as backup to Junior Wells, but Samuel Charters persuaded Vanguard to record the guitarist in his own right, reasoning that a college market which was now exposed to the pyrotechnics of Eric Clapton and Mike Bloomfield might be receptive to an "authentic" Chicago guitar hero. Guy's first album, *A Man and the Blues*,[15] came out in 1967, and its sensitive arrangements and generous, expansive sound engineering gave the young virtuoso the time and space to explore the songs and develop his solos in a way that had always been denied to him in previous studio sessions. Otis Spann was at his quietly authoritative best on these sides, the calmly professional Wayne Bennett lent support on rhythm guitar, A. C. Reed led the horns, while Jack Myers and Fred Below kept the ship steady.

With its B. B. King covers, a couple of originals, and a beautifully underplayed version of Mercy Dee Walton's "One Room Country Shack," Buddy Guy's first album was pretty much straight-up blues. His second was not.

There was no blues in the R&B charts in 1968, but there were plenty of songs by Otis Redding, Aretha Franklin, Marvin Gaye, and James Brown. For Guy's second album, Vanguard's confidence was high enough to release a live set, *This Is Buddy Guy!*,[16] recorded in Berkeley, California, which provided an up-close and startling taste of Guy's performance style, with its instrumental call-and-response routines, screaming soul vocals, and tight, funky arrangements from a band that boasted a five-piece horn section. It certainly worked for me. There was also a seminal rendition of Guitar Slim's "The Things That I Used to Do."

That wasn't where Guy's future lay, however. In Chicago, he and Junior Wells had teamed up formally as a double act and were given a residency at Pepper's Lounge on East Forty-Third Street, a hundred yards from the future Checkerboard. As purveyors of up-tempo Chicago blues to receptive white audiences, the pair of them played festivals and enjoyed TV appearances, more recording opportunities, and concert dates from New York to San Francisco. Guy was selected in 1969 for a blues package promoted by the State Department to undertake a concert tour in Africa, part of a U.S. government "hearts and minds" push. By the end of the 1960s he was almost famous. Rock musicians spoke of his technique with awe and studied it. Live audiences and television viewers were thrilled by his raw, blues-rock virtuosity. The Rolling Stones invited Guy and Wells, plus band, to support their 1970 European tour.

• • •

The Guy-Wells Band in 1970 was one of the best Chicago combos ever assembled, comprising Guy's regular sidemen A. C. Reed and Jimmy Conley on saxophones, Ernest Johnson on bass, Roosevelt Shaw on drums, and Buddy Guy's brother Phil on rhythm guitar. While in Europe they cut an LP at Michel Magne's studio at Château Herouville, near Paris, under the leadership of piano veteran and Paris resident Memphis Slim. Released as one half of the double album *Old Times, New Times*[17]—the other disc was piano blues, shared, along with some hokey recorded reminiscences, between Slim and Roosevelt Sykes—it was a successful set, by turns exuberant, relaxed, and intense, and notable for how the spotlight fell, for the first time, more on Guy than on Wells. Producer Philippe Rault, like Charters, understood that his audience for these performances—as Bruce Iglauer said—regarded blues as a branch of rock music. Guitar was king. Within weeks the duo were recording again, this time ripping up Tom Dowd's

Criteria Studio in Miami, laying down tracks for the 1972 Atlantic album *Buddy Guy and Junior Wells Sing the Blues*.[18] With contributions from Dr. John and half of "Derek and the Dominos"—Carl Radle and Jim Gordon, plus a subdued and respectful Eric Clapton on rhythm guitar—this LP helped to cement the Guy-Wells template that would build their live reputation over the next decade. Although both were great showmen and instrumentalists, neither was known for his writing. They had their signature songs—"The Things That I Used to Do," "Help Me"—but in essence their act was a blues revue, soulful but not soul music, performing covers and standards for rock crowds. The irrepressible harp player did most of the singing, took the occasional solo, and then stepped back to make way for the man with the guitar.

It was a winning formula. The band's touring schedule routinely took in Europe and North America, and appearances in Chicago became less important. The club scene was changing, in any case. While North Side bars began to book blues acts to cater for the college crowd, the traditional blues scene in the black neighborhoods had entered its terminal decline, even as Guy opened his own club in the heart of the South Side in 1972.

It was there that he recorded the live album *The Dollar Done Fell*[19] in 1979, released the following year on JSP. Buddy's brother Phil played rhythm guitar alongside Little Phil Smith, and with J. W. Williams on bass and Ray Allison on drums, Guy launched into a killer set from the small stage of the Checkerboard Lounge, combining elements of soul, blues, and funk with pure, unabashed rock. Along with an obligatory "The Things That I Used to Do," it was mainly original material—songs of hurt and disappointment, some wry, some plaintive, some way too long—and although some of his singing was uneven, Guy's instrumental work packed a powerful charge, heightened by melodramatic, off-mike vocalizing over the top of the guitar. Wild variations in volume created drama and tension. Periods of near-silence clashed with flurries of extraordinary virtuosity. The band was excellent. Phil Guy's playing in particular was beautifully structured and coherent. Together the sidemen built a formidably rational edifice against which Guy's solos crashed like a storm surge, heading out into dangerous musical territory, over-bending through to the next semitone and beyond—a technique of such plain aural wrongness that it only underscored a raw intensity of feeling—before flooding back as an unstoppable, lashing tidal wave of sound.

As an artifact, *The Dollar Done Fell* was faithful to my 1979 memories of the club's laid-back atmosphere, with banter between the stage and a neighborhood audience who talked all the way through. The place even sounded authentically half-empty. While the music was frequently breathtaking, in other respects it was an indifferent record that could have benefited from tighter direction. The sound and the mixing never overcame the acoustic limitations of the room. One song just seemed to peter out through lack of interest. But that didn't matter. As a monument to the power of Guy's playing, it was priceless. And for me, as a reason to return to Chicago, it proved compelling.

In B. B. King's *Live at the Regal* set—a live album as perfect as *The Dollar Done Fell* was flawed—the Memphis blues singer didn't even play guitar on all the songs. But in Buddy Guy's performances, the guitar took center stage. With its emphasis on the instrumental, this act—and this album, for all its faults—announced the arrival of this Chicago bluesman as a fully fledged rock guitar hero.

• • •

If you knew where to look, it was possible to see Guy perform pretty regularly in Chicago: just not in his own club. Up in the northern suburbs, Biddy Mulligan's tended to attract a noisy rock crowd whose hollers and whoops would probably have been even more annoying had the club booked acts that involved any subtlety or introspection. But they never did. Dancing was encouraged. Even elderly blues performers knew they had to turn the volume up when they played at 7644 North Sheridan Road. There were ice cubes in the urinal, with a sign above explaining that they were 'hardly ever used in drinks.' Cover charge could be as much as five dollars, yet the place was sometimes so packed you could be standing a few feet from the stage and still not see anything, particularly if the object of your attention was sitting down, as John Lee Hooker or Willie Dixon were wont to be. The atmosphere was perfect for Buddy Guy and Junior Wells.

One hot July night I made the long, rattling journey north on the L and arrived midway through their first set. Wells was almost civil in his dealings with the noisy young crowd, while Guy grinned a lot and made faces at the girls. Together they were loud, soulful, and funky. Solo, Guy's playing was vicious in its single-minded pursuit of the riff. In midflight he would wince, stop, flex his left hand—pure showmanship—only to begin again, even faster, even louder. The crowd loved it. So did I.

Guy and Wells were also regulars at ChicagoFest and would usually headline the blues stage on at least one night. I watched them bring the curtain down on the ten-day event in 1979, with Guy dressed in an immaculate white jacket—perhaps the same one he was wearing on the cover of my *Live in Montreux* LP[20]—and Wells in an embroidered suede coat and huge fedora. They featured on Navy Pier again in 1982, powering through a tight set that included "Driving Wheel" and the inevitable "Help Me" in front of a lubricated festival audience that was overwhelmingly white, thanks to a black boycott urged by Jesse Jackson in protest at recent city appointments. Beyond the stage lights, Chicago's skyline reflected in the dark mirror of the lake as Guy's solos soared into the night air, incendiary and redemptive.

In a city full of great guitar players, these glimpses of Buddy Guy's transcendent talent merely stimulated demand. No one could play or pack a venue like he did. Each week in *The Reader* there was the mocking promise:

CHECKERBOARD LOUNGE, 423 E. 43rd: Tonight and Saturday, Buddy Guy.

Every trip on a clanking L train down into the sinister shadows of the South Side was a triumph of hope over experience. One Friday evening in the middle of August I stepped off the street and into the Checkerboard's increasingly familiar neon glare, noting the formidable figure of Big Time Sarah behind the bar, up for no nonsense, and the club's proprietor, Buddy Guy himself, sitting near the door with the card players. They didn't look up. Off to the left on the bandstand, Phil Guy was wrapping up his first set, with Fred Grady guesting on the drums and J. W. Williams playing bass. A can of Old Style was a dollar ninety. That had to be a promising sign. Sure enough, Phil announced that his brother would be stepping up on stage after the break. I chose a table right at the front. The place was almost empty apart from a smattering of locals and the usual excited Swedes or Italians in the corner.

Phil got the second set under way with "Garbage Man Blues" from his new album[21] and then segued the band quietly into the unmistakable opening of "Stone Crazy." Brother Buddy wandered over from his poker game and listened from the side for a while, then vanished into the back of the club and came out wheeling his amplifier. He plugged it in as the band continued to play around him, then strolled off again and came back with his guitar. He had a beer in his hand and asked the waitress for a shot of bourbon, no ice. "I like my whiskey like my women—straight up," he winked, downing the first shot, and then a second. And when we were sitting comfortably, he began.

"People come up to me and say the blues is dead," he announced, serious now. "Well it ain't dead as long as I'm alive. You just have to try and deal with people every day, and you'll have the blues." Phil and the band were simmering in the background. "The blues don't sound good until late at night. If you don't believe me, get high and go home and turn on your record player." He nodded toward J. W. on the bass and launched into a raucously orthodox version of B. B. King's "You Upset Me Baby" in a pure, gospel tenor:

Well, she's thirty-six in the bust, twenty-eight in the waist,
Forty-four in the hip, she got real crazy legs
You upset me baby, yes you upset me baby
Well, like being hit by a falling tree—woman, what'd you do to me?

He stopped, and stopped the band, and let go with a piercing solo, straight out of *Live at the Regal* in the key of G, while Phil restrained the other musicians from joining in. Then he cut it dead.

"That was how B. B. King does it," said Guy, into the sudden silence, sweat beginning to glisten on his forehead in the close summer air. "This is how Lightning Hopkins used to do it." As if from the open window of some Houston speakeasy, Guy's green Guild Starfire picked out the wiry old Texan's distinctive, cruising bass lines and percussive open treble, note-perfect, as he sang the first few lines of "Mojo Hand":

> I'm goin' to Louisiana, get me a mojo hand
> Gonna fix my woman so she can't get no other man

Then a change of pace—a Jimmy Reed song, one I couldn't place but unmistakable in its half-asleep delivery, lazy lope, and easy chord changes, which Guy immediately pursued with the primordial boogie of John Lee Hooker, with a few words of "Boogie Chillen" thrown over the top. And a pause. The room was quiet, the sparse audience rapt. Women called out and Buddy Guy laughed and answered in kind. He had our attention. He was enjoying himself. He marveled wide-eyed at Big Time Sarah's skills as a manager, in booking so many acts for a forthcoming benefit show: "I couldn't have done it," he exclaimed. "She calls up and says 'come and play Sunday, and I'll do you a favor later.' I don't know what kind of favor she means—do you? Is she a taxi driver?" The place was cracking up. Behind the bar, Sarah raised a warning eyebrow and allowed herself a smile.

"That was the first song I learned," said Guy, serious again. "This was the next." It was, of course, "The Things That I Used to Do." I couldn't say how often I had heard it, but I had never heard it like that: inspired, impassioned, flawless. Guy's guitar was three feet from my head and he was looking down at me as he played, smiling. I knew it was nothing to do with me. I knew he was a showman and I knew that in all probability he had done this act a hundred times before. But to me at that moment it seemed like a private performance, a secret initiation into everything that went into the making of a master. I smiled back, and then realized I was laughing. This one set paid for all those earlier, empty trips down to the Checkerboard. This was what I came for.

When it was all over, with Sarah and the waitress wiping tables and gathering up glasses, I went over to Buddy Guy on my way out to tell him how great I thought the show had been. Suddenly tired, he was perched on a stool and leaning on the bar with just a beer for company. He looked up at me through half-closed, heavy eyes and smiled that smile of his. "Thanks, man. I appreciate it."

It was worth the wait.

Fade to Black

When I went to Chicago in 1982 it was with a vague idea of writing an epitaph for the blues, but when I sat down at my typewriter, it seemed more complicated than that. That its best days were behind it was clear enough. Most of the great artists whose work defined the genre were long gone before I arrived: Howlin' Wolf in 1976, Little Walter in 1968, and Sonny Boy Williamson just as the British blues boom was getting under way, long before I ever heard of him.

I never saw Muddy Waters when I was in Chicago because by then his health was failing, so I was thankful to have once seen him perform in London, at the Rainbow in Finsbury Park.[1] That gig was memorable for a fight that broke out in the stalls, right in front of the great man, between a couple of irate longhairs who were clearly unversed in the art of violence. Muddy looked down at them from his stool with wry amusement, but never let up playing his Telecaster. When the show ended and he began the long, slow walk to the wings, someone threw a long-stemmed rose onto the stage. Muddy stooped to pick it up and waved it, in an elegant and moving farewell.

The remaining Southern-born musicians working in Chicago's blues clubs were also fading away, and with them went our connections with legendary figures from the past. When you shook hands with Big Walter Horton, you were shaking a hand that had shaken Robert Johnson's; Floyd Jones's father used to work with Charley Patton. Louis and Dave Myers remained active, and Jimmy Rogers was still an occasional presence in B.L.U.E.S, but it was a rare evening when you heard an unfamiliar song or something genuinely new coming out of a guitar or harmonica. Yet every musician I asked would invariably answer that the blues would never die, and even though their protestations sometimes carried a whiff of desperation about them, it was nevertheless true that the music could be heard all over the city, played by musicians of all ages and backgrounds. Some of them were better than others, but in general the blues in Chicago in 1982 sounded pretty good. It was too soon for an obituary.

With the summer over and my money exhausted, I flew back to London and surveyed the piles of notes, tapes, photographs, and records I had accumulated, with little idea of what to do with them all. Not knowing what sort of book I wanted to write, I couldn't start, let alone finish it. Besides, I needed to get a job.

Jimmy Dawkins wrote me a letter: "Thanks for the photos. I been a little busy on the road with band. And I was down a bit—I had a stroke—so now up. Will tour Europe in May. My LP on Isabel won the Jazz & Blues Grand Prix for 1982 in Paris. Was nominated for the Best Blues of 82 by the W. C. Handy Awards in Memphis, Tenn—so that makes me happy. I'm waiting on Album Records for the release of the LP we cut live in Paris, May 1982—I think I love that work of me + artists like Leake and Queen Sylvia etc. 'bout as well or better than any record in years." He signed it: "Eazy—your friend, Jimmy Dawkins."

I went back to Chicago several times over the next few years, on one occasion for a bizarre magazine assignment to interview martial arts star Chuck Norris and football legend Walter Payton Jr., who were involved in a powerboating stunt on the lake. But mostly I went to see friends and catch up with the music. With a driver's license I was able to rent a car, and I discovered companies like Fender Benders and Rent-a-Wreck who had fleets of elegantly wasted rustheaps for hire, half a block long. Cruising down to the South Side in a rumbling 1973 Chevrolet Caprice was pure joy compared with the anxious trial of waiting at dark bus stops and lonely L stations at three in the morning.

On these trips I listened to many of my favorite musicians again, like Johnny Littlejohn and Magic Slim, and saw Robert Junior Lockwood for the first and only time, at a new blues festival in Grant Park. I went to the Checkerboard Lounge, and there was Buddy Guy at the bar, holding court for friends and fans. He didn't get up to play. But I did see him perform a couple of days later at the Chicago Historical Society in Lincoln Park, in a brightly lit theater complete with classical decor, air-conditioning, a proscenium arch and ladies in hats. It was two o'clock in the afternoon. Guy looked down from the stage with a nervous smile at the sea of elderly, well-to-do white folks and confessed, "I'm not used to playing this early in the day." But somehow he and the band managed to fabricate a soulful blues groove, and even after they asked him to turn the volume down he put on a great show.

Perhaps the highlights of these later visits were two astounding evenings in 1985, listening to Otis Rush in the Kingston Mines: performances of instrumental virtuosity and raw emotional power. But visiting Chicago for a few days or a week at a time just wasn't the same. Maybe I was conscious of having moved on while the Chicago blues had not, but there was also regret at no longer being even a peripheral part of that nocturnal world. Reluctantly, I was forced to count myself among the burgeoning ranks of blues tourists, whose well-intentioned enthusiasm was slowly but surely eroding the atmosphere of even the most intimate clubs.

The first bluesman I saw in Chicago was Floyd Jones. On one of my last visits to B.L.U.E.S he was helped up onto the stage, looking rather frail and elderly, to do a couple of songs. Sunnyland Slim was at the piano and Eddie Taylor on the guitar, and with these two old friends behind him he sat with his Fender bass, eyes closed behind thick glasses, and sang "Going Down Slow":

> I have had my fun, if I never get well no more
> I have had my fun, if I never get well no more
> All of my health is failing, Lord, I'm going down slow

Theresa's closed in 1983 and Buddy Guy sold his stake in the Checkerboard two years later. On the North Side in 1987 Rob Hecko and Bill Gilmore opened a new venue, B.L.U.E.S Etcetera, on West Belmont Avenue. It was much bigger than the original bar, and on my sole visit, in 1989, to see a rare Chicago performance by Clarence Gatemouth Brown, it was packed to the rafters with young white men who whooped and shrieked like chimpanzees. It reminded me of those dismal Son Seals gigs in the Wise Fools Pub, when the crowd's undiscriminating enthusiasm in witnessing a black man playing a guitar seemed more to do with some dimly perceived and oppressively patronizing notion of "authenticity" than with any appreciation or enjoyment of what he was trying to do. Back in 1982 there was a remedy: go somewhere more congenial. Seven years later, that simple solution no longer seemed to be available. From what I could see, all the clubs were like that now.

There were opportunities closer to home. I took friends to see Albert King at a half-empty Astoria[2] on London's Charing Cross Road, but the virtuoso string-bender was in a bad mood, preoccupied with scolding his sidemen, and seemed sadly bored by the music he was playing. John Mayall and his band played a big London Jazz Festival gig, but a stage act that might have worked in his adopted California left the local crowd bemused. It wasn't his music that lingered in my memory so much as the sight of a sixty-one-year-old Englishman dancing on stage in a sleeveless tee shirt and leather trousers. Fortunately, Sonny Rollins was on the same bill. Even a hardworking Buddy Guy doing his level best to conjure up a club atmosphere in the echoing void of the Royal Festival Hall[3] was more wearisome than inspiring and ultimately just seemed rather noisy. "What a racket," my musician friend Dave muttered wryly.

Bobby Bland came to the Hammersmith Odeon. I knew his music from the *Together . . .* live albums[4] he made in the mid-1970s with B. B. King and was eager to see a blues singer whose huge popularity remained almost entirely confined to black American audiences. His smooth nightclub act, with its big band, sharp suits, seductive patter and a marked lack of guitar heroics was straight out of the Apollo or the Regal. It was sentimental, highly polished, self-consciously sophisticated and, to the London blues fans who packed the venue—young, male, and white—about as familiar as Chinese opera. Bland's distinctive gurgling scream at the emotional crux of a song—a stylistic affectation that must have melted a million ladies' hearts back home—had the bearded young man sitting next to me sniggering with embarrassment.

There was always B. B. King. Constantly on tour, he never disappointed, and he cropped up in the most unexpected venues: some of the best blues photographs I ever took were of him playing at the Fairfield Halls, in suburban Croydon. Buddy's brother Phil Guy played an excellent gig at the 100 Club,[5] the basement bar on Oxford Street. He had put on weight since I last saw him in the Checkerboard Lounge, but he did a terrific show. The actress Helen Mirren was in the audience and ended her evening dancing on a table. It was a good night.

In 1983 David Bowie released his *Let's Dance* album. This featured the Texan guitarist Stevie Ray Vaughan and thereby introduced a new generation of listeners to the sound of Albert King. One side effect of this was to foster the notion among these new fans that the blues was a style of rock guitar. At the same time a young musician named Robert Cray emerged from the West Coast as a new blues hopeful. *Bad Influence* was a polished and heavily promoted soul-blues album, which didn't do much for me but undoubtedly helped drag the blues back into the spotlight.

Lurrie Bell's friend and bandmate Eli Murray breezed through in May 1985. He had a different hairstyle, a reefer jacket from Jimi Hendrix's Sergeant Pepper period, a more flamboyant guitar technique and a new name, Elisha Blue. Taking advantage of one of Richard Branson's more enlightened publicity stunts, he had been able to earn his passage to the United Kingdom on a Virgin Atlantic flight by busking onboard with a twelve-string guitar. *Blues Unlimited* magazine had lined up some gigs for him, supported by the Devon guitarist Julian Piper. Eli said he was moving to Amsterdam. Ron Abrams was already there, he thought, and doing well. "The blues deserves to stay around, and I wanna have something to do with that," he told me. "I won't be playing Delta, I'll be doing what I think belongs today. That's why I had so many problems in the U.S., they wanted me to play like somebody else—'Hey man, play this like Louis Myers and the Aces.' I said I'm not Louis Myers and the Aces! But at the time I wasn't sure who I was."

I introduced Eli to English ale[6] at my local in south London, where his outlandish looks were a hit with the children in the pub garden. The thoughtful and humorous young man of a few years before had acquired an angry edge: "I'm not going to sell myself cheap, man. I don't know when I'm going back. You get a negative attitude from guys in Chicago: 'You're not gonna make it, you're going to stay here with us, we're all going to hell together.'" He sounded bitter but seemed optimistic. Since I last saw him, Eli had played in John Lee Hooker's band at ChicagoFest: "He said to me, 'Now listen there, young man, don't you fuck up now or I'm gonna hook ya!' But he didn't hook me off the stage. I was playing next to Eddie Taylor, watching. I didn't know fuck all about what *he* was doing."

A few days later I rode my motorcycle down the A303 to Devon, where Eli played three gigs in three nights, backed by Julian Piper's capable band, the Junkyard Angels. Eli's performances blew the young West Country crowds away. Just hearing him tuning up had the audience scurrying in from the bar, mouths agape. They queued for autographs. Julian Piper, no slouch on the Stratocaster himself, confessed to being in awe of Eli's technique, not having seen its like, he said, since he sat next to Mick Jagger in a smoky club off Piccadilly in 1966 to hear the newly arrived Jimi Hendrix. Just before Eli's final Devon performance, at an agricultural college in the middle of nowhere, a young woman approached me at the bar, breathless and shy: "Are you with Elisha? Were you there last night? Isn't he *wonderful*?"

• • •

On a business trip to Düsseldorf in about 2002 I spotted a torn poster pasted to the wall outside a basement jazz club. The grey concrete capital of North Rhine-Westphalia would present a dreary prospect on a sunny spring morning, so crunching through snow in the evening gloom of a German January while searching for some decent live music was like witnessing the death of hope. But there on the poster was a name I recognized, and a photo: Steve Freund. I hadn't thought about him for years. The gig was long past, but the idea of him playing the blues in Düsseldorf lifted my spirits: for a short while, anyway. Then I pushed open the door and descended the stairs, resigned to another night of frothy beer, trad jazz, and comedy sousaphone.

Steve Freund was Sunnyland Slim's key sideman. I remembered him as a thoughtful and well-read guitarist with superb technique, just as likely to underline a phrase with a carefully framed sequence of chords as to let fly with a soaring solo. In 1982 he was thirty years old and one of the best players in town: solemn young blues fans, in thrall to the guitar, would sit and watch his fingers intently.

Some years after that dreary Düsseldorf evening I caught up with him in Belgium, where the promoter had paired him with a blues and boogie piano player, Gene Taylor. They sounded as if they had been playing together for years. During the final set at the Cafe Merlo in Brussels, I noticed that the crowd of middle-aged couples rocking their heads at the bar had melted away, to be replaced by a row of solemn young men, in thrall to the guitar, watching Freund's fingers intently.

He no longer lived in Chicago. By the early 1990s many of the older blues-men had gone, and the city's blues scene was changing, Freund explained. "For the most part it was really crappy gigs: the same old stuff over and over, and I was just tired of it. They weren't interested in the traditional stuff any more." Actually they probably were—it was just that tourists in search of an authentic Chicago blues experience had a different idea of "traditional." For Freund it meant playing "Hoochie Coochie Man" and "Sweet Home Chicago" every night.

So he moved to California. "Being a white musician back in Chicago in that black blues world, you're basically being judged by other white people," he remembered. "They're the ones who own the nightclubs and the ones who are booking the events, and they're the ones who can make or break you."

Freund had been steeped in the blues since he was very small, albeit unknowingly, thanks to the elderly janitor in his family's apartment building. "He was from the Deep South, and he lived in the bowels of the building, kept live chickens in there. It was real country—he would kill 'em and cook 'em, and he used to play these old records." Even at one remove this was more of a rural Mississippi childhood than most Jewish kids from Brooklyn could claim, and the old music—Bessie Smith and Louis Armstrong, he worked out later—made a permanent impression.

"It's a spiritual commitment," said Freund. "I dare say I could get a guy out of Berklee School of Music and put the music in front of him and he would play it note for note, but what I want to know is, what's going on in the person's mind. When I play the blues I'm spiritually connected, and I'm sure B. B. King is, I'm sure Peter Green is, and all the old guys. They don't even have to think about it."

• • •

In 2002 Carlo Rotella brought out a book called *Good with Their Hands*, a collection of essays that included a long and thoughtful piece about Buddy Guy.[7] I wondered if this kind of attention from a fan who was an academic—as opposed to a fan with a typewriter like Mike Rowe or a fan who was a journalist like Robert Palmer—was a sign of both how far the blues had come and how far it had gone. Perhaps now that the music had been around long enough to have been thoroughly chewed over by several generations of writers, it was deemed to have arrived as a serious subject, worthy of academic attention. But maybe it was also starting to be seen as a form that had run its course: a cultural artifact, no longer a living thing. As if installed behind glass, the blues could safely be studied from all angles and wasn't going to suddenly jump up and do something unexpected.

Rotella had a sharp and entertaining style. It never quite shook off the dust of academia—Muddy Waters was apparently a "first-wave, postwar codifier," while a group of people standing around outside a club became "a living portrait of the overlap between industrial and postindustrial blues synthesis"—but he was a longstanding and perceptive fan of Buddy Guy.

In his essay he set out to counter critics who accused the guitarist of dumbing down his playing in order to appeal to rock fans. The critics' argument was that as Guy got more famous in the 1980s and 1990s and started increasingly to appear in front of white fans who knew more about rock than blues, he changed his style to suit them, rather than staying true to himself. Descriptions like "white noise" were bandied about. Writers used phrases like "too many notes."

The style in question was the one I heard with my friend Dave at that Royal Festival Hall gig in about 1998, and it was pretty damn noisy. But although when I went to that concert I hadn't seen or heard Guy for at least ten years, it didn't come as a complete surprise to me, and as Rotella rightly pointed out, neither would it have done to anyone else who owned Guy's Alligator Records album *Stone Crazy*.[8] He had been playing like that for a long time. Maybe just not quite so much.

Stone Crazy was a great and very noisy album. So was the U.K. label JSP's less great but more noisy *The Dollar Done Fell*. They were both recorded in 1979. But whereas the professionally produced Alligator opus was about Guy's struggle, in Rotella's words, to "rein in his guitar playing just enough to sustain or at least gesture at the traditional balance of voice and guitar," the unsupervised and chaotic JSP effort—recorded live at the Checkerboard Lounge and produced by Buddy Guy himself—attempted no such feat. Neither was there much evidence on the scary British album that Guy "attends to compulsory figures before attempting quintuple axels." He just launched straight into a high-wire act with no net.

Rotella's point was that the critics were wrong. Guy had been doing the white noise stuff for years, and *Stone Crazy* caught him on the cusp between blues guitar hero and rock guitar god: "You can hear Guy's dueling impulses to both establish and push past an interesting generic limit." Well, maybe you could, but not because it was 1979 and Guy was in the process of developing his style, as Rotella suggested, but because there was an experienced producer in the studio telling the musician to behave.[9] Remove the professional producer and put Guy in charge, turn the Checkerboard into a makeshift and acoustically suspect recording studio for the night, and you got the kind of mad, indulgent musical mayhem that the critics, years later, started complaining about.

Far from creating this frayed, nihilistic style in response to the enthusiasm of white rock fans who had been too young to see Hendrix play live, the evidence of *The Dollar Done Fell* is that Buddy Guy first confronted his artistic demons, and first started playing rock, in the safety of his own South Side club.

· · ·

After twenty-something years in London I upped sticks with my family and moved down to the West Country, settling in an old English market town close to that agricultural college where Elisha blew his young audience away all those years ago. It was also not far from my old university and its phenomenal music archive, where I used to sit wearing headphones and gaze out of the window while listening to scratchy blues 78s.

Live music in my new hometown's pubs tended to be either rock 'n' roll, modern jazz, or folk, so I was surprised one evening to discover a young white Englishman who sat on a stool with a guitar and harmonica and played in the style of the old Delta bluesmen. The intensity of his performance was balanced by a disarming and wryly humorous self-deprecation. Introducing the song "Outside Woman Blues," he said: "This is a Joe Reynolds song made famous by Cream in the late sixties. But I hate Cream. Sorry." Another time he informed his bemused audience: "This is a Robert Johnson tune that I've changed a little bit, for the worse."

Tall, angular and bespectacled, Thomas Ford was twenty-eight years old and grew up listening to his father's Canned Heat records. When he picked up a guitar at the age of fifteen, he wanted to play like Son House. "The stuff that my old man was listening to became a starting point," he told me. "I don't listen to much stuff past then: my interest was in going back." And back he went, all the way to the 1920s: he claimed Tommy Johnson as an influence, and cited Tommy McClennan as his favorite Delta bluesman. "People go on about Robert Johnson," he explained, "but Tommy Johnson was ten years before, singing in a real high falsetto voice." Ford's favorite album featured Canned Heat's Alan Wilson playing in the 1960s alongside the recently rediscovered Son House: "Amazing," he said. "The thing with the Delta blues is there's so much of it to discover, so many different players."

With his instincts as an entertainer, his undoubted technical ability and his fascinating repertoire, Ford had regular gigs in small venues like the bar where I first saw him, which he was able to fit in around his day job at the local university. In recent summers he had also enjoyed success at blues festivals in Europe, where he had found audiences who appreciated the history of the music. But in England it was different: "There's a real thing in the U.K. about blues-rock," he said. "I can't stand it. I can't get a gig at a blues festival in the U.K. for love nor money. They just want rock musicians."

In a country where the paths of blues and rock converged decades ago, Thomas Ford's music seemed not so much anachronistic as defiant. The blues they liked in England had much younger roots—Little Walter, B. B. King, Muddy Waters—while Ford preferred the songs that these men had learned from. His performances were as much pastiche as homage—the sort of thing John Hammond Jr. and Dave Van Ronk used to do at folk clubs in the early 1960s—but Ford also wrote his own material. "Mississippi Fred McDowell Blues," which name-checked Bo Diddley, Blind Blake, Son House and the Reverend Gary Davis as well as Alan Wilson, was based on a surreal dream populated by the old musicians he had clearly spent a little too much time thinking about. A blues song about old bluesmen, written by a white Englishman and sung, by him, in the style of those very artists: postmodern, or what?

It's a lot easier to find the blues today than it used to be. In 1982, to stumble across someone like Thomas Ford in small town in England would have been unimaginable. The blues today is not the esoteric, unfashionable, and hard-to-find cultural touchstone that it seemed to be when I was a young fan. It's everywhere, accepted as a commodity for use in advertising, not just as a soundtrack to lend a rootsy authenticity to the sales message but as part of the narrative. Cars, beer, and mobile phones have all received the blues treatment. In Britain we enjoyed a turn by Lonnie Brooks in a beer commercial, which suggested that if he hadn't been such a talented musician, he could have made a good living as a comedy actor. The blues is now so mainstream, according to Carlo Rotella, that they play Fenton Robinson's "I'm Going to Chicago" as Muzak at O'Hare Airport. I read Rotella's investigation of the touristification of the blues in modern Chicago with appalled fascination.[10] It certainly wasn't like that in 1982.

• • •

These days whenever I think about the troubling business of "authenticity," I remember a magazine story I wrote about the potter Bernard Leach. He was an Englishman who drew his inspiration from the Far East, first in the raku tradition of Japan and then in the Song dynasty wares of medieval China, which he idealized for their spontaneity, unselfconsciousness, and simplicity of form. He spent much of the rest of his life trying to achieve these ideals in his own work, and he inspired thousands of others to do the same.

As part of my research I went to talk to an elderly potter, living locally, who used to know Leach, and there was a question I couldn't resist asking her. Some years before, I had found myself in a picturesque Hampshire market town where there was an antiques shop and, a few doors down, an art gallery. The antiques shop had an ancient Chinese tea bowl for sale, green-glazed, with fluted sides and just the sort of unassuming elegance that inspired Leach. The art gallery had a virtually identical bowl for sale at the same price, only theirs was made by a contemporary English ceramicist, who had signed it: there was his distinctive seal on the foot. The coincidence was extraordinary. Each was the work of a master craftsman: one an anonymous Chinese potter from Yaozhou, and the other a famous disciple of Bernard Leach. There was no material difference between the two pots, except for the trifling matter of a thousand years. Yet only one was "authentic."

I told the story to my potter and asked: if she could only have one of them, which would she choose?

"Oh, that's easy," she said, amused. "You must just choose whichever is the better pot."

Chicago Blues Gigs, 1979, 1982, 1985

For reasons that escape me now, in 1979, long before I thought of writing this book, and in 1985, long after I put it to one side, I still kept notes of all the gigs I went to in Chicago. So here they are, for what they're worth, deciphered from miscellaneous scraps of paper, along with my schedule for the summer of 1982, when I did most of my research. They offer an exhausting, if not exhaustive, idea of the variety and quality of the music that was available in the city during the period.

Not all of the acts listed here were headlining: band members or anyone sitting in whose contribution seemed noteworthy are also included.

1979

July 10	Floyd Jones, Playboy Venson, B.L.U.E.S.
	Roy Hightower, Kingston Mines.
July 11	Lee Jackson; Sunnyland Slim, S. P. Leary, Billy Branch, B.L.U.E.S.
July 12	Son Seals, Phil Guy, Big Moose Walker, Wise Fools Pub.
July 13	Jimmy Walker, Billy Branch, Big Walter Horton, B.L.U.E.S.
July 14	Eddie Shaw & The Wolf Gang, incl. Hubert Sumlin, Biddy Mulligan's.
July 15	J. B. Hutto & the New Hawks, Wise Fools Pub.
July 16	Homesick James, Floyd Jones, Playboy Venson, Snooky Pryor, B.L.U.E.S.
July 17	Floyd Jones, Sunnyland Slim, Jimmy Walker, Snooky Pryor, Homesick James, Playboy Venson, B.L.U.E.S.
July 18	Magic Slim, Wise Fools Pub.

July 19	Eddie Clearwater, Lavelle White, Blues Valley All Stars, Kingston Mines.
	Eddie Taylor, Good Rockin' Charles, B.L.U.E.S.
July 22	Big Walter Horton, Floyd Jones, Little Joe Berson, Homesick James, Playboy Venson, B.L.U.E.S.
July 23	Joe Daley Jazz Quorum, Orphans, 2462 N. Lincoln Avenue.
July 25	Lee Jackson, Sunnyland Slim, B.L.U.E.S.
July 28	Erwin Helfer, Odie Payne, Big Time Sarah, B.L.U.E.S.
July 29	Big Walter Horton, Pinetop Perkins, S. P. Leary, Steve Freund, Little Joe Berson, B.L.U.E.S.
August 1	Big Moose Walker, S. P. Leary, B.L.U.E.S.
August 2	Left Hand Frank, Dimestore Fred, Kingston Mines.
	Blind John Davis, B.L.U.E.S.
August 3	Johnny Littlejohn; Lightning Hopkins, ChicagoFest.
	Jimmy Johnson, Lavelle White, Addie Lee, Kingston Mines.
August 5	James Cotton, ChicagoFest.
August 7	Brewer Phillips and Ted Harvey, Billy Branch, John Embry, B.L.U.E.S.
August 8	Willie Dixon, Billy Branch, ChicagoFest.
August 9	Albert Collins; Jimmy Johnson; Fenton Robinson, ChicagoFest.
	Eddie Shaw and the Wolf Gang, incl. Hubert Sumlin, B.L.U.E.S.
August 12	Buddy Guy and Junior Wells, ChicagoFest.
August 15	Carey Bell and Lurrie Bell, Wise Fools Pub.
	Lovey Lee, Hubert Sumlin, B.L.U.E.S.
August 19	Buddy Guy, Checkerboard Lounge.
August 22	Jeanne Carroll, Jimmy Moorelander, Smokey Smothers, B.L.U.E.S.
	Albert Collins, Wise Fools Pub.
August 26	Playboy Venson, Maxwell Street.
	Big Walter Horton, Floyd Jones, Playboy Venson, B.L.U.E.S.
August 27	Lefty Dizz, Jimmy Johnson, Checkerboard Lounge.
	Sammy Lawhorn, Theresa's Tavern.
August 28	Bill Warren, B.L.U.E.S.
	Lonnie Brooks, Wise Fools.
August 29	Carey Bell and Lurrie Bell, Kingston Mines.
	New Hawks with Good Rocking Charles, Smokey Smothers, B.L.U.E.S.
August 30	Luther Allison, Biddy Mulligan's.
	J. B. Hutto & the New Hawks, B.L.U.E.S.
August 31	Left Hand Frank, Jimmy Rogers, Frank Bandy, Alabama Red, Big Time Sarah, B.L.U.E.S.
September 1	Blind John Davis, Fred Below, B.L.U.E.S.
	Magic Slim, Checkerboard Lounge.

1982

June 2	Eddie Shaw and the Wolf Gang, B.L.U.E.S.
	Jimmy Johnson, Kingston Mines.
June 3	Hubert Sumlin, Chico Chism, Johnny Littlejohn, B.L.U.E.S.
	Lefty Dizz and Shock Treatment, Kingston Mines.
June 4	43rd Street Band, Sports Corner.
	Erwin Helfer, Big Time Sarah, B.L.U.E.S.
June 5	Lonnie Brooks, Biddy Mulligan's.
	Otis Clay, Detroit Jr., Kingston Mines.
June 6	Pinell Curry Benefit: Hip Linkchain, Johnny Dollar, Big Time Sarah, Buddy Scott, Jimmy Johnson, Sunnyland Slim, Steve Freund, Koko Taylor, Emmett Maestro Sanders, Lonnie Brooks, B.L.U.E.S.
June 8	Louis Myers, 43rd Street Blues Band, Checkerboard Lounge.
	Hip Linkchain, B.L.U.E.S.
June 9	Jimmy Johnson, Kingston Mines.
June 10	43rd Street Blues Band, Checkerboard Lounge.
	Brother Mud, Theresa's Tavern.
June 11	Mighty Joe Young, Biddy Mulligan's.
	Lefty Dizz, Valerie Wellington, Detroit Jr., Kingston Mines.
June 13	Kansas City Red, Sunnyland Slim, Steve Freund, Fred Below, B.L.U.E.S.
	Lavelle White, Bob Levis, Aron Burton, Kingston Mines.
June 15	Buster Benton, Willie Kent, Johnny Dollar, B.L.U.E.S.
June 16	Jimmy Dawkins, Queen Sylvia Embry, Johnny Dollar, B.L.U.E.S.
June 18	Son Seals, Wise Fools Pub.
June 19	Magic Slim, B.L.U.E.S.
	Chicago Slim, Kingston Mines.
June 20	Smokey Smothers, Queen Sylvia Embry, Little Smokey, Big Time Sarah, Hip Linkchain, B.L.U.E.S.
	Luther Allison, Kingston Mines.
	Sunnyland Slim, B.L.U.E.S.
June 24	Little Arthur Donkin, Scotty and the Bad Boys, Steve Freund, B.L.U.E.S.
	Hubert Sumlin, Chico Chism, Lefty Dizz, Kingston Mines.
June 25	Sunnyland Slim, Johnny Littlejohn, Delta Fish Market.
	Lefty Dizz, Johnny Dollar, B.L.U.E.S.
	Jimmy Johnson, Valerie Wellington, James Cotton, Kingston Mines.
June 26	Willie Dixon, Billy Branch, Biddy Mulligan's.
	Lefty Dizz, B.L.U.E.S.
	Jimmy Johnson, Valerie Wellington, Kingston Mines.

June 30	Jimmy Dawkins, B.L.U.E.S.
	Johnny Dollar, Kingston Mines.
July 1	John Lee Hooker, Biddy Mulligan's.
	Johnny Dollar, Sugar Blue, Kingston Mines.
July 2	Junior Wells, Kingston Mines.
	Mama Yancey, Erwin Helfer, B.L.U.E.S.
July 3	Junior Wells, Lurrie Bell, Kingston Mines.
July 4	Lavelle White, Valerie Wellington, Kingston Mines.
July 6	McFarland-Ford Band, Valerie Wellington, Johnny Howard, Kingston Mines.
July 7	Lavelle White, Ronald Abrams, Johnny Dollar, Kingston Mines.
July 8	S.P. Leary, Playboy Venson, Floyd Jones, Homesick James, Harmonica George, Blind John Davis, B.L.U.E.S.
	Hubert Sumlin, Chico Chism, Sammy Fender, Kingston Mines.
July 9	Louis Myers, Dave Myers, Fred Below, Johnny Big Moose Walker, B.L.U.E.S
	Luther Allison, Kingston Mines.
July 10	Luther Allison, Eddie Clearwater, Valerie Wellington, Kingston Mines
	Max Roach Quartet, Jazz Showcase at the Blackstone Hotel.
July 14	Fenton Robinson, Wise Fools Pub.
	Ronald Abrams, Kingston Mines.
July 15	Fenton Robinson, Wise Fools Pub.
	Jimmy Dawkins, Johnny Littlejohn, Detroit Jr., B.L.U.E.S.
	Hubert Sumlin, Chico Chism, Kingston Mines.
July 16	Magic Slim, B.L.U.E.S.
	Lefty Dizz, Kingston Mines.
July 17	Jimmy Rogers, Carey Bell, B.L.U.E.S.
	Lefty Dizz, Kingston Mines.
July 18	Lefty Dizz, Lincoln Avenue Street Fair.
	Smokey Smothers, Sunnyland Slim, Johnny Littlejohn, B.L.U.E.S.
July 19	Lefty Dizz, Sammy Lawhorn, Muddy Waters Jr., Checkerboard Lounge.
	Hip Linkchain, Mad Dog Lester Davenport, B.L.U.E.S.
July 22	Eddie Taylor, Johnny Littlejohn, B.L.U.E.S.
	Hubert Sumlin, Chico Chism, Kingston Mines.
July 23	Johnny Littlejohn, Delta Fish Market.
July 24	Buddy Guy and Junior Wells, Biddy Mulligan's.
July 26	Junior Wells, Johnny Dollar, Foree Superstar Montgomery, Taste Entertainment Center.
July 27	Little Brother Montgomery, Sue Conway, B.L.U.E.S.
July 29	Blind John Davis, S. P. Leary, B.L.U.E.S.
	Hubert Sumlin, Chico Chism, Sugar Blue, Kingston Mines.

July 31	Sunnyland Slim, Johnny Littlejohn, Fred Below, B.L.U.E.S.
August 1	Johnny Twist, South Shore Country Club.
	Sunnyland Slim, Johnny Littlejohn, B.L.U.E.S.
August 4	McFarland-Ford Band, Luther Allison, ChicagoFest.
August 6	Buddy Guy and Junior Wells, with Phil Guy, Steve Ditzell, ChicagoFest.
	Lefty Dizz, B.L.U.E.S.
	Son Seals, Kingston Mines.
August 8	Smokey Smothers, Sunnyland Slim, Illinois Slim, Mad Dog Lester Davenport, Steve Cushing, B.L.U.E.S.
	Sammy Fender, Lavelle White, Valerie Wellington, Kingston Mines.
August 9	Sonny Terry and Brownie McGhee, ChicagoFest.
August 10	Jimmy Rogers, Hip Linkchain; Albert Collins, ChicagoFest.
August 11	Albert Collins, Koko Taylor, Son Seals, Emmett Maestro Sanders, Stages.
	Hip Linkchain, Big Time Sarah, B.L.U.E.S.
	Mark Hannon, Lucky Lopez, Kingston Mines.
August 12	Otis Blackwell, Willie Dixon, Phil Guy, Sugar Blue, Koko Taylor, Jimmy Witherspoon, Stages.
	Carey Bell, Lurrie Bell, James Cotton, Emmett Maestro Sanders, Piano C Red, Kingston Mines.
August 13	Buddy Guy, Phil Guy, Checkerboard Lounge.
August 14	Jimmy Dawkins, Willie Kent, B.L.U.E.S.
	Larry Davis, Kingston Mines.
August 15	Sunnyland Slim, Steve Freund; Sonny Rollins; Willie Dixon, ChicagoFest.
August 17	Eddie Taylor, Willie Kent, Smokey Smothers, B.L.U.E.S.
August 18	Magic Slim, B.L.U.E.S.
	Jimmy Johnson, Gene Pickett, Kingston Mines.
August 19	Brewer Phillips and Ted Harvey, B.L.U.E.S.
	Carey Bell, Sugar Blue, Kingston Mines.
August 20	Lefty Dizz, Kingston Mines.
August 21	Lefty Dizz, Kingston Mines.
August 22	Billy Branch, Lurrie Bell and the SoB Band, Wicker Park Greening Festival.
August 23	Johnny Dollar, Taste Entertainment Center.
August 24	Johnny Dollar, B.L.U.E.S.
	Joe Kelley, Sugar Blue, Kingston Mines.
August 25	Jimmy Johnson, James Cotton, Kingston Mines.
August 26	Eddie Shaw and the Wolf Gang, Kingston Mines.
August 27	Billy Branch, Lurrie Bell and the SoB Band, New Living Room.

August 28	Jimmy Johnson, B.L.U.E.S.
	Sugar Blue, Kingston Mines.
August 30	Lacy Gibson, B.L.U.E.S.
August 31	Buster Benton, Willie Kent, B.L.U.E.S.
	Joe Kelley, Bob Anderson, Kingston Mines.
September 1	Billy Branch, Lurrie Bell and the SoB Band, Biddy Mulligan's.
September 2	Lee Shot Williams, Kingston Mines.
September 3	Eddie Cleanhead Vinson, KOOL Jazz Festival, Grant Park.
	Johnny Dollar, Ronald Abrams, B.L.U.E.S.
	Lefty Dizz, James Cotton, Louis Myers, Checkerboard Lounge.
	Detroit Jr., Bootsy's Show Lounge.
September 4	Billy Branch, Lurrie Bell and the SoB Band with Jimmy Walker, KOOL Jazz Festival, Grant Park.
	Lonnie Brooks, Johnny Dollar, Kingston Mines.
September 5	Alberta Hunter; Miles Davis, KOOL Jazz Festival, Grant Park.
	Sunnyland Slim, Steve Freund, Fred Below, B.L.U.E.S.
	Sammy Fender, Lavelle White, Valerie Wellington, Kingston Mines.
September 6	Billy Branch, Lurrie Bell and the SoB Band, House of J Lounge.
	Lefty Dizz, John Embry, Checkerboard Lounge.
September 7	Hip Linkchain, B.L.U.E.S.
	Johnny Dollar, Kingston Mines.
September 8	John Primer, Michael Robinson, Jerome Binder, B.L.U.E.S.
	Mark Hannon, Kingston Mines.
September 9	Condition Blue with Jim Smith, Robert Covington, and Lefty Dizz, West End.
	Smokey Smothers, Little Smokey, Mad Dog Lester Davenport; Byther Smith, B.L.U.E.S.
	Lee Shot Williams, Kingston Mines.
September 10	Johnny Littlejohn, James Cotton, Delta Fish Market.
	Jimmy Johnson, Kingston Mines.
September 11	Koko Taylor, Son Seals, Lonnie Brooks, Emmett Maestro Sanders, On Broadway.
	Jimmy Johnson, Kingston Mines.
September 12	Sunnyland Slim's Birthday Party: Sunnyland Slim, Jimmy Walker, Fred Below, Bonnie Lee, S. P. Leary, Blind John Davis, Lefty Dizz, Erwin Helfer, B.L.U.E.S.
September 14	Cub Coda, Brewer Phillips, Ted Harvey, Louis Myers, B.L.U.E.S.
September 16	Lavelle White, Kingston Mines.
	Magic Slim, Biddy Mulligan's.
September 17	Willie Dixon, John Watkins, Sugar Blue, Little Arthur Donkin, Biddy Mulligan's.

September 18	Syl Johnson, Buddy Scott, Checkerboard Lounge.
	Pete Allen, New Excuse Lounge.
September 19	Magic Slim, Louis Myers, Pete Allen, Florence's Lounge.
	Sunnyland Slim, B.L.U.E.S.
September 20	Sammy Lawhorn, Pee Wee Madison, Muddy Waters Jr., Louis Myers, Theresa's Tavern.
	Homesick James, John McDonald, B.L.U.E.S.
September 21	Buster Benton, B.L.U.E.S.
September 22	Magic Slim, B.L.U.E.S.
September 23	Little Bobby and Spice, Theresa's Tavern.
	Steve Freund, B.L.U.E.S.

1985

May 31	Otis Rush, Kingston Mines.
June 1	Otis Rush, Kingston Mines.
June 4	Sunnyland Slim, Eddie Taylor, Floyd Jones, B.L.U.E.S.
	Lavelle White, Kingston Mines.
June 5	Jimmy Johnson, B.L.U.E.S.
	Magic Slim, Kingston Mines.
June 6	Magic Slim, Checkerboard Lounge.
	Muddy Waters Jr., Kingston Mines.
	43rd St Band, Little Joe Berson, Michael Robinson, Kingston Mines.
June 7	Koko Taylor, Chicago Blues Festival, Grant Park.
	Magic Slim, B.L.U.E.S.
	Lonnie Brooks, Kingston Mines.
June 8	Sunnyland Slim, Steve Freund, Robert Junior Lockwood, Chicago Blues Festival, Grant Park.
	Billy Branch, J. W. Williams & The Chi-Town Hustlers, Rosa's Lounge.
	Jimmy Johnson, Steve Freund, Robert Covington, Lilly's, Lincoln Avenue.
June 9	Buddy Guy, Chicago Historical Society, Lincoln Park.
	Sunnyland Slim, B.L.U.E.S.
	Billy Branch, Kingston Mines.
June 11	Johnny Littlejohn, Eddie Taylor, Steve Freund, B.L.U.E.S.

Notes

Prologue: Blues Fell This Morning

1. The national speed limit at the time, an energy-saving measure signed into law by Richard Nixon in 1974. It lasted until 1987.

2. B. B. King used the phrase on his *Live at the Regal* LP.

3. "I want you to squeeze my lemon till the juice runs down my leg" came from Robert Johnson's "Traveling Riverside Blues." The Led Zeppelin song also lifts elements from Howlin' Wolf's "Killing Floor" and Albert King's "Crosscut Saw." "Lemon Song" was credited on the album (*Led Zeppelin II*) to Page, Bonham, and Plant. Wolf's publishers successfully sued. On the other side of the album Willie Dixon's "Bring it on Home" (written for Sonny Boy Williamson) was credited to Page and Plant. This sort of thing used to really annoy me. Still does, actually.

4. It's perhaps a little unfair to single out one singer. Like all popular music, the blues tended to latch on to good ideas and wear them out.

5. CBS album 22135, released 1970.

6. *Mississippi Delta Blues Vol 2*, Arhoolie 1042, 1967. Recorded in the field by George Mitchell.

7. *Texas Sharecropper and Songster*, Arhoolie F1001, 1960.

8. Three volumes, Vanguard VRS-9216, 9217, and 9218, and regularly re-released.

9. Survivors from the short-lived English skiffle era, and Cliff Richards's backing band. To my generation, the last word in musical dreariness.

10. Three volumes, 1979, Alligator AL 7701, 7702, and 7703, followed in 1980 by three more (7704–6). Regularly re-released.

11. The club, which is still there, punctuates its name in a variety of ways. The punctuation used here and throughout the book is that seen on the club's original wooden sign.

Chapter 1: Sunnyland Slim's Birthday Party

1. The guitar was a 1971 SG Special. The bridge was engraved with the name of the previous owner, Walter Verdun Jr. If you see it, feel free to get in touch: I lost it in a burglary in about 1987. And in fact the paper bag itself attracted attention on the bus, from two young men who assumed it contained drugs and that I was a dealer. They were very nice about it.

2. *Chicago Blues* by Mike Rowe. Originally published as *Chicago Breakdown* in 1973, by the Eddison Press, London.

3. Chicago's "alternative" weekly newspaper, a pioneer of free circulation, first published in 1971. Still going.

4. Information from listings in *The Reader*, September 24, 1982. The nine clubs were: Biddy Mulligans (7644 North Sheridan Road), B.L.U.E.S (2519 North Halsted Street), the Checkerboard Lounge (423 East Forty-Third Street), Domino Lounge (2352 West Roosevelt Road), the Kingston Mines (2548 North Halsted Street), Minstrels (6465 North Sheridan Road), Theresa's Tavern (4801 South Indiana Avenue), West End (1170 West Armitage Avenue) and the Wise Fools Pub (2270 North Lincoln Avenue).

5. Pepper's Lounge, 503 East Forty-Third Street. Moved to 1321 South Michigan Avenue in 1971. Big John's, 1638 North Wells Street. Closed 1966. Paul Butterfield's band also played there a lot. Mother Blues, 1305 North Wells Street. Primarily a folk club. Closed 1970s. Owned by Lorraine Blue (d. 2000).

6. By Sheldon Harris, published by Arlington House, 1979. A stupendous work of scholarship.

7. *Smokey Smothers Sings the Back Porch Blues*, King LP 779, 1962.

8. "Things Ain't What They Used to Be"/"Black Cat Girl," Rooster R48. Smokey Smothers, vocal and guitar; Mad Dog Lester Davenport, harmonica; Illinois Slim, guitar; Big John Trice, bass; Steve Cushing, drums.

9. In 1982 I saw just two white headliners in B.L.U.E.S: Scotty and the Bad Boys, and Cub Coda, who was fronting Hound Dog Taylor's old band, the Houserockers. The pianist Erwin Helfer also played there regularly, but usually as an accompanist. The Kingston Mines tended to book more white acts. Late one night I sat at the back of the Mines having a beer with a waitress called Kitty, who was on her break. Up on stage a white rock guitarist, Joe Kelley, was playing his Flying Vee for the almost empty room, backed by the All Stars. At the table next to ours Joe's girlfriend had been entrusted with a tape recorder, and Joe had told her to press the Pause button after each song rather than waste tape on the gaps. Toward the end of the set, as we got talking, it transpired that somehow she had got out of synch. At the end of each song she had been pressing Play, and as the band counted down to the next one she pressed Pause. She had, in effect, made a tape of the gaps. After a little encouragement she too saw the funny side, but we weren't able to observe Joe's reaction: just before the set ended Kitty thought it wise to get back to work, and I decided to take a stroll over to B.L.U.E.S.

10. "Brownskin Woman" (Hy-Tone 32) and "The Devil Is a Busy Man" Hy-Tone 33.

Chicago, 1948. Sunnyland Slim, vocal and piano; Lonnie Johnson, guitar; Andrew Harris, bass.

11. Named for the circuit inscribed by the L tracks around the city center.

12. The earliest example I have heard (in the BBC TV film *Blues America*, dir. Mick Gold) of this kind of folkifying of the blues for white audiences was in 1938 at the Spirituals to Swing concert, organized by John Hammond at the Carnegie Hall in New York, when the urbane Chicagoan Big Bill Broonzy had to dress as some sort of farm hand to stand in for the recently deceased Robert Johnson.

13. Actually, I think he was seventy-seven years old.

14. New Orleans jazz bandleader based in Chicago from 1918 to 1927, now chiefly remembered as an employer and mentor of Louis Armstrong.

15. Concentrated on the South Side, caused by competition for jobs and housing between the existing European migrant population and newly arrived black economic migrants from the South. The spark that set them off was an incident on a segregated swimming beach. The disturbances lasted a week; thirty-eight people died. In the predominantly Irish Bridgeport district, the Hamburg Athletic Club orchestrated some of the gang violence against blacks. Future Chicago mayor Richard J. Daley was a member of the club at the time.

16. By Peter Schwendener. Edition of August 27, 1982.

Chapter 2: Can Blue Men Sing the Whites?

1. British radio comedians from the 1950s: Harry Secombe, Spike Milligan, Michael Bentine and Peter Sellers. Very popular in their day, which was some time before mine.

2. Peter Cook and Dudley Moore, British comedy duo. Cook (1937–1995) was a merciless satirist, Moore (1935–2002) a gifted jazz pianist who also had some success as a comic actor in Hollywood.

3. English musicians and surrealists: Vivian Stanshall, Neil Innes, Roger Ruskin Spear, Rodney "Rhino" Desborough Slater, "Legs" Larry Smith and others.

4. At the Saville Theatre, 135 Shaftesbury Avenue, October 29, 1967.

5. Red Lightning R008, released 1972. Walter Horton accompanied by Robert Nighthawk, and Paul Butterfield accompanied by Smokey Smothers, Jerome Arnold and Sam Lay. Sessions recorded at Big John's, Wells Street, 1963.

6. Published by Eddison Press, London, 1975. Quote is from p. 61.

7. Published by the University of Chicago Press, 1966. It won the university's prize for the best master's thesis of 1963–64.

8. Promoters of the American Folk Blues Festival, a European roadshow put together with Memphis Slim (who lived in France) and on-the-spot help in Chicago from Willie Dixon, who was working for Chess Records at the time. Very important in developing the European popularity of the blues. The first one was in 1962. It ran annually until 1970 and lasted intermittently until the mid-1980s.

9. Published by Doubleday, New York, 1980.

10. Sidney Bechet performed in London in 1919 and reputedly bought his first soprano saxophone at Lafleur's on Wardour Street.

11. If, instead of the inestimable Chicago bluesman, Barber had introduced to British fans and musicians Clarence Gatemouth Brown, say, or Robert Junior Lockwood, the history of popular music might have turned out very different.

12. Decca ACL 1130. In spite of the title, a studio album.

13. Decca LK 4804.

14. Wonderful jazz, blues, and folk record shop in London, founded by Doug Dobell (1917–1987) at 77 Charing Cross Road and later also at 10 Rathbone Place. Closed in the late 1980s.

15. Legendary London music venue. Opened in the late 1950s on Oxford Street, then moved to Wardour Street, and finally to Charing Cross Road.

16. Then as now, a noted center of the music business in London and full of musical-instrument shops. Surprisingly short.

17. Elektra EKL-294. Liner notes by Pete Welding.

18. A wealthy enclave of Chicago's South Side, which includes the university.

19. Elektra EKL-315.

20. One of the first "supergroups": Eric Clapton (guitar), Jack Bruce (bass), Ginger Baker (drums). Toured exhaustively, especially in the United States, made several albums, and eventually expired at the end of 1968. Directly responsible for a lot of terrible later music.

21. Delmark DS-612.

22. At the time the main branch of the record store was at 11 West Grand Avenue.

23. Chess LP 1444. Personnel includes Pat Hare (guitar), James Cotton (harmonica), Francis Clay and Willie Smith (drums), Andrew Stephenson (bass) and Otis Spann (piano).

24. Same personnel as *Muddy Waters Sings Big Bill* (minus Willie Smith). The pre-eminent Chicago blues band, and a performance that set the standard for all subsequent imitators.

25. *Blues on the South Side*, Homesick James (Prestige 7388); *More Blues on the South Side*, Billy Boy Arnold (Prestige 7389) and *The Blues Never Die!*, Otis Spann (Prestige 7391).

26. Testament T-2203.

27. If these folk-music audiences were happier with the polished pastiche of John Hammond Jr.'s country blues than with the rustic efforts of real old bluesmen, I felt that they clearly couldn't have been troubled by "authenticity" in the way that many blues fans were. But maybe the folkies didn't expect it: the origins of much of their music were lost in the mist, whereas in 1982 the man who wrote "You Can't Lose What You Ain't Never Had" was still living out in Chicago's western suburbs. Someday, I thought, when there are no real old bluesmen left, the whole authenticity debate will simply evaporate. Maybe.

28. A thirty-five-hundred-seat art deco former cinema, opened in 1932. One of London's principal concert venues from the 1960s through to the 1980s.

29. On early versions of the record sleeve he was listed as "Friendly Chap," since Koester thought, wrongly, that Guy was under contract to Chess at the time.

30. Double live album by the Allman Brothers Band (Capricorn SD 2-802) that contains the inevitable *longueurs* interspersed with awe-inspiring musicianship and some of the finest electric blues guitar playing ever committed to tape.

31. Covered by the Grateful Dead on their eponymous first album, 1967.

32. The song starts: "I was born in Chicago in nineteen and forty one. My father told me, 'son, you'd better get a gun.'" To be fair, Butterfield didn't actually write it.

33. At the Newport Folk Festival, July 1965. His electric *Highway 61 Revisited* album came out at the end of August.

34. Delmark DS-647.

35. *Magic Sam Live*. Delmark DL-645/646. Released 1981. Recorded live at the Alex Club, 1963, and at the Ann Arbor Blues Festival, 1969.

36. Delmark DS-643. Recorded live at Hibiya Park, Tokyo, 1975. Released 1978. An absolute jewel of a record.

37. Recorded November 21, 1964, released by ABC Records in 1965. If you've only got space for one blues album, you might want to make it this one.

Chapter 3: At the Court of King Luther

1. In his magnificent *Deep Blues* (Viking, 1981), 266–67.

2. *Fast Fingers*. Delmark DS-623.

3. Straight and surprisingly long. On a clear day, the only thing that prevents you from seeing one end of Halsted Street from the other is the curvature of the earth.

4. An expression used to describe racial segregation laws in force in the South from the nineteenth century until the 1960s.

5. One of the most celebrated examples of a white band helping to boost the career of a blues musician was the Rolling Stones' invitation to Howlin' Wolf to appear with them on the American TV show *Shindig* in 1965.

6. During Luther Allison's ChicagoFest gig, August 4, 1982.

7. It perhaps wasn't quite as sudden a shift as Linkchain remembered, but the blues at that time was definitely in decline as hit-making music. You could still find Freddie King, Jimmy Reed, and B. B. King in the R&B charts in 1961, but you were more likely to encounter James Brown, Sam Cooke, or Etta James. The last time the Chicago blues really impacted the listings was back in 1955, when Little Walter's "My Babe" and Priscilla Bowman's "Hands Off" both reached number one.

8. Teardrop 001, 1981. The label was originally set up by Frank Bandy specifically to record the album.

9. *Johnny Littlejohn's Chicago Blues Stars*, Arhoolie 1043.

Chapter 4: Peeling Potatoes at Carey Bell's

1. Hound Dog Taylor and the Houserockers were among the most popular bands in Chicago, and famously the first to be recorded by Bruce Iglauer's Alligator Records. Hound Dog died in 1975.

2. Bluesway BLS-6079.

3. *Big Walter Horton with Carey Bell*, Alligator 4702, 1972.

4. Bruce Iglauer, boss of Alligator Records.

5. *Son of a Gun*, by Carey Bell and Lurrie Bell, Rooster R2617.

6. The United States was in recession. At the time of my interview with Bell, unemployment nationally was over 10 percent, and much higher in individual pockets such as Rockford, Illinois, which reached 25 percent in mid-1982. Inflation had been in double figures for three years.

7. A classic blues harmonica technique, imitating the mournful note of a steam train's whistle, invariably on a dark night in the middle of nowhere.

8. The annual ten-day music, burger, and beer bonanza on the city's dilapidated Navy Pier, which ran from 1978 to 1983, was organized and heavily branded by the mayor's office. It was one of the cultural highlights of the city summer, with seven music stages, numerous entertainment areas and dozens of food stalls, all for six dollars a day admission (five dollars in 1979). Most of the blues performers booked were based in the city, but the festival also provided opportunities to see some of those who didn't come to Chicago very often. Albert King played an excellent set in 1979, and I also saw Lightning Hopkins from right down in the front, close enough to shake his hand. Folk-blues stars Sonny Terry and Brownie McGhee put on a show at the 1982 Fest, which was memorable not just for the way their drummer, a lanky white boy with long hair, played the drums with a pair of springy padded coat hangers and the cymbals with a hammer, but also for the fact that the two elderly musicians obviously couldn't stand each other. Every time McGhee began a solo Terry would launch into one on his harmonica, cutting across him and drowning out the guitar. McGhee would stop and let his partner carry on, and then next time it would happen all over again. This occurred so often that after a while I realized it wasn't just inept and unprofessional, but quite deliberate, and that Terry's hurt, baleful expression seemed to be a shameless attempt to portray himself as the poor, wronged, blind man. McGhee also tried for our sympathy: "I'm trying to play, but he won't let me!" he complained, exasperated. They had known each other for forty years and had been a successful double act for most of that time. It had clearly been a little too long.

9. The band originally also had Willie Dixon's son Freddie Dixon on bass, which helped to justify the name. In 1982 the SoBs' usual bassist was the ubiquitous J. W. Williams, while Freddie played in his father's band, along with another brother, piano player Arthur Dixon.

10. Released in July 1982 and reached number 4 on the Billboard "Hot Black Singles" chart and number 8 in the U.K. singles chart. It was the first hip-hop record most people

had ever heard. The incident described, driving through the South Side listening to two young, black, blues musicians arguing about it, seemed such a gift for a writer that I can distinctly remember thinking, "no one's going to believe this."

11. A traditionally Irish area separated from the black South Side by the Dan Ryan Expressway. Deliberately, some said: the road was built during Richard J. Daley's tenure.

12. Published in 1971. Mike Royko was a *Daily News* journalist. Where lesser writers might only have been able to howl with rage, the masterful Royko dissected the bloated and corrupt and racist "Chicago machine" of Mayor Richard J. Daley with intelligence and humor. A timeless classic of political reportage. Daley was Chicago's mayor from 1955 to 1976.

13. 1625 East 67th Street.

14. Edition of October 5, 1978. Later reprised in *Deep Blues* (1981).

15. "Chicago's most beautiful cocktail bar," 167 North State Street.

16. This happened more than once. It seems artistic standards weren't always a priority at Chess Records.

Chapter 5: Turning the Tables at WXOL

1. WXOL renamed itself WVON in 1983.

2. Financial support for ex-military personnel, which included college tuition fees.

3. "Stoop Down Baby" was a favorite number.

4. It wasn't even the single off the album: that honor went to a song called "Cheating in the Next Room." The album reached number 17 and remained in the charts for two years.

5. By Blind Lemon Jefferson, 1927. Not generally believed to be about an actual snake.

6. Story from *Bluesland, Portraits of Twelve Major American Blues Masters*, edited by Pete Welding and Toby Byron, p. 43.

7. It was "Wee Wee Hours."

8. According to the BBC TV film *Blues America*, directed by Mick Gold.

9. Chicago's three-thousand-seat Regal Theater was on the corner of Grand Boulevard (now South Parkway) and Forty-Seventh Street. It opened in 1928, closed down in 1968, and was demolished in 1973.

10. Apparently some disagreement with the German record producer Siegfried Christmann.

11. One of the very first blues publications, launched in England in 1963. It lasted until 1987.

12. The longest of the three *Living Blues* obituaries of Big Walter Horton was by David Whiteis, and the other two were by *Living Blues* co-editor Jim O'Neal, and Alligator Records' Bruce Iglauer.

13. From the album *Johnson's Whacks*, Delmark DS-644.

14. Rooster R2615.

15. *Grand Slam*, by Magic Slim and the Teardrops, Rooster R2618.

16. Rooster R2616.

17. Now broadcast online at WDCB.

18. According to Doc, the only excuse Lee Shot could offer was to claim that he wasn't sure he was booked, and so he had decided not to turn up. I suspected that the singer was dismayed by the thin crowd for the second gig and didn't want to perform for an empty room.

19. 1604 West Van Buren Street.

20. Argo LP 4031, later re-released under various titles, including *Blues from Big Bill's Copa Cabana* (Chess CH 9181). My own 1967 copy is on Pye Records' Marble Arch imprint (MAL 724), titled *Festival of the Blues*. The backing band were: Dave Myers (bass), Jarrett Gibson and Donald Hankins (saxophones) and Fred Below (drums). There was also a track by Sonny Boy Williamson, a first outing for "Bring It on Home," which was studio-recorded and spliced in later with dubbed applause, as was one of Buddy Guy's.

21. Also appears on the album *Muddy Waters Folk Singer* as "My Home Is in the Delta."

22. So said Paul McCartney at a press conference, according to legend, after the Beatles were asked what they wanted to see in the United States. I haven't been able to find a clip to confirm it.

Chapter 6: Fried Mississippi Catfish Blues

1. *Lefty Dizz feat. Big Moose Walker*, Black & Blue GP 346, 1979. Recorded in Chicago at the Paul Miller Studio, engineered by Harry Brotman.

2. Dizz did two songs on *Spivey's Blues Showcase*, Spivey 1017, 1975, and played as guest guitarist on Spivey 1023, 1980. Victoria Spivey (1906–1976) was a successful blues singer in the 1920s and 1930s whose later record label was noteworthy for the spectacularly amateurish nature of its sleeves.

3. Wells must eventually have come to some agreement with ChicagoFest's organizers, because he and Buddy Guy were booked that summer and played a very fine show.

4. *Blues People*, by LeRoi Jones (who later called himself Amiri Baraka), published by Morrow, 1963.

5. The writer David Whiteis read an early draft of this and suggested an alternative interpretation: "Junior was a proud and resolutely urbane man; nonetheless, in an all-black setting, or at least a setting where he wasn't being paraded as an 'authenticity' exhibit for a white writer, he never denied his roots. In fact, at Theresa's he used to point to a Depression-era photograph of a little boy in a sharecropping family, on the wall behind the stage, and claim that it was actually a picture of himself as a child. It seems to me that he was reacting against Metcalfe's attempt to exhibit him for this white interloper." Faced with this "implied racial condescension," Whiteis continued, Junior "probably gritted his teeth and put up with it when playing in predominantly white venues, but never expected to have to deal with it so close to home."

6. Itself a pretty faithful homage to John Lee Hooker.

7. Some sources say Dizz was in the air force. I didn't ask him myself, but Sammy Lawhorn told me Dizz was an infantryman.

8. Carl Jones Records recorded Earl Hooker, Homesick James, and Detroit Junior, among others, and was the first label to record Hound Dog Taylor. Jones (1913–1985) had been a singer and worked as a barman at Theresa's.

9. This was Bobby "Top Hat" Davis. His son grew up to become Eric "Guitar" Davis, who was murdered in 2013.

10. The average waiting time between rides was much longer in the United States than in the United Kingdom, but the length of the average ride was much longer, too. People in the United States also seemed more generous and hospitable, but it might just have been that longer rides gave them more opportunities to buy me lunch.

11. But not with impunity: Wyman and two of his fellow Stones were arrested and fined for the offence, which took place in Essex in 1965.

12. For years the interior of my local London arts cinema, the Ritzy in Brixton, was decorated with amateurish painted murals. One of them, near the door on the left-hand wall, was of Big Walter, copied, I think, from the much-reproduced Marcel Imsand photograph, with harmonica, microphone, and cigarette. I never tired of pointing it out to my friends whenever *The Blues Brothers* was shown there.

Chapter 7: Comparing Hangovers at Alligator

1. I was thinking of Johnson's "Terraplane Blues," but the line also occurs in his "Sweet Home Chicago."

2. This rift must eventually have been patched up, because in the 1990s Alligator released four Luther Allison albums.

3. Alligator 4701. It was followed three years later by *Natural Boogie* (4704) and finally by a posthumous live album, *Beware of the Dog* (4707), in 1976.

4. Jazz Record Mart alumni included Jim and Amy O'Neal, Charlie Musselwhite, Pete Welding, Mike Bloomfield, and many others.

5. Chess LP 1501, 1965. The first of a series of Chess reissues as the label repackaged its gold mine of 78s and 45s for new, white, album-buying folk fans in the pre–British-invasion era. (An earlier "Best of" compilation, Chess LP 1427, was released in 1958.) Not to be confused with *Muddy Waters Folk Singer* (Chess LP 1483, 1964), an acoustic album that was an attempt to repackage the man himself for a folk music audience.

6. 3730 North Clark Street. On another occasion at Stages when I went along to see Willie Dixon, Otis Blackwell was the support act. The writer of many rock 'n' roll classics, including "All Shook Up," "Fever," and "Great Balls of Fire," had a laconic way of introducing his songs: "I'd like to thank Elvis, again, for recording this one . . ."

7. *Big Walter Horton with Carey Bell*, Alligator 4702, 1972.

8. As a movement, "disco sucks" certainly had legs. Nearly sixty thousand people turned up to Dahl's bonfire of inanity at Comiskey Park, and chaos duly ensued.

9. *Midnight Son*, Alligator 4708, 1976; *Live and Burning*, Alligator 4712, 1978; *Chicago Fire*, Alligator 4720, 1980.

10. A so-called "diddley bow." A bottle would be used for a bridge.

11. Published by Omnibus, 1971. Highly recommended.

12. *I Got What It Takes*, Alligator 4706, 1975; *The Earthshaker*, Alligator 4711, 1978; *From the Heart of a Woman*, Alligator 4724, 1981. Taylor also recorded an album on the French label Black & Blue in 1973, and Chess had earlier released a singles compilation.

13. *Ice Pickin*, Alligator 4713, 1978.

14. *Broke and Hungry*, Capitol ST-403. Lonnie Brooks's first album, released under the name of Guitar Junior.

15. *Sweet Home Chicago*, Black & Blue 554.

16. *Bayou Lightning*, Alligator 4714; *Turn on the Night*, Alligator 4721.

17. *Somebody Loan Me a Dime*, Alligator 4705, 1974, and *I Hear Some Blues Downstairs*, Alligator 4710, 1977.

18. But not permanently: in 1984 there was a third Alligator album by Fenton Robinson: *Nightflight*, 4736.

19. From an accident in a cotton gin, I was told.

20. The French production was packaged by Alligator as *Raw Magic*, 4728. The Rooster album was *Grand Slam*, R2618. Both excellent, but there is a very appealing roughness around the edges of the Rooster effort.

Chapter 8: Louis Myers's White Eldorado

1. A DVD of this 1981 performance at the Checkerboard was released in 2012.

2. He had played a gig in France the night before and had another in Wisconsin the following day. He looked knackered.

3. The neighborhood bears that name again today. But I never heard it used in 1979 or 1982.

4. Blues fans from Europe were not an uncommon sight, and I noted their arrival in July and August as one might mark the first migrating birds. Many of them were musicians, who would sit in when they could. Some stayed.

5. Advent 2809. A worthwhile album by a blues great, backed by excellent session musicians.

6. Johnny Dollar was a big man who looked like he could take care of himself, and he had an arrogant manner that could sometimes seem aggressive. But a lot of it was bluster. Standing around outside B.L.U.E.S in the early hours one morning with him and his girlfriend Barbara, who worked behind the bar, we watched from across the street as a young harmonica player had an argument with his girlfriend. Suddenly the girl whacked the musician on the side of the head with her umbrella and ran off down Halsted. He looked a little sheepish, and as he walked after her Johnny Dollar remarked laconically to Barbara: "If that was you, you know what would happen. Casualty ward." Barbara glanced at me and rolled her eyes.

7. The Muck Muck Man was variously known as Yochanan, The Man from the Sun, and The Space Age Vocalist. He was a rock 'n' roll singer, a Maxwell Street character and a sometime collaborator with jazz extraterrestrial Sun Ra.

8. It is a sign of the respect accorded to Muddy Waters that Theresa Needham should call him that. She was two years older than him.

9. When Sammy Lawhorn wasn't being a sleepy drunk, he could be charming company, and Theresa Needham was right about his musical accomplishments. He was from Arkansas and had served with great distinction in Muddy Waters's band. He could play incisive electric lead guitar when required, but he was most memorable when playing solo, country-style blues, which he did with great subtlety and feeling. I never saw anyone better. I once spent a pleasant half-hour with him at a table in Theresa's, talking and sharing his bottle of gin. He was modest about his music, forty-seven years old, and had the civilized knack of appearing as interested in me as I was in him. He'd served in Korea as an aerial photographer in a navy reconnaissance squadron, he explained, had been injured in the side by anti-aircraft fire, and lost part of his left thumb. He received a pension of nine hundred dollars a month.

10. Published by Barrie and Rockliff, 1969, and subsequently by Penguin. It accompanied the CBS double album of the same name.

11. A major Chicago venue at 6200 South Cottage Grove Avenue, with an ornate Louis XVI interior. Opened 1922, demolished 1967.

12. That is if my compilation LP was anything to go by (*I Was Walking through the Woods*, Buddy Guy, Chess LP 409, 1970). I have heard subsequent reissues on CD that attempt to bring the guitar more to the foreground.

13. *Sonny Boy Williamson*, Chess 427004, 1976. A double LP set of twenty-four songs with liner notes by Cub Coda.

14. *Chicago Anthology*, Sunnyland KS-101, 1970. Fourteen songs by Homesick James, Big Walter Horton, Prez Kenneth, Smokey Smothers, Poor Bob Woodfork, L. C. McKinley, and Snooky Prior, with compendious notes by Mike Leadbitter.

15. Vanguard VSD-79272, 1967.

16. Vanguard VSD-79290, 1968.

17. Barclay 920 332/333, 1972

18. Atlantic SD 33-364, 1972. A session set up by Eric Clapton, a Buddy Guy fan.

19. JSP 1009, 1980.

20. *Buddy Guy & Junior Wells Live in Montreux*, Black & Blue 33.530. Recorded July 9, 1978, with Jimmy Johnson, Jack Myers, and Odie Payne.

21. *The Red Hot Blues of Phil Guy*, JSP 1047, 1982.

Epilogue: Fade to Black

1. Important London rock venue that hosted numerous major concerts during the 1960s and 1970s. Originally opened in 1930 as a cinema called The Astoria. Now headquarters to a Brazilian religious cult.

2. Large London venue originally built in the 1920s as a cinema. Closed 2009 and demolished.

3. Iconic twenty-five-hundred-seat South Bank venue, opened in 1951. One of the first concert halls with scientifically designed acoustics, which didn't cope especially well with Buddy Guy.

4. Bobby Bland and B. B. King *Together for the First Time . . . Live* (MCA 2-4160 DS 50190), 1974, and *Together Again . . . Live* (MCA27102), 1980.

5. Famous London venue, still in business, originally established in 1942. Mainly known for its historic jazz connections, but various punk bands played there in the 1970s.

6. Young's ordinary bitter, which was then still brewed in Wandsworth, a few miles away. Eli seemed to like it.

7. University of California Press, 2002.

8. Alligator 4723, released 1981. Originally Isabel WE 341, *The Blues Giant*. Recorded in France, produced by Didier Tricard.

9. The same effect appears to be evident in the albums Guy has recorded since signing to the Silvertone label in 1991.

10. See Rotella's "Too Many Notes" essay in *Good with Their Hands*.

Biographical Notes

People are listed under the names by which they're best known. Where those names include real (or apparently real) surnames, they are listed by surname (for example: Hill, Big Bill). Nicknames and stage names are listed according to their first word (as in Lefty Dizz [Walter Williams]). Given names are, of course, listed alphabetically by surname, last name first (Davis, Larry).

Abrams, Ronald: outstanding guitarist who worked in Johnny Dollar's band and is believed to have moved to Europe in the 1980s.

Allen, Albert "Pete": d. Chicago, 2008. Exceptional guitar player who often worked alongside Magic Slim.

Allison, Bernard: b. Chicago, 1965. Blues guitarist and singer. Son of Luther Allison. Based in France.

Allison, Luther: b. Widener, Arkansas, 1939; d. Madison, Wisconsin, 1997.

Bandy, Frank: bass player with Hip Linkchain's band, among others. Founder of Teardrop Records.

Barber, Chris: b. Welwyn Garden City, Hertfordshire, 1930. British jazz bandleader famous for bringing blues musicians over from America in the late 1950s.

Bell, Carey: b. Macon, Mississippi, 1936; d. Chicago 2007. Harmonica player and bandleader.

Bell, Lurrie: b. Chicago, 1958. Guitarist and singer. Son of Carey Bell.

Below, Fred: b. Chicago 1926; d. Chicago, 1988. Drummer. Played in the army with Lester Young, on numerous Chess Records sessions, and in the 1950s was a key member of crucial Chicago blues band The Aces. In 1982, arguably the best blues drummer in Chicago.

Benton, Arley "Buster": b. Texarkana, Arkansas, 1932; d. Chicago 1996. Guitarist and bandleader.

Big Bill Broonzy (Lee Conley Bradley): b. Scott, Mississippi, 1893; d. Chicago 1958. Guitarist and singer. A bridge between the solo country blues and the postwar urban blues band styles, he was a hugely successful and influential recording artist who inspired and mentored many younger musicians.

Big Time Sarah (Streeter): b. Coldwater, Mississippi, 1953; d. Chicago, 2015. Singer.

Bishop, Elvin: b. Glendale, California, 1942. Blues and rock guitarist. Moved in 1959 to study at the University of Chicago; taught by Smokey Smothers and played in Paul Butterfield's band before going solo in 1969.

Bland, Bobby "Blue": b. Rosemont, Tennessee, 1930; d. Memphis, 2013. Superstar blues singer on the chitlin circuit who cut his first singles in 1951 and recorded constantly thereafter.

Bloomfield, Mike: b. Chicago, 1943; d. San Francisco 1981. Guitar player, already a recognized talent when he joined Paul Butterfield's band in 1964. Collaborated with Bob Dylan and played on the famous electric set at Newport Folk Festival in 1965. Formed Electric Flag in 1967. Worked as a solo artist through the 1970s. Died of a drug overdose.

Bonnie Lee (Jessie Lee Frealls): b. Bunkie, Louisiana, 1931; d. Chicago, 2006. Jazz and blues singer who collaborated with Sunnyland Slim and Willie Kent.

Boyd, Eddie: b. Clarksdale, Mississippi, 1914; d. Helsinki, Finland, 1994. Piano player, singer and songwriter. Lived in Finland from 1970.

Branch, Billy: b. Great Lakes, Illinois, 1951. Harmonica player, bandleader, and educator.

Brooks, Lonnie (Lee Baker Jr.): b. Dubuisson, Louisiana, 1933. Guitarist, singer, bandleader, and Alligator recording artist.

Brown, Clarence "Gatemouth": b. Vinton, Louisiana, 1924; d. Orange, Texas, 2005. Phenomenal, eclectic, Texan multi-instrumentalist.

Burnside, R. L.: b. Harmontown, Mississippi, 1926; d. Memphis, 2005. Wonderful "country blues" singer and guitarist, recorded in 1967 by Arhoolie but had to wait until the 1990s for recognition and commercial success.

Burton, Aron: b. Senatobia, Mississippi, 1938. Bass player, singer, and songwriter who served in the bands of Freddie King, Junior Wells, and Albert Collins, among others.

Butterfield, Paul: b. Chicago, 1942; d. Hollywood, California, 1987. Singer and harmonica player of inestimable significance in popularizing the Chicago blues with white audiences. Died of a drug overdose.

Charters, Samuel: b. Pittsburgh, Pennsylvania, 1929; d. Arsta, Sweden, 2015. Music historian, producer, and writer.

Chess, Leonard: b. Motal, Poland, 1917; d. Chicago, 1969. Club owner and record executive, co-founder of Aristocrat and then Chess Records with brother Phil (b. 1921). Sold the company in 1969.

Clapton, Eric: b. Ripley, Surrey, 1945. Influential English singer and guitarist.

Copeland, Martha: dates unknown. Singer from the "classic blues" era who recorded between 1923 and 1928.

Cotton, James: b. Tunica, Mississippi, 1935. Harmonica player and bandleader famous for his work as a sideman with Howlin' Wolf and, especially, Muddy Waters.

Crawford, Ernest "Big": b. 1891 (or 1892, or 1897); d. Memphis, 1956. String bass session musician chiefly remembered for his contributions to Muddy Waters's early Chess recordings.

Davis, Blind John: b. Hattiesburg, Mississippi, 1913; d. Chicago, 1985. Singer and piano player.

Davis, Cyril: b. Denham, Buckinghamshire, 1932; d. 1964. One of the earliest British blues harmonica players. Formed Blues Incorporated with Alexis Korner in 1961.

Davis, Larry: b. Kansas City, Missouri, 1936; d. Los Angeles, 1994. Recorded "Texas Flood" on Duke in 1958 (accompanied by Fenton Robinson on guitar) and made an album for Rooster in 1982.

Dawkins, Jimmy: b. Tchula, Mississippi, 1936; d. Chicago, 2013. Singer and guitarist first recorded by Delmark in 1969, associated with Chicago's West Side.

Detroit Junior (Emery Williams Jr.): b. Haynes, Arkansas, 1931; d. Chicago, 2005. Pianist and songwriter who worked with Howlin' Wolf.

Dixon, Willie: b. Vicksburg, Mississippi, 1915; d. Burbank, California, 1992. Singer, bass player, Chess and Cobra Records producer and prolific songwriter.

Eckstine, Billy: b. Pittsburgh, Pennsylvania, 1914; d. Pittsburgh, 1993. Singer and bandleader of the swing era.

Eddie Clearwater (Edward Harrington): b. Macon, Mississippi, 1935. Singer and guitarist, part of Chicago's West Side scene in the early 1950s. First recorded 1958; from 1980 made several albums for Rooster and Alligator.

Embry, "Queen" Sylvia: b. Wabbaseka, Arkansas, 1941; d. 1992. Singer and bass player, married to guitarist Johnny Embry.

Estes, "Sleepy" John: b. Nutbush, Tennessee, 1899; d. Brownsville, Tennessee, 1977. Country blues singer who first recorded in 1929, tracked down by Bob Koester and Samuel Charters in 1962.

Ford, Thomas (Thomas Langsford): b. Plymouth, England, 1985. Guitarist and singer.

Freund, Steve: b. New York, 1952. Guitarist and singer. Sideman to Big Walter Horton and Sunnyland Slim.

Green, Peter (Peter Allen Greenbaum): b. London, 1947. Excellent blues guitar player who went on to become a founding member of the successful rock group Fleetwood Mac with fellow Bluesbreakers alumni Mick Fleetwood and John McVie. Struggled with schizophrenia through the 1970s and 80s, and has since played with the Peter Green Splinter Group and Peter Green and Friends.

Guitar Slim (Eddie Jones): b. Greenwood, Mississippi, 1926; d. New York, 1959. Singer, guitarist, and seminal figure in electric blues and rock 'n' roll.

Guy, George "Buddy": b. Lettsworth, Louisiana, 1936.

Guy, Phil: b. Lettsworth, Louisiana, 1940; d. Chicago Heights, Illinois, 2008. Excellent guitarist and bandleader, but chiefly famous for being Buddy Guy's younger brother.

Hammond, John, Jr.: b. New York, 1942. Guitarist and singer. Son of producer, blues talent scout, and historian John Hammond (1910–1987).

Harvey, Ted: b. Chicago, 1930. Drummer with Hound Dog Taylor and the Houserockers.

Helfer, Erwin: b. Chicago, 1936. Blues and boogie-woogie piano player, proprietor of Red Beans Records. Long-time accompanist to singer Mama Yancey.

Hendrix, James Marshall "Jimi": b. Seattle, 1942; d. London, 1970. Ultimate blues and rock guitar player.

Hill, Arzell "Z. Z.": b. Naples, Texas, 1935; d. Dallas, Texas, 1984. Soul blues singer whose greatest success was the 1982 album *Down Home*.

Hill, "Big" Bill: b. England, Arkansas, 1914. Blues promoter and disc jockey.

Hip Linkchain (Willie Richard): b. Jackson, Mississippi, 1936; d. Chicago, 1989. Singer, bandleader, and guitarist.

Homesick James (John William Henderson): b. Somerville, Tennessee, 1910 (or 1914); d. Springfield, Missouri, 2006. Singer and slide guitarist. Member of Elmore James's band for some years.

Hooker, Earl: b. Quitman County, Mississippi, 1929; d. Chicago, 1970. Revered guitar virtuoso.

Hooker, John Lee: b. Coahoma County, Mississippi, 1917; d. Los Altos, California, 2001. Blues legend who made his first recordings in 1948 and remained a successful and inspirational performer until the end of his life.

Hopkins, Sam "Lightning": b. Centerville, Texas, 1912; d. Houston, 1982. Influential singer and guitar player who learned from Blind Lemon Jefferson and recorded prolifically, starting in 1946.

Horton, "Big" Walter: b. Horn Lake, Mississippi; 1918; d. Chicago, 1981. Revered harmonica player who grew up in Memphis and moved to Chicago in the early 1950s. Backed virtually everyone from the 1930s to the 1970s. Seldom worked as a bandleader but did record for Sam Philips in 1951 and made an album under his own name on Argo in 1964: *The Soul of Blues Harmonica*, with Buddy Guy, Jack Myers, and Willie Smith.

House, Eddie James "Son": b. Lyon, Mississippi, 1902; d. Detroit, 1988. Influential singer and slide guitarist who first recorded in 1930 and had a second career at folk and blues festivals in the 1960s.

Howlin' Wolf (Chester Burnett): b. White Station, Mississippi, 1910; d. Hines, Illinois, 1976. One of the blues greats and a force of nature. When Sun Records' Sam Phillips first heard the Wolf, he said, "This is where the soul of man never dies."

Humes, Helen: b. Louisville, Kentucky, 1909; d. Santa Monica, California, 1981. Successful and much-recorded blues and swing singer who worked with Count Basie.

Hutto, Joseph Benjamin "J.B.": b. Blackville, South Carolina, 1926; d. Harvey, Illinois, 1983. Master of the slide guitar.

Iglauer, Bruce: b. Ann Arbor, Michigan, 1947. Founder and owner of Alligator Records.

James, Elmore: b. Richland, Mississippi, 1918; d. Chicago, 1963. Hugely influential singer and slide guitarist who first recorded in Jackson in 1951.

James, Nehemiah "Skip": b. Bentonia, Mississippi, 1902; d. Philadelphia, Pennsylvania, 1969. Blues singer and guitarist who recorded first in 1931 and then again after his "rediscovery" in the 1960s. One of the greatest.

Jefferson, Blind Lemon: b. Couthman, Texas, 1893; d. Chicago 1929. Popular, successful, and influential blues singer and guitarist.

Johnny Dollar (John Sibley): b. Greenville, Mississippi, 1941. Singer, guitarist, and bandleader. Brother of Lefty Dizz. Served in the military until age thirty, played in covers bands before moving into blues. Recorded albums for Isabel in 1980, the B.L.U.E.S R&B label in 1986, Wolf in 2000.

Johnny Littlejohn (John Wesley Funchess): b. Lake, Mississippi, 1931; d. Chicago, 1994. Superb blues singer and guitarist highly respected in Chicago but little recorded.

Johnny Twist (John Williams): singer and guitarist. Few biographical details available. He had a shop called Old Dusty's on Forty-Third Street almost opposite the Checkerboard Lounge. The shop sold records and tapes, and a variety of miscellaneous items, including wigs.

Johnson, Jimmy (James Earl Thompson): b. Holly Springs, Mississippi, 1928. Singer, guitarist, and keyboard player.

Johnson, Lonnie: b. New Orleans, 1899; d. Ontario, Canada, 1970. Prolific and highly influential blues singer and guitar player.

Johnson, Robert: b. Hazlehurst, Mississippi, 1911; d. Greenwood, Mississippi, 1938. Archetypal Delta blues singer and slide guitarist whose phenomenally good 1930s recordings, released on LP by Columbia in the 1960s, proved hugely influential on the white blues and rock movement. A vacuum of sketchy biographical information at that time was filled by frenzied mythmaking.

Johnson, Syl (Sylvester Thompson): b. Holly Springs, Mississippi, 1936. Blues, R&B, and soul singer, guitarist, and harmonica player. Brother of Jimmy Johnson.

Johnson, Tommy: b. Terry, Mississippi, 1896; d. Crystal Springs, Mississippi, 1956. Important early Delta blues recording artist on the Paramount and Victor labels. Composer of "Canned Heat Blues" and "Big Road Blues."

Johnson, Willie: b. Senatobia, Mississippi, 1923; d. Chicago, 1995. Seminal guitarist whose recordings with Howlin' Wolf in the early 1950s wrote the opening chapter of heavy rock.

Jones, Floyd: b. Marianna, Arkansas, 1917; d. Chicago 1989. Singer, guitarist, and bass player. His 1947 sides "Stockyard Blues" and "Keep What You Got" on Marvel are regarded as some of the earliest Chicago blues on record. Also wrote "Hard Times," "School Days" and "On the Road Again."

Jones, LeRoi (Everett LeRoi Jones, Imamu Amiri Baraka): b. Newark, New Jersey, 1934; d. Newark, New Jersey, 2014. Writer, poet, dramatist and critic. Author of *Blues People*, 1963.

Jordan, Louis: b. Brinkley, Arkansas, 1908; d. Los Angeles, 1975. Phenomenally successful bandleader, singer, and songwriter in the 1940s, and one of the originators of R&B.

Kansas City Red (Arthur Lee Stevenson): b. Drew, Mississippi, 1926; d. Chicago, 1991. Drummer.

Keil, Charles: b. Norwalk, Connecticut, 1939. Anthropologist, ethnomusicologist and professor; author of *Urban Blues*.

King, Albert (Albert King Nelson): b. Indianola, Mississippi, 1923; d. Memphis, 1992. Guitar legend.

King, Freddie: b. Gilmer, Texas, 1934; d. Dallas, Texas, 1976. Guitar legend.

King, Riley "B.B.": b. Berclair, Mississippi, 1925. Blues legend. Probably the most influential guitar player of all time, in any genre.

Kirkland, Frank: b. Washington D.C., 1927; d. 1973. Much in demand bass player whose work can be heard on numerous Chess, Delmark, and Vanguard recordings.

Koester, Bob: b. Wichita, Kansas, 1932. Owner of the Jazz Record Mart and founder of Delmark Records.

Korner, Alexis: b. Paris, 1928; d. London, 1984. Musician, bandleader, and club owner. One of the founding fathers of British blues, notably with Cyril Davis in Blues Incorporated.

Lawhorn, Sammy: b. Little Rock, Arkansas, 1935; d. Chicago 1990. Superb guitarist, best known as a member of Muddy Waters's band from 1964 to 1973.

Leadbelly (Huddie Ledbetter), b. Louisiana 1888; d. New York 1949. Prolific folk and blues musician and recording artist.

Leary, S.P.: b. Carthage, Texas, 1930; d. Chicago, 1998. Drummer. Toured with T-Bone Walker in the 1940s and later backed both Howlin' Wolf and Muddy Waters.

Left-Hand Frank (Craig): b. Greenville, Mississippi, 1935; d. Los Angeles, 1992. Singer and guitarist.

Lefty Dizz (Walter Williams): b. Osceola, Arkansas, 1937; d. Chicago 1993. Singer and guitarist.

Lightning Slim (Otis Hicks): b. St Louis, Missouri, 1913; d. Detroit, Michigan, 1974. Louisiana-based singer and guitar player who recorded through the 1950s on Excello and enjoyed success with white audiences later in his career.

Lipscomb, Mance: b. Navasota, Texas, 1895; d. Navasota, Texas, 1976. Musician and farmer discovered and recorded by Arhoolie in 1960.

Little Milton (James Milton Campbell): b. Inverness, Mississippi, 1935, d. 2005. Singer, guitarist, and blues superstar on the chitlin circuit.

Little Walter (Jacobs): b. Marksville, Louisiana, 1930; d. Chicago, 1968. Seminal harmonica player who played with the Muddy Waters band before enjoying huge commercial success in his own right.

Lofton, Cripple Clarence: b. Kingsport, Tennessee, 1897; d. Chicago, 1957. Early boogie-woogie pianist and singer, and composer of the Willie Mabon hit "I Don't Know."

Lovie Lee (Edward Lee Watson): b. Chattanooga, Tennessee, 1909; d. Chicago, 1997. Piano player and singer who worked with Carey Bell and Muddy Waters and recorded a session for Alligator Records' *Living Chicago Blues* series.

Lyons, Willie James: b. Alabama 1938; d. Chicago, 1980. Singer and guitarist who worked mainly as a sideman, although he did record an album for Isabel in 1979.

Mabon, Willie: b. Hollywood, Tennessee, 1925; d. Paris, 1985. Singer and piano player best known for "I Don't Know," which stayed at no. 1 in the R&B charts for eight weeks in 1952.

Magic Sam (Sam Maghett): b. Grenada, Mississippi, 1937; d. Chicago, 1969. West Side guitarist and singer whose recorded output does scant justice to his phenomenal talent.

Magic Slim (Morris Holt): b. Torrance, Mississippi, 1937; d. Philadelphia, 2013. Guitarist, singer, and bandleader.

Margolin, Bob: b. Brookline, Massachusetts, 1949. Guitarist. Played in Muddy Waters's band from 1973 to 1980 and can be seen in the film *The Last Waltz*.

Mayall, John: b. Macclesfield, Cheshire, 1933. Singer, multi-instrumentalist, and pivotal member of the British blues boom; his band, the Bluesbreakers, served as an academy for numerous musicians.

McClennan, Tommy: b. Durant, Mississippi, 1905; d. Chicago, 1961. Delta blues singer and guitarist who recorded on Bluebird, 1939–42. Composer of "Cross Cut Saw Blues," among others.

McTell, Blind Willie: b. Thomson, Georgia, 1898; d. Milledgeville, Georgia, 1959. Prolific and influential singer and guitarist who recorded for various labels through the 1920s and 1930s.

Melrose, Lester: b. Sumner, Illinois, 1891; d. Lake, Florida, 1968. One of the most significant prewar Chicago record producers, particularly associated with Bluebird Records.

Memphis Slim (John Chatman, aka Peter): b. Memphis, 1915; d. Paris, 1988. Piano player, bandleader, singer, and songwriter. First recorded in 1940, collaborated with Big Bill Broonzy and Willie Dixon, moved permanently to Paris in 1962.

Montgomery, Eurreal "Little Brother": b. Kentwood, Louisiana, 1906; d. Champaign, Illinois, 1985. Renowned piano player and singer.

Muddy Waters (McKinley Morganfield): b. Issaquena, Mississippi, 1913; d. Westmont, Illinois, 1983. Singer, songwriter, guitarist, and bandleader. The godfather of Chicago blues.

Murray, Eli (Elisha Blue): guitarist. Friend and associate of Lurrie Bell, last heard of en route to Amsterdam in 1985.

Myers, Dave: b. Byhalia, Mississippi, 1926; d. 2001. Pioneer electric bass player, brother of Louis, and founder member of The Aces.

Myers, Jack: b. 1936, d. 2011. Influential electric bass player who collaborated with Buddy Guy, Earl Hooker, Sonny Boy Williamson and others.

Myers, Louis: b. Byhalia, Mississippi, 1929; d. Chicago, 1994. Guitarist, harmonica player, and singer. Brother of Dave and founder member of The Aces.

Needham, Theresa: b. Meridian, Mississippi, 1912; d. Chicago, 1992. Club owner: Theresa's Lounge, 1949–1983.

Nighthawk, Robert (Robert Lee McCollum): b. Helena, Arkansas, 1909; d. Helena, Arkansas, 1967. Respected and moderately successful singer and guitarist.

Oliver, Paul: b. Nottingham, England, 1927. Architect, academic, and hugely important blues writer and researcher.

Patton, Charley: b. Edwards, Mississippi, 1887–91; d. Indianola, Mississippi, 1934. Singer, guitarist and "father of the Delta blues."

Payne, Odie, Jr.: b. Chicago, 1926; d. Chicago 1989. Superb drummer who worked with virtually everyone, most notably Elmore James, Muddy Waters, Sonny Boy Williamson, and Chuck Berry.

Payton, Dion: b. Greenwood, Mississippi, 1950. Singer, guitarist, and leader of the 43rd Street Blues Band.

Peetie Wheatstraw (William Bunch): b. Ripley, Tennessee, 1902; d. St Louis, Missouri, 1941. Popular and influential blues singer and guitarist who first recorded in 1930.

Perkins, Joe Willie "Pinetop": b. Belzoni, Mississippi, 1913; d. Austin, Texas, 2011. Blues and boogie-woogie piano player famous for his association with Muddy Waters.

Phillips, Brewer: b. Coila, Mississippi, 1924; d. Chicago, 1999. Guitarist with Hound Dog Taylor and the Houserockers.

Pryor, James Edward "Snooky": b. Lambert, Mississippi, 1921; d. Cape Girardeau, Missouri, 2006. Harmonica player, one of the pioneers of electric amplification.

Race, Wesley: b. Wichita, Kansas, 1947. Writer and producer. Early investor in Alligator Records.

Rachell, James "Yank": b. Brownsville, Tennessee, 1910; d. Indianapolis, 1997. Country blues guitar and mandolin player.

Rainey, Ma (Gertrude Pridgett): b. Columbus, Georgia, 1886; d. Rome, Georgia, 1939. "The Mother of the Blues," one of the first of the "classic" blues singers to record, in 1923.

Richard, Cliff (Harry Webb): b. Lucknow, India, 1940. British rock 'n' roller who scored his first hit in 1958.

Robinson, Fenton: b. Greenwood, Mississippi, 1935; d. Rockford, Illinois, 1997. Singer and guitar player who recorded in the late 1950s for Meteor and Duke, and later for Alligator.

Robinson, Freddy (Abu Talib): b. Memphis, 1939; d. Lancaster, California, 2009. Blues and jazz guitarist who worked with Howlin' Wolf, Little Walter, and Jimmy Rogers; studied at the Chicago School of Music before moving to Los Angeles in the 1960s to join Ray Charles's band.

Robinson, Michael: b. 1957; d. Chicago, 2007. Stupendously good guitarist who played in the Tuff Enuff house band at Theresa's Lounge and worked alongside Koko Taylor, among others.

Rogers, Jimmy: b. Ruleville, Mississippi, 1924; d. Chicago, 1997. Wonderful old-school singer, guitarist and songwriter who worked with Muddy Waters and also recorded in his own right for Chess.

Rush, Otis: b. Philadelphia, Mississippi, 1935. Singer and utterly stupendous guitarist: one of the seminal stylists of blues and rock.

Rushing, Jimmy: b. Oklahoma City, 1901; d. New York, 1972. Blues, jazz and swing singer, long associated with Count Basie's band.

Sain, Oliver: b. Dundee, Mississippi, 1932; d. St. Louis, 2003. Renowned St. Louis musician, bandleader, and producer who played drums for Sonny Boy Williamson and Howlin' Wolf, wrote "Don't Mess Up a Good Thing," and launched the careers of Little Milton, Bobby McClure, and Fontella Bass.

Scott, Kenneth "Buddy": b. Goodman, Mississippi, 1935; d. Chicago, 1994. Singer and guitarist, leader of the band Scotty and the Rib Tips.

Seals, Frank "Son": b. Osceola, Arkansas, 1942; d. Chicago, 2004. Singer and guitarist who made a total of nine albums, eight of them on Alligator.

Shakey Jake (Harris): b. Earle, Arkansas, 1921; d. Forrest City, Arkansas, 1990. Singer, songwriter, and harmonica player who often worked with nephew Magic Sam.

Shaw, Eddie: b. Stringtown, Mississippi, 1937. Saxophonist who worked in Howlin' Wolf's band from 1972 and took it over on Wolf's death in 1976, renaming it the Wolf Gang.

Shaw, Eddie "Vaan" Jr.: b. 1955. Guitarist, singer, and songwriter, son of Eddie Shaw.

Shines, Johnny: b. Memphis, Tennessee, 1915; d. Tuscaloosa, Alabama, 1992. Delta blues singer and guitarist who traveled with Robert Johnson and later settled in Chicago.

Smith, Bessie: b. Chattanooga, Tennessee, 1894; d. Clarksdale, Mississippi, 1937. One of the most popular singers and recording artists of the "classic" era: the "Queen of the Blues."

Smith, Willie "Big Eyes": b. Helena, Arkansas, 1936; d. 2011. Drummer and harmonica player best known for his long association with the Muddy Waters band.

Smothers, Albert Abraham "Little Smokey": b. Tchula, Mississippi, 1939; d. Chicago 2010. Guitarist and singer.

Smothers, Otis "Big Smokey": b. Lexington, Mississippi, 1929; d. Chicago 1993. Guitarist and singer.

Spann, Otis: b. Jackson, Mississippi, 1924; d. Chicago, 1970. The leading postwar blues piano player. Member of Muddy Waters's band from 1952 to 1968; also recorded as a solo artist.

Spann, Pervis: b. Itta Bena, Mississippi, 1932. "The Blues Man": disc jockey and promoter.

Strachwitz, Chris: b. Gross Reichenau, Germany, 1931. Moved to the United States in 1947. Founder of Arhoolie Records in 1960.

Sugar Blue (James Whiting): b. New York City, 1949. Harmonica player who first recorded for the Spivey label in 1970 and 1975; moved to Chicago in 1982.

Sumlin, Hubert: b. Greenwood, Mississippi, 1931; d. Wayne, New Jersey, 2011. Famed for his groundbreaking work as Howlin' Wolf's guitarist from 1954 until Wolf's death in 1976.

Sunnyland Slim (Albert Luandrew): b. Quitman County, Mississippi, 1906; d. Chicago 1995. Prolific singer and piano player who was a mainstay of the Chicago blues for forty years.

Sykes, Roosevelt: b. Elmar, Arkansas, 1906; d. New Orleans, 1983. Pioneer blues and boogie-woogie piano player who first recorded in 1929.

Taylor, Eddie: b. Benoit, Mississippi, 1923; d. Chicago 1985. Outstanding guitarist, famed for his work as a sideman with Jimmy Reed, Elmore James, and others. His *I Feel So Bad* album on Advent is well worth seeking out.

Taylor, Gene: b. Los Angeles, 1952. Singer and piano player. Learned his trade very young in California, backing musicians like T-Bone Walker and Big Joe Turner. A member of Canned Heat in the mid-1970s and later The Fabulous Thunderbirds. Based in Belgium.

Taylor, Koko (Cora Walton): b. Shelby, Tennessee, 1928, d. Chicago, 2009. Singer. Chess and Alligator recording artist.

Taylor, Theodore "Hound Dog": b. Natchez, Mississippi, 1915; d. Chicago, 1975. Singer and slide guitarist, leader of The Houserockers; first artist to record on Alligator Records.

Thompson, Alfonso "Sonny": b. Centerville, Mississippi, 1923; d. Chicago, 1989. Pianist, bandleader, session musician and producer best known for his work with the King and Federal labels.

Thornton, Big Mama: b. Ariton, Alabama, 1926; d. Los Angeles, 1984. Blues singer famed for her hit with the song "Hound Dog" in 1952. Also played drums and harmonica.

Tolbert, Israel: b. Montgomery, Alabama, 1939; d. 2007. Southern soul-blues artist and DJ whose big hit was "Big Leg Woman" in 1971.

Turner, Big Joe: b. Kansas City, 1911; d. Inglewood, California, 1985. Pioneer jump blues, swing, and rock 'n' roll singer.

Walker, Aaron Thibeaux "T-Bone": b. Linden, Texas, 1910; d. Los Angeles, 1975. Electric guitar pioneer and seminal blues guitar stylist. First recorded in 1929, but it is his 1940s Capitol and Black & White recordings and his sides for Imperial in the early 1950s that are appreciated as some of the most important blues records ever made. Blind Lemon Jefferson was a family friend.

Walker, Jimmy: b. Memphis 1905; d. Chicago 1997. Blues and boogie-woogie piano player.

Walker, Johnnie "Big Moose": b. Stoneville, Mississippi, 1927; d. Chicago, 1999. Piano player who backed Earl Hooker, Elmore James, Muddy Waters, Junior Wells, Otis Rush, and many others. Later in his career he recorded in his own right for Alligator and JSP.

Welding, Pete: b. Philadelphia, 1935; d. Alta Loma, California, 1995. Blues historian, writer, and producer. Founder of Testament Records.

Wellington, Valerie (Valerie Hall): b. Chicago, 1959; d. Maywood, Illinois, 1993. Singer. Recorded a couple of albums, appeared in stage productions, and even had a film role in a short but memorable career.

Wells, Amos Blakemore "Junior": b. Memphis, Tennessee, 1934; d. Chicago, 1998. Singer and harmonica giant, member of the Muddy Waters band, co-founder of The Aces with Dave, Louis Myers, and Fred Below, and later famed for a longstanding partnership with Buddy Guy.

White, Booker T. Washington "Bukka": b. Aberdeen, Mississippi, 1909; d. Memphis 1977. Country blues singer and guitarist who recorded first in the 1930s and then again in the 1960s after being tracked down by folklorists. I always assumed the phonetic "Bukka" nickname was transcribed by some gormless white blues researcher who hadn't heard of Booker T. Washington, but in fact it first appears on the labels of his 1930s Vocalion 78s.

White, Josh: b. Greenville, South Carolina, 1914; d. New York, 1969. Singer, guitarist, and civil rights activist. First recorded in 1930 and became a prominent member of the 1950s folk music movement.

White, Lavelle: b. Amite City, Louisiana, 1929. Blues and soul singer and songwriter who first worked in Houston and recorded as Miss La-Vell on Duke in the late 1950s and early 1960s. Moved to Chicago in 1978.

Williams, Henry Lee "Shot": b. Lexington, Mississippi, 1938; d. 2011. Singer. Cousin to Otis "Smokey" Smothers, Albert "Little Smokey" Smothers, and "Mad Dog" Lester Davenport.

Williams, Joe: b. Cordele, Georgia, 1918; d. Las Vegas, 1999. Blues and jazz singer who worked with Coleman Hawkins, Lionel Hampton, and Count Basie; first recorded in the 1940s.

Williams, Big Joe: b. Crawford, Mississippi, 1903; d. Macon, Mississippi, 1982. Country blues singer, songwriter, and guitarist who first recorded in the 1930s and saw some success on the coffeehouse and festival circuit in the 1960s. One of the first artists to record for Delmark Records.

Williams, Robert Pete: b. Zachary, Louisiana, 1914; d. Rosedale, Louisiana, 1980. Country blues singer and guitarist. First recorded in 1961, on Arhoolie.

Williamson, John Lee "Sonny Boy": b. Jackson, Tennessee, 1914; d. Chicago, 1948. "Father of modern blues harp," major recording artist, and prolific songwriter, perhaps best remembered today for having his name stolen by Alec Miller.

Williamson, Sonny Boy (Alec Miller): b. Tallahatchie County, Mississippi, c. 1912; d. Helena, Arkansas, 1965. Singer and harmonica player. One of the giants of postwar blues who also wrote some of its most enduring songs.

Witherspoon, Jimmy: b. Gurdon, Arkansas, 1920; d. Los Angeles, 1997. Blues, jazz, and R&B singer who first recorded in the 1940s.

Yancey, Mama (Estella Harris): b. Cairo, Illinois, 1896; d. Chicago, 1986. Singer, who married boogie-woogie piano player Jimmy Yancey in 1925 and performed with him until Yancey's death in 1951. Later used several other accompanists, notably Erwin Helfer.

Young, Johnny: b. Vicksburg, Mississippi 1918; d. Chicago, 1974. Singer and guitarist who arrived in Chicago in 1940 and worked with Sonny Boy Williamson (the first) and Muddy Waters. Also played mandolin.

Index

ALAN HARPER is a journalist and magazine editor. He was born in Scotland, brought up in Africa, educated in England, and lives in Devon with his wife, two sons, and a dog.

MUSIC IN AMERICAN LIFE

"Happy in the Service of the Lord": Afro-American Gospel Quartets in Memphis
  Kip Lornell

Paul Hindemith in the United States   *Luther Noss*

"My Song Is My Weapon": People's Songs, American Communism, and the Politics
  of Culture, 1930–50   *Robbie Lieberman*

Chosen Voices: The Story of the American Cantorate   *Mark Slobin*

Theodore Thomas: America's Conductor and Builder of Orchestras, 1835–1905
  Ezra Schabas

"The Whorehouse Bells Were Ringing" and Other Songs Cowboys Sing
  Collected and Edited by Guy Logsdon

Crazeology: The Autobiography of a Chicago Jazzman   *Bud Freeman, as Told
  to Robert Wolf*

Discoursing Sweet Music: Brass Bands and Community Life in Turn-of-the-Century
  Pennsylvania   *Kenneth Kreitner*

Mormonism and Music: A History   *Michael Hicks*

Voices of the Jazz Age: Profiles of Eight Vintage Jazzmen   *Chip Deffaa*

Pickin' on Peachtree: A History of Country Music in Atlanta, Georgia
  Wayne W. Daniel

Bitter Music: Collected Journals, Essays, Introductions, and Librettos
  Harry Partch; edited by Thomas McGeary

Ethnic Music on Records: A Discography of Ethnic Recordings Produced
  in the United States, 1893 to 1942   *Richard K. Spottswood*

Downhome Blues Lyrics: An Anthology from the Post–World War II Era
  Jeff Todd Titon

Ellington: The Early Years   *Mark Tucker*

Chicago Soul   *Robert Pruter*

That Half-Barbaric Twang: The Banjo in American Popular Culture   *Karen Linn*

Hot Man: The Life of Art Hodes   *Art Hodes and Chadwick Hansen*

The Erotic Muse: American Bawdy Songs (2d ed.)   *Ed Cray*

Barrio Rhythm: Mexican American Music in Los Angeles   *Steven Loza*

The Creation of Jazz: Music, Race, and Culture in Urban America   *Burton W. Peretti*

Charles Martin Loeffler: A Life Apart in Music   *Ellen Knight*

Club Date Musicians: Playing the New York Party Circuit   *Bruce A. MacLeod*

Opera on the Road: Traveling Opera Troupes in the United States, 1825–60
  Katherine K. Preston

The Stonemans: An Appalachian Family and the Music That Shaped Their Lives
  Ivan M. Tribe

Transforming Tradition: Folk Music Revivals Examined   *Edited by Neil V. Rosenberg*

The Crooked Stovepipe: Athapaskan Fiddle Music and Square Dancing
  in Northeast Alaska and Northwest Canada   *Craig Mishler*

Traveling the High Way Home: Ralph Stanley and the World of Traditional
  Bluegrass Music   *John Wright*

Carl Ruggles: Composer, Painter, and Storyteller   *Marilyn Ziffrin*

Never without a Song: The Years and Songs of Jennie Devlin, 1865–1952
  Katharine D. Newman

Together Let Us Sweetly Live   *Jonathan C. David, with photographs by
    Richard Holloway*
Live Fast, Love Hard: The Faron Young Story   *Diane Diekman*
Air Castle of the South: WSM Radio and the Making of Music City
    Craig P. Havighurst
Traveling Home: Sacred Harp Singing and American Pluralism   *Kiri Miller*
Where Did Our Love Go? The Rise and Fall of the Motown Sound   *Nelson George*
Lonesome Cowgirls and Honky-Tonk Angels: The Women of Barn Dance Radio
    Kristine M. McCusker
California Polyphony: Ethnic Voices, Musical Crossroads   *Mina Yang*
The Never-Ending Revival: Rounder Records and the Folk Alliance   *Michael F. Scully*
Sing It Pretty: A Memoir   *Bess Lomax Hawes*
Working Girl Blues: The Life and Music of Hazel Dickens   *Hazel Dickens and
    Bill C. Malone*
Charles Ives Reconsidered   *Gayle Sherwood Magee*
The Hayloft Gang: The Story of the National Barn Dance   *Edited by Chad Berry*
Country Music Humorists and Comedians   *Loyal Jones*
Record Makers and Breakers: Voices of the Independent Rock 'n' Roll Pioneers
    John Broven
Music of the First Nations: Tradition and Innovation in Native North America
    Edited by Tara Browner
Cafe Society: The Wrong Place for the Right People   *Barney Josephson, with
    Terry Trilling-Josephson*
George Gershwin: An Intimate Portrait   *Walter Rimler*
Life Flows On in Endless Song: Folk Songs and American History   *Robert V. Wells*
I Feel a Song Coming On: The Life of Jimmy McHugh   *Alyn Shipton*
King of the Queen City: The Story of King Records   *Jon Hartley Fox*
Long Lost Blues: Popular Blues in America, 1850–1920   *Peter C. Muir*
Hard Luck Blues: Roots Music Photographs from the Great Depression
    Rich Remsberg
Restless Giant: The Life and Times of Jean Aberbach and Hill and Range Songs
    Bar Biszick-Lockwood
Champagne Charlie and Pretty Jemima: Variety Theater in the Nineteenth Century
    Gillian M. Rodger
Sacred Steel: Inside an African American Steel Guitar Tradition   *Robert L. Stone*
Gone to the Country: The New Lost City Ramblers and the Folk Music Revival
    Ray Allen
The Makers of the Sacred Harp   *David Warren Steel with Richard H. Hulan*
Woody Guthrie, American Radical   *Will Kaufman*
George Szell: A Life of Music   *Michael Charry*
Bean Blossom: The Brown County Jamboree and Bill Monroe's Bluegrass Festivals
    Thomas A. Adler
Crowe on the Banjo: The Music Life of J. D. Crowe   *Marty Godbey*
Twentieth Century Drifter: The Life of Marty Robbins   *Diane Diekman*

Henry Mancini: Reinventing Film Music   *John Caps*
The Beautiful Music All Around Us: Field Recordings and the American Experience
     Stephen Wade
Then Sings My Soul: The Culture of Southern Gospel Music   *Douglas Harrison*
The Accordion in the Americas: Klezmer, Polka, Tango, Zydeco, and More!
     Edited by Helena Simonett
Bluegrass Bluesman: A Memoir   *Josh Graves, edited by Fred Bartenstein*
One Woman in a Hundred: Edna Phillips and the Philadelphia Orchestra
     Mary Sue Welsh
The Great Orchestrator: Arthur Judson and American Arts Management
     James M. Doering
Charles Ives in the Mirror: American Histories of an Iconic Composer   *David C. Paul*
Southern Soul-Blues   *David Whiteis*
Sweet Air: Modernism, Regionalism, and American Popular Song
     Edward P. Comentale
Pretty Good for a Girl: Women in Bluegrass   *Murphy Hicks Henry*
Sweet Dreams: The World of Patsy Cline   *Warren R. Hofstra*
William Sidney Mount and the Creolization of American Culture
     Christopher J. Smith
Bird: The Life and Music of Charlie Parker   *Chuck Haddix*
Making the March King: John Philip Sousa's Washington Years, 1854–1893
     Patrick Warfield
In It for the Long Run   *Jim Rooney*
Pioneers of the Blues Revival   *Steve Cushing*
Roots of the Revival: American and British Folk Music in the 1950s   *Ronald D. Cohen
     and Rachel Clare Donaldson*
Blues All Day Long: The Jimmy Rogers Story   *Wayne Everett Goins*
Yankee Twang: Country and Western Music in New England   *Clifford R. Murphy*
The Music of the Stanley Brothers   *Gary B. Reid*
Hawaiian Music in Motion: Mariners, Missionaries, and Minstrels   *James Revell Carr*
Sounds of the New Deal: The Federal Music Project in the West   *Peter Gough*
The Mormon Tabernacle Choir: A Biography   *Michael Hicks*
The Man That Got Away: The Life and Songs of Harold Arlen   *Walter Rimler*
A City Called Heaven: Chicago and the Birth of Gospel Music   *Robert M. Marovich*
Blues Unlimited: Essential Interviews from the Original Blues Magazine
     Edited by Bill Greensmith, Mike Rowe, and Mark Camarigg
Hoedowns, Reels, and Frolics: Roots and Branches of Southern Appalachian Dance
     Phil Jamison
Fannie Bloomfield-Zeisler: The Life and Times of a Piano Virtuoso
     Beth Abelson Macleod
Cybersonic Arts: Adventures in American New Music   *Gordon Mumma, edited with
     commentary by Michelle Fillion*
The Magic of Beverly Sills   *Nancy Guy*
Waiting for Buddy Guy   *Alan Harper*

The University of Illinois Press
is a founding member of the
Association of American University Presses.

University of Illinois Press
1325 South Oak Street
Champaign, IL 61820-6903
www.press.uillinois.edu